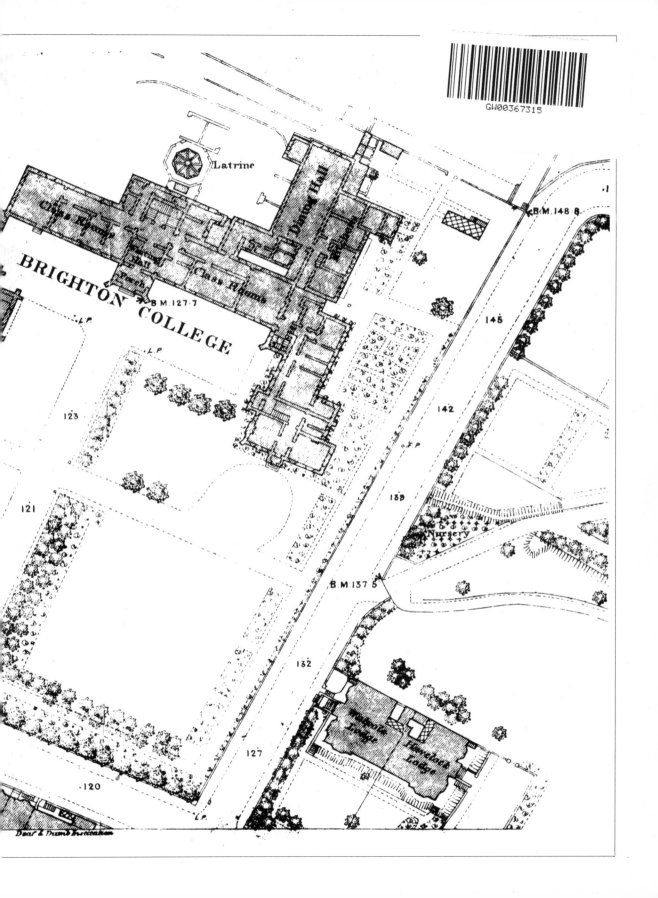

GW00367315

Latrine

Dining Hall

BRIGHTON
COLLEGE

B.M 127.7

B M 148 8

.1

145

142

139

Nursery

123

121

B.M 137 5

132

127

.120

Deaf & Dumb Institution

BRIGHTON COLLEGE
1845-1995

To Clementine,

Brighton College will

always be a part of you.

Wishing you health, happiness

& success in the future.

Keep singing!

with best wishes from

Alison Withers & all the

girls in Williams House

20ᵗʰ March 2009

BRIGHTON COLLEGE
1845-1995

Martin D.W. Jones

Phillimore

MCMXCV

1995

Published by
PHILLIMORE & CO. LTD.,
Shopwyke Manor Barn, Chichester, West Sussex

© Martin D.W. Jones, 1995

ISBN 0 85033 978 2

Printed and bound in Great Britain by
BUTLER & TANNER LTD.
Frome and London

Contents

Preface

Four Histories of the school have been published, but all are out of print and copies are scarce. Arthur Belcher's in *The Brightonian* (November 1948 and February 1949) was exceedingly brief and is now almost impossible to get hold of. Philip Burstow's *A History of Brighton College* (1957) and my own *Short History* (1986) sold out soon after publication. This new History, published to mark the College's sesquincentenary, aims to supplement and amplify each of its predecessors. As one who has known Brighton College for only 18 years, I am exceedingly conscious of my dependence on the generous assistance of so many whose memories could together span half the school's life. I should have liked to list them one by one, but I hope that they will accept this the briefest of acknowledgements of my debt for letters and conversations, for entertaining me with tales of salad days, for cautioning me with stories of very hell, and for saving me from many an error.

All interested in the story of Brighton College stand in the shadow of Philip Burstow, who saved so many historic papers from the boilers in 1950, who classified them in the Archives he instituted, who systematically gathered in so many more and then went to press, setting out the first clear narrative of College History. His book was published despite official obstruction and only after substantial censorship. I am happy to record a very different experience. Encouraged initially by Norman Frith, this volume has enjoyed the active patronage of Bill Blackshaw and Stephen Cockburn. A special debt of gratitude is also owed to my wife, Jenny. For years she has borne with equanimity my preoccupation with long-dead schoolmasters. Her encouragement has been vital—and only she could have turned my crabbed manuscripts into neatly wordprocessed typescript.

Traditional school histories are little more than annals, lacking objectivity and cloyingly sentimental. To those who expect in these pages the rosy glow of reminiscence—and do not find it—I make no apology. A history must examine structures and themes, as much as personality and events. The school must not be isolated from the social and educational contexts of its times. If this book has a theme, it is the significance of change, not the importance of continuity. Soon after I began work, Norman remarked to me: 'Of course, nothing of value ever changes in a public school.' From a Historian that was a curious remark, and this book demonstrates why. Nothing is immutable. Few traditions are as ancient as we like to think. Institutions fear change, and schools are no exception. The story of the successful may well be one of sluggish, even unwilling adaptation. But to survive is to change, even if sleight of hand then disguises what has occurred under the mask of continuity. The story of Brighton College has been one of an extraordinary resilience, of survival against great odds; that is why there is so much in this book about the size of the roll and the state of the finances. Only if we measure those difficulties can we understand why Brighton College has been so successful and, yes, praise those to whom this school owes so much.

Part I

Principals

Arthur Macleane	August 1846
Henry Cotterill	February 1851
John Griffith	September 1856
Charles Bigg	September 1871

Introduction

Jane Austen and Walter Scott were dead. Gilbert was nine and Sullivan three. Oscar Wilde, Conan Doyle and Rudyard Kipling were yet to be born. Victoria and Albert had been married but five years. The penny post was still almost a novelty. The transporting of convicts to Australia had just ceased, but soldiers and beggars were still flogged, and executions took place in public. There would be no compulsory schooling for another 25 years, and then only to the age of thirteen. Men wore top hats, women crinolines and bonnets. These were the days of the foundation of Brighton College—before the Great Exhibition, before the publication of *The Origin of Species*, before either Gladstone or Disraeli was prime minister. The year was 1845.

Being a Victorian was about doing. On the edge of the Victorian era, Britain was a state rich in confidence, looking to the future and anxious for progress. The Victorians were full of energy, moral and intellectual as well as physical and industrial. Theirs was, in Asa Briggs' memorable phrase, the age of improvement. Not a few thought civilisation to be on the brink of perfection. The first Victorians were also a generation in revolt. Driven by that seriousness shot through with indignation which underpinned the first stirrings of provincial bourgeois morality, their new wholesome family domesticity repudiated (what they saw as) the shallow, godless ways of their Regency parents. The nation must be purged of the boozing, gambling, leering, farting world that was Georgian England—and to do that successfully the chief imperative was to reform the uppermost stratas of society. If they set the right tone, regeneration would trickle down and transform the nation. The high Victorians were thus embarked upon a crusade. Irreligion was a growing worry. The 1851 census of religious worship shocked polite society with its discovery that only 60 per cent of the English attended church, in Brighton barely 52 per cent. Everything would depend upon the moral fibre and religious character of the next generation of gentlemen, the mainstay of the realm. Education would therefore be seen as fundamental to the cause, but in that endeavour there would be no rôle for the state. Few then regarded the provision of education (at any level) as any part of the state's function. Neither did they look to the church itself, which centuries back had lost its monopoly of educational provision. Rather, individual christian citizens would help state and church by founding schools where sound religion was cherished.

This Victorian mission needs, however, to be set within a larger frame for it was heir to late 18th-century middle-class attempts to reform the ancient grammar schools. Those initiatives had ground to a halt and, by the 1820s, frustration was beginning to foster radical thinking. Dr. Arnold might be transforming Rugby (1828-41), but the old public schools would not do. They were fiercely attacked (not always justly) for having too narrow a curriculum, using out-of-date teaching methods, offering primitive facilities, providing inadequate food and charging excessive fees. Traditional English secondary education had been found wanting. As an alternative, there were plenty of private academies, eminently respectable in their clientèle and sometimes purveyors of a first-rate education. But such establishments were also judged unsatisfactory because, the personal property of their headmaster, they tended to be ephemeral, were short of capital and often ill-equipped, especially for the teaching of science. As in religion and in architecture, a new mood was abroad in education. All three were animated by revivalist fervour. From 1825, therefore, a new type of secondary school began to appear: the proprietary school. These institutions marked the cutting edge of the new, reflecting substantial demand from the fast-prospering, fast-growing and increasingly self-confident professional and middle classes, the moneyed product of industrialisation. Educational need was changing.

The proprietary schools had no choice but to offer the traditional classical curriculum of the old public and grammar schools. Without that, access to the universities was impossible and a fundamental middle-class aspiration would have been frustrated. But there was another reason why upwardly-mobile businessmen supported Latin and Greek as essential components within the curriculum. Through study of the Classics, their sons would acquire gentility. While the momentous if modest political reforms of the 1820s and 1830s had revealed the power of the bullish manufacturing class, they equally demonstrated that there would be no revolution in England. Industrialisation had generated great wealth, now admitted to political influence. But the new group was still denied acceptance by polite society. They were not regarded as true gentlemen. In response, they pushed harder for admission, aped the ruling oligarchy and took up fox hunting. Their own claim to gentlemanly status might remain questionable, but they could use education as a social stepping stone for their heirs. With Latin and Greek, their boy could go to Oxford, enter the church or be commissioned into a smart regiment. Education would make him a gentleman. Money would be made respectable.

But these hard-headed men wanted more. They demanded a complementary 'modern' curriculum to make that education serve the new god of utility: mathematics, modern languages, science. In the words of the College's Annual Report on 1853, it was necessary 'to engraft on a Liberal Education that practical knowledge which is required to meet the altered circumstances of the present day'. Until the 1820s, it had been available only in the first-rate academies of the protestant dissenters. But the universities, the professions and politics all required membership of the established church. Here was the market niche for the proprietary schools, offering a progressive curriculum in an Anglican context.

The way in which that new mixed curriculum would be delivered was equally representative of the time. Groups of like-minded individuals would band together in joint-stock companies to set up a new school. The shares sold would provide the capital for buildings and equipment while the permanence of a company would remove the capriciousness and short-termism of headmasters concerned only to make a profit. With such a background, it should come as no surprise to find that these new schools were urban and primarily for 'day scholars'. None were official church foundations, although almost all were affiliated to the established church. A few were experimental, making attendance voluntary or forbidding corporal punishment.

The 1830s and 1840s witnessed the heyday of the proprietary schools. They spread across the kingdom until most towns of even reasonable size had one. If between 1840 and 1844 Liverpool, Cheltenham, Fleetwood and Marlborough all saw the need, it was not going to be long before someone proposed a similar foundation in Brighton. After all, it was then the fastest growing metropolis in England. The first attempt came in 1837, but Brighton Proprietary Grammar School never got off the ground. When another scheme was floated in 1845, the town responded more positively, as did Glasgow that same year.

The very vigour of these precocious newcomers forced the gothic ramparts. It would be the new schools which captured and then dominated the market. And it was they who created that quintessential feature of 19th-century England: the Victorian public school. For a while, forget the stereotypical image that term conjures: a boarding school, planted deliberately in the countryside for good air, for playing fields and far from sin. Boarding was not as yet particularly fashionable with the middle classes. But it was coming, and fast. Founded at a moment of transition, Brighton was the last of the great urban proprietary schools.

THE PROPOSED COLLEGE AT BRIGHTON.

SIR,

We beg to inform you that a Meeting of Gentlemen favourable to the Establishing of a Proprietary College at Brighton, will be held at the Town Hall, Brighton, on Monday next, the 24th day of November instant, at Three o'clock precisely, to receive a Report from the Provisional Committee appointed at the Preliminary Meeting, held on the 27th day of October last, and to adopt such measures thereupon as may seem expedient. The favour of your attendance is requested.

We have the honour to be, Sir,

Your obedient humble servants,

W. A. SOAMES, } Hon. Secs.
EDWARD CORNFORD, } pro tem.

Brighton,
18th November, 1845.

Part I

Principals

Arthur Macleane	August 1846
Henry Cotterill	February 1851
John Griffith	September 1856
Charles Bigg	September 1871

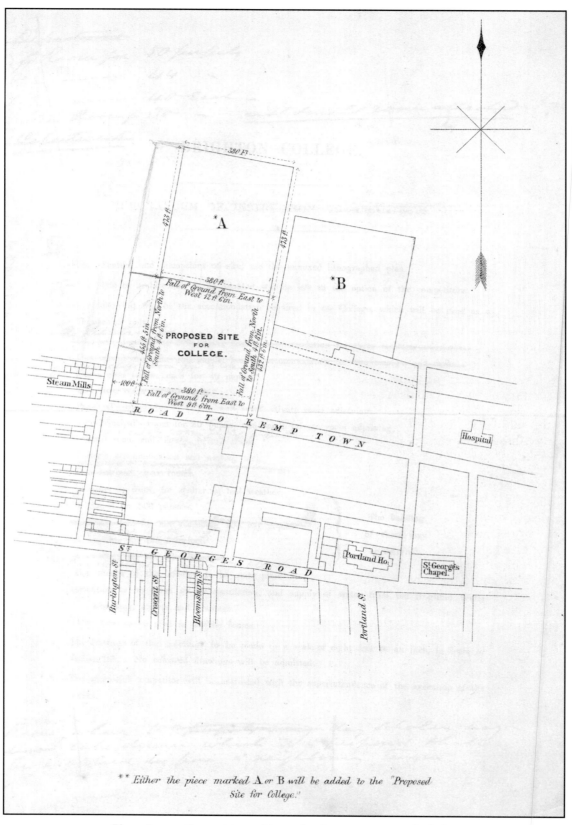

– *One* –

1845-1848

Sons of the morning

To inspire others with a dream and induce them to give of their time, their talent and their money, to sustain that enthusiasm and bring it to fulfilment is given to few. In that capacity lies greatness and one such was William Aldwin Soames, our forgotten founder. He it was who, in the words of his memorial tablet in chapel, 'conceived the idea of Brighton College and in the year 1845 took the principal part in founding it'. He drafted the College's constitution and deed of foundation. He gathered around him a nucleus of enthusiasts to form the initial committee. He organised the private and public meetings to canvass support. He enlisted the original share-holders, and then he took office as the College's inaugural treasurer, joint honorary secretary and trustee. His was the idea and the driving force to bring Brighton College to birth. He himself bought the very first four shares and thereafter served his creation most faithfully, sitting on the Council to within a fortnight of his death in 1871. In June 1859, he even assumed personal liability for the College's £6,000 mortgage when it became clear that funds were insufficient.

Whether Soames was typical of those behind the new public schools is difficult to say for no systematic research seems to have been carried out on their founders: Rossall (1844) was the brainchild of a hotelier; Clifton (1862) was conceived by the Mayor of Bristol; Malvern (1862) the idea of a factory manager. By contrast, Lancing (1848), Hurstpierpoint (1849), Cranleigh (1863) and Framlingham (1864) were all founded by Anglican clergymen. Of a family which during the 18th century had prospered through trade, business had by the 1830s been relegated to secondary significance for our Mr. Soames behind the property interests bought into with its profits. On top of extensive land in Brighton, he owned nearly thirty smart London freeholds and leaseholds in areas like New and Old Bond Streets, Oxford Street, Fleet Street and High Holborn. He was a substantial *rentier*, living the life of a gentleman, and when he died was possessed of a personal fortune of around £150,000 (perhaps £4.5 million today). According to family tradition, it was his personal maxim to divide his annual income into thirds: one part he spent, one part he invested, one part he gave away in charity—this in an era when income tax never exceeded 1s. 7d. in the pound.

We know also that he was active on the committees of several Brighton charities working to ameliorate the severe poverty of the town's extensive slums. He was a regular donor to St Mary's Hall which offered a free education with board and lodging for the daughters of impoverished Anglican clergymen (and outside the town to St John's School which, in London and then Leatherhead, offered the same to clergy sons). With his brother, back in the 1820s, he had established and built the

William Aldwin Soames

village school near their then home at Cottered in Hertfordshire. Presumably, signifi-cant philanthropy stemmed from deep religious conviction. A staunch evangelical within the established church, he was churchwarden of All Souls on Eastern Road and a committee member of the Brighton and East Sussex Auxiliary Religious Tract Society. From surviving poll books, even his politics can be known. Occasionally he did not vote, but when he did he stood with that minority of Brighton burgesses casting both their votes for a Tory candidate. Soames was the catalyst. He possessed the capital and the drive to found the school entirely by himself. But his intention was very different from that of Rev. Dr. Woodard with Lancing and Hurstpierpoint. Soames would be no sole founder. He intended Brighton College to be proprietary, not private, and thus he wanted (rather than needed) a collective effort within the town. In consequence, as the Council itself acknowledged 14 years after his death, 'he sacrificed some of his own interests to secure the cooperation of persons specially suited to aid the College'. When he had found and brought those persons together, he was more than happy to take but one seat at its Council table; after all, this was *the* age of the committee, *the* heyday of the joint-stock company. He seems first to have enlisted a local solicitor, Edward Cornford, and his own parson Richard Snowdon Smith (perpetual curate of All Souls). Together they then approached the vicar of Brighton, Henry Wagner. Preliminary conversations led to a formal private meeting on 7 July 1845 involving all these gentlemen, together with the perpetual curate of St Peter's, Thomas Cooke, and one of Wagner's curates, Thomas Coombe, at which

it was deemed desirable and practicable to establish a College at Brighton on Church of England principles for the education of the sons of noblemen and gentlemen. Some minor points were discussed—such as the nature of education, the terms, the site, the capital, the officers and it was determined to have a general meeting on the subject as soon as many gentlemen who were likely to take interest in the Design should be returned to Brighton.

Rev. Henry Venn Elliott

Wagner's attitude to the College remains a mystery. His endorsement was essential, and that he seems to have given readily. But his associations with the infant College were minimal. His only specific action on its behalf would appear to have been his undertaking to write to Windsor in search of royal patronage. Certainly he took no formal part in College affairs. He never owned any shares and, as far as is known, never attended College functions. While his Tory views gave him a firm link with the College promoters, his churchmanship did not. But then neither did Richard Snowdon Smith's, who introduced to All Souls the first surpliced choir in Brighton. Whatever the reason, it was for Wagner a curious position to adopt. Indifference to the institution seems very unlikely, for him. Perhaps it was a vote of confidence. If so, it was a rare compliment from so testy and overbearing a man. Of the other five midwives present at that July meeting, Cooke and Coombe disappeared at once, leaving the original nucleus of Soames, Cornford and Smith.

Other local worthies soon joined them as active agents of the project: Sir Thomas Blomefield, Rev. Henry Venn Elliott, the perpetual curate of St Mark's and founder of St Mary's Hall, and Lord Alfred Hervey, one of the town's two MPs and younger brother of the Marquis of Bristol. All six would in time serve on the inaugural College Council. Resident just beyond the town at Stanmer Park, the Earl of Chichester agreed to become the president. The right kind of names were of inestimable value to a project such as this. The founders of Rossall and Malvern were even unseated because, as a hotelier and a factory manager respectively, they were not gentlemen and were thus deemed unworthy of their foundations. The College's constitution, therefore, made provision for the great and good to be associated with the institution.

Appropriately for a school rooted so firmly to the Church of England, the Bishop of Chichester accepted the position of patron and the vicar of Brighton became one of four vice patrons–the other three being General Sir Adolphus Dalrymple, Hon. Charles Hanbury Tracy and Colonel George Wyndham (respectively a baronet and former MP, the heir to a new barony and, reputedly the richest man in the kingdom, the illegitimate son of an earl). Considering Brighton's contemporary place in the front rank of gathering places for the élite of the kingdom, they made a respectable but by no means outstanding group. That is revealing. Had Soames and his colleagues noticed what was happening to Brighton? In December 1845, still fired with that initial passion which accompanies any enterprise, they had written to Queen Victoria asking 'that Her Majesty will graciously consider to become the Patron of the Proposed College'. But, as royal patronage had set the ultimate seal of respectability on the town from 1783, so its withdrawal had profound consequences for its attraction to society.

The request for royal patronage came too late. Influenced by Prince Albert, Victoria had that very year decided against the Royal Pavilion as wholly unsuitable for the young, expanding royal family. It was too small, too open to public gaze and too reminiscent of dissolute Uncle George. Thus it was that the Keeper of the Privy Purse wrote back, politely declining the College's invitation with a rather lame excuse: 'the Queen could not comply ... without subjecting herself to considerable embarrassment from applications of a similar nature which Her Majesty had been obliged to decline'. As the College solicitor noted dryly but accurately many years later, their application had been 'innopportune'. The Queen wanted nothing more to do with Brighton. When the crown went (to Osborne, purchased in 1845), so too did most of the aristocracy, hurrying also to escape the excursion trains which from 1844 were bringing hordes of London day-trippers who spent little, cluttered the promenades and lowered the tone. Fashionable Brighton was under attack.

Such were the founder and his closest allies. What of their foundation? Of a series of private meetings held between June and October 1845 we know practically nothing. The infant project only begins to come into focus with a public meeting held in the National School on 27 October. There it was formally decided that a College be established:

> for the purpose of providing an efficient course of education for the sons of gentlemen comprising religious and moral instruction in strict conformity with the principles and doctrine of the Established Church, the Greek, Latin, Hebrew, and modern languages and literature; History, Geography, Mathematics, Naval and Military and such other branches of knowledge as it may be found practicable and advantageous to introduce. And that the College be divided into two departments–the Senior and the Junior.

To that meeting some 120 local gentlemen were invited, including the town's entire Anglican clergy and most of its medical and legal practitioners. Three comments sum up the feeling of that occasion. First, the local solicitor, property developer and clerk to the town commissioners, Thomas Attree: 'I have ever thought that a College would be to Brighton the greatest public boon that could be conferred on it, and when I see the course things are taking, I look forward, as a well-wisher of my native town, in confident expectation of all the good I dreamt of years ago to be effected ... I will not compliment you or my friend Soames, tho' I have such a fair field for it'. Second, the Earl of Chichester: 'It has long been considered by residents in this County that a public College is needed on a scale and character worthy of the County'. Third, the founder himself: 'If in other towns, College Institutions succeeded, Brighton has a very great and peculiar recommendation for a College which would extend to the nobility and gentry of the town the benefits of a sound education sufficient for the universities or any other walks in life.'

Brighton must indeed have seemed an ideal site. The early Victorians were exceedingly health-conscious and Brighton had become a renowned spa town famed for good air and curative waters. While the reasons for pupils coming to the College were never systematically recorded, chance references indicate several boys being transferred from Eton, Rugby and Harrow for health reasons. There must have been more and certainly it was a qualification the College was keen to promote. Dr. George Hall, appointed Honorary Physician in 1846, played an important rôle in determining the exact site on which the new school should be built and the VIth Annual Report commended 'the rare healthiness of the locality'. The railways too could also be expected to play a significant rôle. The opening of lines to Shoreham (1840), London (1841), Lewes and Hastings (1846) would do much to make the new College, in Soames' words, 'attractive to youth from other parts of the kingdom not yet endowed with such an establishment.' From the start, it was intended that Brighton College, unlike many proprietary schools, would have a significant boarding element alongside the day scholars.

Underpinning everything, however, were the town's credentials for social respectability. Handsome squares and crescents, supplemented by a few individual villas, had been built on a large scale within the previous 20 years. These offered a standard of genteel town housing, ideal for the middle classes to buy and for the aristocracy to rent during the season. That was to be fundamental to the new College. Despite the railway and a readiness to admit boarders, Soames wanted 'the benefits of a good education to be united with all the advantages of home influences'. So too did his most active supporters. All five of the key group behind the foundation (and three more on the fringe) had moved to Brighton within the previous ten years and had young families with sons not yet at school. All eight sent all of their boys to Brighton College. In other words, Soames and his allies were not merely thinking of the benefit to their town. They were at (or close to) that stage when they would have to settle their children's schooling. Rejecting the still largely discredited public schools, they had the money and initiative to set up their own school, shaped the way they wanted it, in their own home town, for their own children. Twenty years later, they would have packed their boys off to boarding school. In the first two years of the College, the proportion of dayboys among new entrants was 46 per cent and 45 per cent respectively. These men were of the last generation untouched by that resolute bias against day-schooling which so straight-jacketed English private education until the 1960s. Nothing could stand in greater contrast to Dr. Woodard who, in founding his Sussex schools, deliberately sought to remove boys from 'the noxious influence of their home'. Did Soames and Woodard know of each other? In their churchmanship, as in their tactics for the reform of the middle classes, there would not have been a meeting of minds.

Table 1.1: The original Council–where they educated their sons

	Council membership	sons already at/left school in 1845	sons under 6 in 1845	sons born 1845+	shares owned
Vice Presidents					
Rev. J.S.M. Anderson	1845-53	0	0	(4M)	1
Sir T. Blomefield	1845-58	(4H)	1BC	0	1
Rev. H.V. Elliott	1845-65	0	3BC	0	4
Lord Alfred Hervey	1845-75	0	(1E)	(4M)	4
Triennial members					
John Bovell	1845-51	0	(1C,1CH)	?	2
Edward Cornford	1845-50	0	4BC	0	4
Rev.Dr. J.H. Jerrard	1845-50	?	?	?	2
Rev. C.E. Kennaway	1845-46	0	(2H)	?	0
Rev. C.D. Maitland	1845-65	(2?)	1BC	0	2
Lt. C. Malden R.N.	1845-49	(2H,1M)	3BC	0	1
Edward Polhill	1845-51	?	?	?	1
Rev. F. Reade	1845-54	0	1BC	?	1
Dr. Samuel Scott	1845-49	0	0	5BC	1
William Soames	1845-71	0	1BC	2BC	4
Rev. R.S. Smith	1845-95	(1M)	1BC	?	1
Rev. J. Vaughan	1845-54	?	(1H)	?	1

Key: BC = Brighton College, C = Charterhouse, CH = Christ's Hospital, E = Eton, H = Harrow,
    M = Marlborough (founded 1843)

The College would be selling to a clearly-defined market niche–not that Soames and his allies would ever have expressed it in such coarse commercial terms. Secondary education before 1902 was confined exclusively to those able to pay for it. Schools like Brighton College were academically selective. Just as important, they imposed social as well as financial and academic tests. In the words of the first Principal, the school was 'designed for persons moving in the upper ranks of society'. That alone explains why Soames and his fellow Council members could not contemplate sending their sons to any of the eleven Sussex grammar schools. It was not the distance to Steyning or Lewes that counted against them, but their admission of the sons of shopkeepers and tenant farmers.

Like the new Liverpool, Cheltenham and Marlborough Colleges, Brighton would have no charitable element within the foundation, funded from the pockets of local benefactors, to educate a fixed number of free scholars. Deliberate social stratification within English education had begun in the later 18th century, when the grammar schools began to exclude their (free) foundation scholars. To that tradition the proprietary schools were true heirs. Although almost all stated they were establishments for the sons of noblemen and gentlemen, that must not be taken at face value. None succeeded in attracting much ancient blue blood. The old aristocracy could rarely be wooed away from the ancient public school. Talk of noblemen should be seen as an attempt to impress the College's real target customers: gentlemen.

What does that word mean? As a term, it was even then as vague in definition as it was common in use. Many fathers in the College's early admission registers are so classified, but it is probable that few came from the old squirearchy. If, despite its occassional fantasies, Brighton College was not to be a school for the aristocracy and county gentry, for whom then did it cater? The registers are of little help but, fortunately, the Principal supplied the Council with a near-complete occupational breakdown of parents:

Table 1.2: Parental Occupations, March 1850

	Boarders	Day scholars
Anglican clergyman	22	6
country gentleman	13	
Indian civil service	11	2
naval/army officer	12	4
solicitor	11	13
merchant	8	
barrister	7	4
widow	5	
county banker	4	
College master	3	1
physician	2	4
MP	1	
architect	1	
manufacturer	1	
retired businessman	1	4
house agent		3
widow keeping school		2
other	3	15
Total	105	58

Brighton College parents were the same men as the lay members of the Council. The school was educating the sons of the respectable (professional) middle classes, the kind of people who, if local residents, were moving into recent housing developments like Montpelier Villas and Crescent, Clifton Terrace, Park Crescent and Powis Square. Some of the new schools even targeted a particular profession: Marlborough, Rossall and Bradfield advertising a bias to the sons of the Anglican clergy, Epsom the sons of doctors. Brighton never forged such a link, although concessionary fees were offered to the sons of the clergy in the early 1880s and again from c.1899, this time with a similar deal for 'the sons of naval and military officers'.

One major occupational area is, however, conspicuous by its absence from the Principal's analysis: trade, that dread activity never to be mentioned in drawing rooms. Early in 1846, the infant College had sought advice from the five-year-old proprietary Cheltenham College on where to draw the social boundary for admissions. What made a 'gentleman' was as much debated in the 19th as it had been in the 18th century. Certainly the term had ceased to be applied exclusively to the landed gentry, and had broadened to include an expanding bourgeois component of bankers, lawyers, doctors and even merchants. That, of course, only muddied the waters further. As Tennyson lamented in 1850: 'the grand old name of gentleman has been defamed and soiled in this land'. Cheltenham's secretary sent detailed advice which Brighton's founders seem to have followed to the letter: 'Gentlemen of small fortune, but of good family' should be welcomed. The crucial group to exclude, he advised, were 'the Sons of Wealthy Tradesmen ... Had we admitted tradesmen in any instance, we must have done so almost without limit–and in the confined circle of shops in Cheltenham, we should have had the sons of gentlemen shaking hands, perhaps, with school-fellows behind the counter, and a fusion of ranks taking place from which the Gentlemen of decided rank and property would derive even less inconvenience, possibly than the Clergymen of confined income or Half-pay Officers'. Character, not the size of the pocket, must be one fundamental. Paternity rather than ability must be the other. Of course, the drawing of a precise line proved as impossible for the College as the country. The third principal sought clarification from the Council in 1862 and, after debate, they permitted him to admit 'the sons of wholesalers, although not of retailers'. Even when the talisman 'for the sons of noblemen and gentlemen' was dropped in 1878, nothing had changed. Five years later, the Council rejected a proposal to accept the sons of tradesmen and it is clear that this policy operated until the bankruptcy of 1893 finally forced a change of policy. The Council itself knew their decree could not be absolute, and conceded in 1862 that the principal should 'use his own discretion on the merits of each case'. From the little we know, a theatre manager was judged beyond the pale, while the manager of a (large) hotel, a (royal) silversmith, a wine merchant and a brewer were all in the 1850-60s deemed capable of being gentlemen. Little by little, therefore, both the concept and its definition moved (like the vote) down the social scale.

The ethos was clear and, as far as was possible, the market defined. Next they needed funds and premises. Substantial capital would be required to found and build a school capable of teaching the new curriculum and rivalling the old public schools. Given that a single munificent benefactor for any school was unlikely, there were two ways to raise the sum necessary: by private subscription or by the sale of shares. Woodard set up Lanc-

---

THE BRIGHTONIAN

FEBRUARY, 1959

EDITORIAL

In *Punch* of September 18th, 1858, appeared these two paragraphs:

SELECT ACADEMY AT BRIGHTON

" We understand that there is at Brighton an Academy which some of our readers might patronise by recommending other people to send their children to it. To this School, a distinguished actor sent his little boy a few months ago. The other day the Master called on the actor to say that he could no longer receive the said little boy, as he had just discovered the nature of his father's profession, and it would injure him among his connections, clergymen and others, were it known that his School contained the son of an actor. He had nothing to say against the boy, who was as good and gentlemanlike a boy as he had ever known.

" What a very select Academy! How much more select a seminary than Eton, Winchester, or any of our Public Schools! We are afraid it is too select for most of our readers to think of sending any boys of their own there. But some of them—perhaps all of them—may know some great snobs, fathers of snobbish families, they may confidently recommend the great snobs to send their little snobs to this select Academy at Brighton, of which the Master expelled the son because the father is an actor. There those little snobs will meet with other little snobs and sons of snobs, who will all, doubtless, be carefully educated in the principles of snobbery."

ing and his other schools by the former route. Soames and his supporters opted for the latter. If to our minds it is an extraordinary notion that a school could be a business company in which shares are bought and sold, to our early Victorian ancestors the idea was both natural and sensible. Like Brighton, Cheltenham, Rossall and Malvern all began as proprietary institutions. At Brighton, each share would cost £25, permitted the nomination of one pupil at any given moment and carried one vote at the annual general meeting of the company, where the governing Council was elected and rules made. Ladies were permitted to vote only by proxy and no individual was permitted to own more than four shares. Sons of non-shareholders would be admitted, but only with the special permission of the Council 'for the purpose of filling up the vacancies should a proprietor fail to nominate', and at an annual premium of £10.

Share ownership by a parent, relative or friend did not bring automatic entry to the school. Prospective pupils had to pass an entrance test in Latin, Greek, reading, writing and the first four rules of arithmetic. Surviving correspondence indicates that failure, even for the sons of the nobility, was not unknown; Macleane rejected a son of the Earl of Leven in October 1847 when he was found 'ignorant of the rudiments of Latin (Greek he has never attempted)'. And there would still be fees to pay: £20 per year for dayboys in the Junior Department, £25 in the Senior (raised in 1854 to £30 if over 17 years); £45 to £65 per year if a boarder, depending on which of the masters' or dames' houses parents chose for their son's lodgings. All figures were exclusive of books and extras: drawing, singing, Italian, Hebrew or Urdu, each of which cost half a guinea per term. Fee levels could themselves be a reason to pick a proprietary school. The architect Sir Thomas Jackson (1850-3) was sent to Brighton College rather than to Harrow, as originally intended, 'because my father [a solicitor] feared the expense'. These sums need, however, a contemporary context. A line regiment subaltern then received £82 per annum, his lieutenant colonel £328 and a major-general £1,095. In the church, a vicar's average income was £300 per annum, a bishop's was £6,700 and the Vicar of Brighton earned £1,041. By contrast, a butler was paid £25-50 per annum and a skilled worker £60-73. An annual season ticket from Brighton to London cost £100.

There seems never to have been any thought of the school beginning only when funds had already been raised, a site purchased and buildings erected. In May 1846, the Council took a three-year lease, at 137 guineas per year, on Lion House, the mansion of 1824-5 at the head of Portland Place. Nineteenth-century Brighton became famous for the legion of educational establishments it could boast. Portland Place was fast becoming an educational ghetto: the 1848 Brighton Directory lists two ladies' academies, a boarding school and a 'preparatory school for gentlemen' as located there. Teaching began in January 1847. But Lion House was only a stop-gap. In September 1846, the Council was of the opinion 'that some portion of the Buildings or Ground of the Palace would be desirable (as being central) for the site of the College'. The Royal Pavilion was then up for sale and Lord Alfred Hervey MP, a College Vice President and a junior Treasury minister, was asked 'to ascertain the intentions of the Government in reference to the disposal of the Palace at Brighton'. His enquiries proved promising:

> I can at once state for the information of the Council of the Brighton College, that it *is* the intention of the Government to dispose of the Pavilion by sale–I think, however, that if any part of the existing structure could be available for the College it might, at the proper time, be purchased at

a very moderate sum as it stands; as the materials, if the Pavilion should be pulled down, would fetch a very small price. By November, the Council was talking of 'an immediate application ... for a Portion of the Palace Grounds'.

Very fortunately, the Queen was not minded to dispose of her seaside Pavilion at the knock-down price Lord Alfred suggested and it was bought by the town for £50,000. Thank goodness Brighton College could not afford it. Beyond the impossibility of upkeep, and the decay that would thus have been inevitable to the exterior, think what generations of bursars and boys would have done to the interior! Instead, the Council had to look around for an area of open land on which to build, which forced them to the edges of the town as it then was. They drew up a shortlist of (as far as we know) four possible locations: one somewhere to the north of St Peter's;

Share certificate of the first Principal

Lion House, Portland Place

eight acres near Black Rock belonging to the Earl of Abergavenny (probably on the cliffs above where the Marina now stands); the block of land bounded now by Walpole Road, Belle Vue Gardens and Eastern Road, which currently has the Junior School at one end and Hawkhurst Court at the other; and the one they finally selected in January 1848. The chosen site was but part of the College estate as we know it today. Situated in one of those dry valleys where the Downs drop towards the sea, delightfully named Bakers Bottom, the land was then divided between market gardens and sheep pasture, located on the Eastern Lane close to but not part of the then highly fashionable Kemp Town, a semi-independent adjunct to Brighton. There was plenty of space. Healthy sea air would sweep in from the promenade. The neighbourhood was genteel. And it may not have been irrelevant that most of the key governors lived close by. Soames' own villa, Tramore Lodge, looked over the valley from what is now Freshfield Road. The Kemp Town area was perhaps a foregone conclusion.

The strange layout of land tenure in Brighton, a visible link back to the medieval strip system, meant that the valley was divided from east to west into a myriad of long narrow 'paul-pieces'. By good fortune, the southernmost 18 were owned by only three gentlemen, comprising together an area of 8.5 acres. These the Council secured leasehold for 99 years in 1847, with right of purchasing the freehold—an option exercised four years later. When it was intended that the school contain 600 pupils, this was an exceptionally tiny site. Malvern began with 14 acres and Lancing with 230, although Cheltenham had initially only 6.7 acres. Subsequent protracted negotiations increased the estate to 11 acres, but every generation has bemoaned the acute shortage of space. Lack of funds to purchase more land during the very brief period it was still available (i.e. up to 1859, when the development of Canning Street began) was part of the reason. The other was William Percival Boxall of nearby Belle Vue Hall who owned rights over most of the rest of the valley and, for reasons unknown, put obstacle after obstacle in the way of the Council for 35 years as it attempted to push northwards and eastwards.

Land had, however, been found and attention could turn to the erection of build-ings. As was then reasonably common with a public project, the Council in January 1848 placed advertisements announcing an architectural competition to design a day and boarding school for 600 boys aged from nine to twenty years. Twenty-one entries were submitted. Runner up and recipient of a 30-guineas premium was the local archi-tect George Somers Clarke. Alas we do not have his design, but his two (later) public buildings in the town show his talent: the (now demolished) Asylum for the Blind further along Eastern Road which was a delectable essay in Venetian Gothic, pure Ruskin, while the Swan Downer Charity School in Dyke Road is so fine a piece of Germanic Gothic as to be of fairy-tale quality. The competition was awarded to George Gilbert Scott, later knighted, the most prolific of High Victorian architects, creator of the Albert Memorial, the Foreign Office, Glasgow University, Bombay University, the *Midland Hotel* at St Pancras Railway Station, St Mary's Cathedral in Edinburgh, and the builder or restorer of a host of churches up and down the kingdom. In 1848, he was not yet a household name, but neither was he any longer obscure. Scott was a workaholic, unable to refuse just one more job or competition. As he himself put it, 'Never pick your subjects. Go in for whatever is on offer, whether you like it or not'.

As always, entries in the competition were submitted anonymously under a pseudo-nym or sign, with the key to that device in a separate, sealed envelope. We can thus

The only extant design rejected by the 1848 competition

SOUTH - WEST - VIEW - OF - BRIGHTON - COLLEGE

WITH PRINCIPALS, VICE-PRINCIPALS AND BOARDING-HOUSES

Gilbert Scott's winning design for Brighton College

presumably dismiss the possibility that the Council picked Scott deliberately, even though one of their own number, Dr. Samuel King Scott, was the architect's younger brother; the doctor was not a member of the sub-committee supervising the competition. We can, however, presume that Gilbert's designs stood out from every other entry for recently he had discovered Pugin, the Camden Society and a wholly new attitude to Gothic architecture: the gospel of a pure, archaeologically correct style, wholly distinct from anything previously attempted. In the opinion of the Council, Scott's proposals were 'the most eligible both in point of Architectural style and internal arrangement ... combining so many excellencies and so completely realising the[ir] wishes'. What he offered, and what they accepted, was a design in the style of the second half of the 13th century, at an estimated cost of £58,000. For 1848, their choice was progressive, even *avant-garde* (which cannot be said of subsequent works commissioned by any of their successors).

From the start, competitors knew that only part of their scheme would be built initially. The Council had suggested £12,000 would be available for the first instalment, and had all 600 shares been sold, there would have been a building capital of £15,000. But shares sales had not been brisk and were already dwindling. The uncomfortable reality the Council faced was that sales had actually realised only £7,034 by December 1848. Thus they had to inform Scott that only half the advertised sum would be available, sufficient only to erect the central building in his scheme, a block of classrooms and studies for the senior masters, which today is known by the prosaic name 'the Main Building'. Wasting no time, tenders were invited and building work began during June, almost three years to the day from the first formal meeting at the National School. Funds remained problematic throughout. Share take-up continued to drop away and in October 1849 the 3 per cent consoles in which part of the capital had been invested showed a loss of 8 per cent. Thus, late in the day, the lean-to pentice along the south front was dropped to save £664; the corbels from which its arches would have sprung are clearly visible to this day.

In every sense, however, Brighton College already existed. In Lion House, teaching had begun on 26 January 1847. Now, 17 months later, there were 126 pupils and here was an opportunity to put the young school on display. So, a day of ceremony and celebration was held on 27 June 1848. Proceedings began in the Town Hall with College Prizegiving. According to *The Brighton Gazette*, 'the hearty cheering with which each successful candidate was greeted by his fellow students exhibited a fine tone of feeling'. Next, the senior praepositor (prefect), James Carey (1847-9), subsequently Archdeacon of Essex, read Greek and Latin verses of his own composition to mark the occasion. These the *Gazette* reporter could not evaluate and instead commented that they 'appeared to give those present who were competent to judge a high opinion of the classical standard of the College'. Elevating speeches were, of course, *de rigueur*. The principal waxed purple about the new building and its architect. 'The Churches and Colleges he had been or might be privileged to raise were associated with everlasting principles, with influences which knew no bounds of time or space'. The Dean of Chichester declared that 'a more gentlemanly body of youths he had never seen and to this point, the *Gazette* asserted, 'he attached great importance'. At that point in the proceedings, carriages were called and everyone adjourned to Bakers Bottom for the Bishop to lay the foundation stone, the boys marching six in a line behind the masters. On site, the College choir chanted Psalm 127 and Bishop Gilbert, assisted by

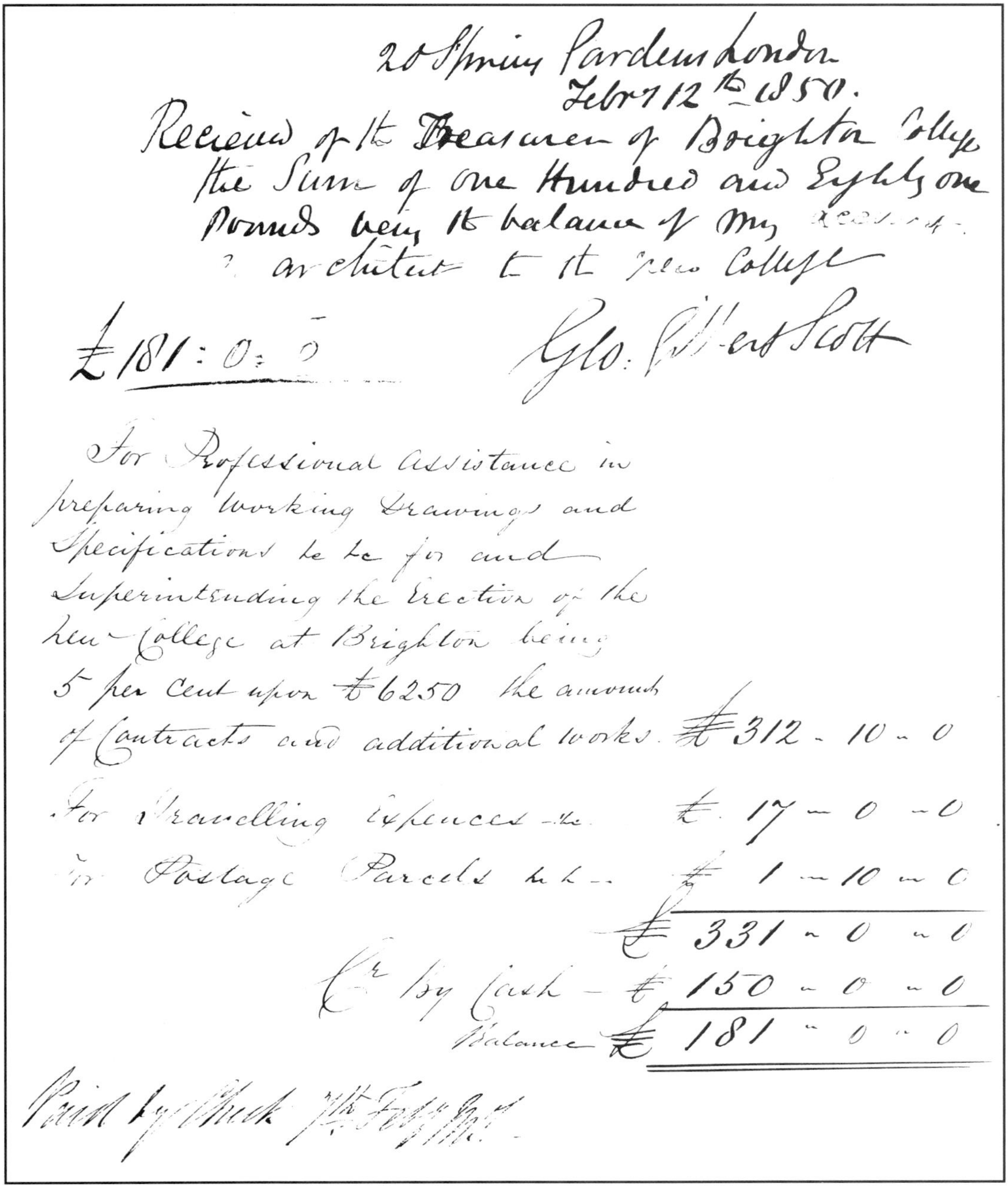

[handwritten bill reproduction]

20 Spring Gardens London
Febry 12th 1850.

Recieved of the Treasurer of Brighton College
the Sum of One Hundred and Eighty one
Pounds being the balance of My Account
? architect to the New College

£181 : 0 : 0   Geo: Gilbert Scott

For Professional Assistance in
preparing working drawings and
Specifications &c &c for and
Superintending the Erection of the
New College at Brighton being
5 per Cent upon £6250 the amount
of Contracts and additional works.   £ 312 - 10 - 0

For Travelling Expences &c   £ 17 - 0 - 0
in Postage Parcels &c &c   £   1 - 10 - 0
                                  ────────────────
                                  £ 331 - 0 - 0
         Cr by Cash -   £ 150 - 0 - 0
              Balance   £ 181 - 0 - 0
                                  ════════════════

Paid by Check 7th Feby 1850

Gilbert Scott's bill

Gilbert Scott, used a specially engraved silver trowel to tap the great block into place. The choir sang again (Farrant's anthem 'Lord for Thy tender mercy's sake'). Prayers were said and the Bishop gave his blessing, together with an extra week to the Midsummer holiday of seven weeks. Everyone was, of course, delighted.

Cartoon drawn by a pupil of the procession to lay the foundation stone, 27 June 1848

Laying the foundation stone, 27 June 1848

Where is that stone? Over the years, people have searched fruitlessly for it, concluding that its inscription must have worn away. The newspaper reports reveal all: it is *inside* the south-west wall of the oriel porch to the Main Building. The stone itself carries no inscription, but underneath lies an engraved brass plate:

> The 1st stone of this College was laid
> On the 27th day of June
> A.D. MDCCCXLVIII
> By the Right Reverend Father in God
> Ashurst Turner Gilbert, D.D.
> Lord Bishop of Chichester

together with a bottle containing coins, papers connected with the College and a copy of *The Times* for the day. One year later, the lease on Lion House was given up and, even though the builders did not move out until September, the Main Building was occupied by staff and pupils for the start of term on 14 August. The sobre Macleane is reported as almost jumping with glee: 'Now we have got the building, thank God! We have got a College, and I am sure it will be our fault if Brighton College is not a blessing to the county.' On that day there were no festivities. No choirs sang. No bishop gave his blessing. Soames and Cornford and Smith, like their Principal, must nevertheless have given thanks. All was safely gathered in.

A selection of Scott's domestic windows [Photos: David Hollinshead]

– *Two* –

1847-1851

The slippery paths of youth

Lady Bracknell took comfort from the belief that 'in England at any rate, education produces no effect whatsoever. If it did, it would prove a serious danger to the upper classes'. At Lion House in Portland Place, around 200 people gathered on a crisp winter's morning in 1847 because they shared a belief in the effectiveness of education and the need of its transforming power on the upper classes. Assembled to mark the opening of Brighton College, the report of those proceedings in *The Brighton Gazette* records how speaker after speaker from the platform of 'influential persons connected with the Institution' addressed a theme which troubled the age of Sir Robert Peel–the want of character in the nation. The Earl of Chichester spoke of the dangers of a wealthy but uneducated gentry. The Principal focused on behaviour, asking whether there was 'any fatal necessity whereby a boy is compelled to be a ruffian'. The Bishop of Chichester urged the parents and boys before him to consider 'that it was not the quantity of knowledge, it was not so much stores of information, as the drawing out, the eliciting, the developing, the strengthening of the faculties of the mind, that should be the purpose of intellectual education'.

Academic success would not be the primary purpose of Brighton College. Nor would anyone (yet) preach the asinine notion, mouthed by Brookes in *Tom Brown's Schooldays* (1858), that it was better to win two housematches than a Balliol scholarship. Ability would in no sense be disparaged; quite the opposite. But the school's first duty was to be as a nursery of christian gentlemen. The nurturing of moral and religious principles was the chief goal of their theory of schooling. The efficacious power of education, on individuals and then on the kingdom, would be its ability to form and mould character. And thus, as the Principal observed, the right kind of school was critical, since 'surely those walls with which are associated the voice of our earliest instruction and development of our earliest feelings are not mere stone'.

For Brighton College, that above all meant its link with the established church. The diocesan bishop was to be its patron, the vicar of Brighton a vice patron. Half of the governing Council were Anglican clergymen. Except for 'teachers of oriental literature and modern languages' (who would be part-time), every member of the teaching staff was required to be a member of the Church of England. As for the Principal, he must be both an ordained cleric and a graduate of Oxford, Cambridge, Durham or Trinity College Dublin (i.e. the Anglican universities). Why Kings College London, which had been teaching for 15 years, was omitted from the list remains inexplicable; Durham had opened its doors only in 1832. But the omission of University College London was most deliberate. From its foundation in 1826, it had outraged many with its exclusion of religious teaching and its refusal to associate with any denomination. Brighton College would have nothing to do with 'the godless of Gower Street'. On such fundamentals the early College was unbending. This was a school which began and ended its day with corporate worship, which went to church on Ascension Day, where boarders attended formal prayers before going to bed and where (until 1888) Council meetings began with prayer. When in 1859 the Principal asked the Council if he could admit two Jewish boys 'of good family', he was instructed to do so 'only provided they submit to the whole discipline of the College'.

If we are to understand Brighton College in its first thirty to forty years, the religious basis of its mission is the point from which we must start. Further, we must recognise the particular Anglican churchmanship which underpinned its ethos. As already noted, Soames was a firm church evangelical. The Rev. Henry Venn Elliott of St Mary's Chapel Rock Gardens (Vice President 1845-65) is held to have been the leader of the church evangelical party in Brighton; his sister was the redoubtable hymn writer, Charlotte Elliott. Stoutly he upheld the principles not only of his illustrious ancestor the Rev. John Venn and the Anglican ginger-group the Clapham Sect which he had led, but of his own mentor the almost legendary the Rev. Charles Simeon. Sir Thomas Blomefield (Vice President 1845-58) was the Brighton Secretary of the Society for the Better Observance of the Sabbath, and Vice President of the Brighton and East Sussex Auxiliary Religious Tract Society; Soames and Edward Polhill (Council 1845-51) were members of its committee. Another Council member, Rev.James Vaughan (1845-54), incumbent of Christ Church Montpelier Road, was the last Brighton cleric to preach wearing a black gown and Geneva bands.

The College President, the third Earl of Chichester (1845-86), was President of both focal organisations for church evangelicals: The British and Foreign Bible Society and The Church Missionary Society, of which the Rev. Henry Elliott and the Rev. Frederick Reade (Council 1845-54) were the local secretaries. These were men of wealth whose morality was rooted in the doctrinal certainties of personal salvation and the atoning power of the cross. Driven by the parable of the sheep and the goats, they knew themselves personally accountable to God. Their religion was outward-looking. While they devoted much time to prayer and Bible study, they were zealous philanthropists. Evangelical in religion and Conservative in politics, men like this fought slavery and worked to improve factory conditions. Until 1861, the Council's annual report always ended with direct acknowledgement of the College's dependence on 'the Sovereign Disposer of events ... well knowing that without His grace there is no excellency, no usefulness, no safety' (1849, 1847). Not until Christmas Term 1902 did the College choir wear surplices. The authorities long regarded amateur dramatics as immoral.

When the Council selected the first Principal and Vice Principal in the summer of 1846, they naturally chose men of the same persuasion. The latter (Henry Cotterill) had as a youth been guided by that most redoubtable of evangelical writers Hannah More, a close friend of his mother. He himself gave up a brilliant career at Cambridge to work in India with the Church Missionary Society. These were anxious days for evangelicals. England was gripped by one of its periodic outbursts of 'no popery', rooted in anxieties about what the Oxford Movement was doing to the nation and whipped to a frenzy by secessions to Rome, most notably John Henry Newman in October 1845. When the College Council selected the Rev. Arthur Macleane in

August 1846, his cause must have been strengthened by one of his testimonials reporting, 'It may not be impertinent to add that he is strongly opposed to certain theological opinions, which, in not a few instances, have lately terminated in avowed Romanism.'

The Council were acting to preserve the Protestant heritage. The choice of Principal was of the utmost importance. Whoever was selected had to be a man of vision, able to inspire and to lead. He had to take the new school and make it a success. He had to make for it a name. The man chosen was aged 34, educated at Winchester (where he was Captain) and Trinity College Cambridge, a proud Scot, married and about to be ordained priest. By our standards he was young. We know that he was youthful in appearance—so much so that Brighton shopkeepers are said to have thought him one of the pupils. But we are the ones who would

Rev. Arthur Macleane

be wrong. All eight College Principals and Headmasters selected before 1914 were aged under forty on appointment. Belcher (1881) and Dawson (1906) were also 34; Bigg (1871) was 30 and Titherington (1895) but twenty-nine. This was no Brighton quirk. Percival was 27 when selected inaugural Headmaster of Clifton (1862), Arnold was 33 when appointed to Rugby (1827). Macleane's testimonials agreed that he was 'a sound and accurate scholar' and possessed of 'a high character for energy and intelligence'. The renowned geologist Professor Sedgwick wrote that he was 'a man of unusual energy of character' and commended his 'knowledge of mankind gained by his converse with the world and its active duties'. Of his 'extremely accurate and elegant scholarship' there can be no doubt. He was placed first wrangler and fourth in the classical tripos of 1845 (i.e. a double first in Maths and Classics) and subsequently edited various classical texts, notably Juvenal, Persius and Horace.

Yet he was surely a curious choice? Out of a field of 42 candidates, at least four of whom were then serving headmasters, the Council picked a man who had never been in a classroom since he himself had left school. When we discover that the same was also true of the first Vice Principal and the third Principal (the Rev. John Griffith, 1856), it is a pattern which could not be imagined today and demands our attention. To launch a school thus would strike us as, at the very least, careless. But we do well to remember that their world was not ours. They did not think it necessary to interview any of the candidates either, not even the final shortlist; the first interviews for the principalship were not held until 1881. Everything was judged on open testimonials (the runners up were Harvey Goodwin, aged 28, subsequently Dean of Ely and Bishop of Carlisle; and George Jacob, aged 37, later Headmaster of Christ's Hospital). By definition then, a clergyman was a teacher. Beyond medicine and the law, training was effectively unknown.

These were still the days when commissions and promotions in the army were not gained by merit but obtained by purchase. In Macleane's case, his unusual background was, in all probability, regarded by the Council as his trump card. After Winchester, he had joined the East India Company, serving 11 years in the sub-continent first as Sheriff of Madras and then Secretary to the Madras Marine Board. When, however, his health had given way, he returned to England and entered Cambridge as a mature student. As Sedgwick noted, here was a man with practical experience of the world. To the utilitarian ethos of the proprietary school promoters, what could have been better?

Teaching began on 27 January 1847, the day after the opening ceremony. There were 47 boys, aged nine to eighteen. The balance of pupils in these earliest years was heavily towards the Junior Department. Two-thirds of the original 47 were aged fourteen or under. Of the 259 who joined between 1847 and 1849, the proportion in the Juniors was three-quarters:

Age Profile of Entrants, 1847-49

Senior Department		Junior Department	
age	number	age	number
19	1	14	32
18	3	13	41
17	12	12	33
16	19	11	35
15	27	10	29
		9	27
	62		197

One of those very first pupils, Professor Sir Thomas Holland (1847- 53), spoke of the 'primaeval days'. Holland reminds us now, as he did the Old Boys' dinner in 1885, how very different the College had to be in 1847:

> We were not a school at all. We had no traditions, no proper fellow-feeling ... We were, I might almost say, a mere set of unlicked cubs, and the difficulty was to put us in some sort of shape ... The first generation had to get on as well as it could.

In the College Archives survives a sprightly description of the College in Lion House from the same voice, this time written from the inside when Holland was 16 years old:

> The entrance to the building is up a broad flight of stone steps under a portico supported by a row of tall pillars. From the entrance hall—a door on the left led to a room over which was inscribed PRINCIPAL. If you had looked in you would probably have seen a dark man in cap and bands, etc., in an easy chair by a long paper-bestrewed table.
> A large room on the left contains the Upper Department, and a larger room the Lower, this latter is reached by a passage which is a continuation of the hall and on which open several small rooms for hats, etc. From the Hall a spiral staircase, whose well extends from the ground floor to a circular lantern in the roof, leads to successive semi-circular landings, on the first are—the Vice Principal's private room—and lecture room—the Council Room, the French and German rooms; on the second the Headmaster of the Lower Department has his private room and classroom, and other assistant classical masters and the mathematical tutor have their respective classrooms ...

Very soon, in consequence of some minor disturbances, an order of praepositors was created, chosen from the highest form who had certain privileges, and certain duties to perform towards maintaining order ...

At mid-summer prizes were distributed in the Lower room–Bishop present, etc. Speeches made–great was the glory of the affair ...

At the close of this half the School was invaded by mumps, ably seconded by influenza–these two produced such an effect on masters and boys that the chief occupants of the School rooms were bare benches–in consequence the half-yearly examination was postponed till after the Christmas holidays.

Macleane enjoyed one advantage permitted to none of his successors–the ability to select, apart from the Vice Principal, every assistant master on his staff. Inevitably he made some mistakes. The worst was undoubtedly the venomous Frederick Metcalfe, Headmaster of the Lower Department, whose vendetta against the Principal is investigated below. But Macleane also found some first-rate men. One was Joseph Newton, the twelfth wrangler of 1847, who stayed at the College until 1888, for the last 31 years as Vice Principal. Another was Thomas Ingram, sub-organist of Ely, whose presence from April 1847 as 'Professor of Music' added singing to the curriculum and music to chapel services. Most remarkable of all must be George Long who had been inaugural Professor of Ancient Languages at the University of Virginia, inaugural Professor of Greek and later Professor of Latin at University College London (which the College did not hold against him), and also co-founder and Honorary Secretary of the Royal Geographical Society. A scholar of international standing and a prolific author, he was Classical Lecturer at the College for 22 years from 1849. How Macleane secured so eminent a scholar remains a mystery but, supported by others, it was his presence that created and then sustained the formidable academic reputation which the young Brighton College rapidly acquired. When in 1881 Henry Cotterill, by that time Bishop of Edinburgh, looked back to the days of Macleane and Long, he claimed 'that the principles of Scholarship which were maintained

were of a superior kind to those which were at that time generally recognised in Public Schools'. Of Long himself, the bishop asserted that his teaching 'was not teaching for present success, not for mere success, but for ripened knowledge in mature life'.

That is borne out from the different perspective of one of Long's pupils, the architect Sir Thomas Jackson (1850-3). His *Recollections* single out from the staff only Macleane and Long for comment. Macleane he describes as

an excellent though formidable master ... rather an awful person who frightened us a good deal. I remember the scorn he would pour on the idiot editors who thought Horace's Lydia and Pyrrha and the rest were real women with whom he was really in love.

But it was Long who held Jackson's esteem. Long was a revolutionary teacher. When editor of *The Quarterly Journal of Education* in the 1830s, he had been a leading advocate of secondary school reform, in particular being violent in his condemnation of teaching within the public schools. At Brighton he had the opportunity to put his theories into practice. The effect his *avant-garde* style had on the young is self-evident:

> He was a dry, shrewd, old lawyer ... caustic and intolerant of nonsense, but he had a real genius for teaching, and the first made me read an ancient author as I should a modern one. On my first going up to him [aged 15] we read Thucydides and Terence. Afterwards, as was natural, he took us into Cicero, his own special subject, and we hunted down that rascal Verres with as much zest as if we had him up in Bow Street or before a judge of the assize. Finding I could draw a bit he set me to copy and catalogue a collection of Graeco-Sicilian coins–or, I should say, sulphur casts of them–from which he would illustrate the subject as each town came up in the course of our study. All this helped us much to realise the actuality of what we were reading about, whereas in the hands of many teachers, it would have remained mere dry bones of words and grammar.

Macleane's staff raise an important issue. Traditional explanations of the rise of the 19th-century public school assert unequivocally the primacy of the influence of Dr. Arnold. A few of the Victorian foundations were indeed little Rugbys, established like monastic daughter houses by staff or pupils who had worked under and imbibed from the good doctor. Rossall took Marlborough as its model, and Marlborough was based on Rugby. But Thomas Holland's reference to 'minor disturbances' which then led to 'an order of praepositors' is most revealing. While it is true that Rugby used that word for its prefects, they were so central to the Arnoldian method that a school established without them must have been unthinkable to any of his acolytes. We have already observed that Brighton looked to Cheltenham.

Neither had a prefectorial system at their beginning. None of the Brighton College Council had any connection with Rugby. Of the seven full-time academic staff under Macleane, three were (like their Principal) products of Winchester. One had been educated at Shrewsbury and another at Macclesfield Grammar School. Two alone had sat at the feet of Arnold: John Smith and George Cotterill. But both were junior masters and both left in 1851. If any school had real influence on early Brighton College, it was Winchester–as was the case with Bradfield and with Woodard's schools. It is very wrong to see the Victorian public schools as of a single tradition, all clones of Rugby.

The school year was, as would then have been the norm, divided into two terms, known as 'halfs'–a system which lasted at Brighton until 1867. The school day began at 9 a.m. with Mattins, followed by lessons until noon when there was an hour's break before lunch. Some played

Professor George Long

games, some worked, some read—the choice was left to the individual. Wednesdays and Saturdays were half holidays and those afternoons were again voluntary time, used for collecting butterflies or fossils or walking on the Downs as much as for playing football or cricket. The other four afternoons saw classes resume at 2 p.m. and continue until 5 p.m. (4 p.m. in November and December), when the day concluded with Evensong. Dayboys were then free to go home, unless they were in the VIth form and therefore preparing for university entrance. In that case, classed as 'half boarders', they stayed on for dinner and had a one-hour lesson with the Principal at 8 p.m. Because of the sizeable dayboy population, there were never pre-breakfast lessons.

Daily and Sunday services posed a tricky problem. Until 1859 the College did not have its own chapel. Neither could the College use the nearby churches, St George's and St Mary's, for both were proprietary chapels. Their pews were thus rented out to locals who thereby enjoyed the exclusive use of 'their' seat; to pay pew-rent was a status symbol. To the rescue came the Rev. Henry Venn Elliott in his capacity as perpetual curate of St Mary's, making arrangements for the College to have use of the adjacent Lecture Room leased to his own church by the College Vice Patron Colonel Wyndham. This the Council had duly 'fitted up for the purpose of divine worship' and licensed by the bishop. At the beginning of every school day, and at the end of the 'non-halfs', the entire College processed down to Rock Gardens for chapel. St Mary's wanted its Lecture Room back by August 1849 and for about a year the College trooped instead to the Royal Pavilion Chapel. The sale of the Pavilion estate in 1850 ejected the College again. Exasperated by such impermanence, as well as the inconvenience of the twice-daily trek, Macleane obtained the Council's permission to use the Main Building's large first-floor vaulted chamber. Although it would remain the school library and Council Chamber, it was converted into a chapel under the guidance of Gilbert Scott. The adaptation must have worked well for, to this day, the room has a natural ecclesiastical feel about it. The saga of temporary chapels provides another reminder of the 'church evangelical' nature of the foundation. Woodard would never have permitted such a situation. But then, the focus of Brighton College's chapel was its pulpit, not its altar. There were no candles, no robed choir, no auricular confession. 'Communion' was celebrated from the north end of the 'table', once a month.

Nobody lived in Lion House except the College porter, Joshua Ponton (1847-59). Boarding pupils lived either in the private house of one of the masters or in one of three 'dames houses', inspected and licensed by the Council; all were in Portland Place or on Marine Parade. College approval was necessary to check more than feeding and laundry. The earliest prospectuses made the specific statement that, in all houses, the fee 'includes a separate bed for each boy'. In 17th- and 18th-century boarding schools it was absolutely normal, even for the rich and titled, for boys to sleep two (or more) to a bed—as they did at home too. From the 1770s, attitudes began to change and separate beds became available, at an extra charge. In the stricter moral climate of the 1840s, that would not do and a care to prevent homosexuality became one of the distinctive features which marked out the new from the old public schools. During the next sixty years or so, anxieties about childhood sexuality would grow to alarming proportions.

The system of living out lasted a long time. While the first on-site House opened in 1853 with the Principal as its master, there would not be another until thirty years later. Pressure to gather all the boys into the private houses of College masters began to be exercised from the 1850s. Licensed dames houses nevertheless remained a feature of life until sometime in the 1870s.

Macleane resigned in January 1851 having held office for less than three and a half years. Arguably, his 41 months were the most critical in the College's history. Had the Council chosen well when selecting their first Principal? Of his attainments as a scholar and of his commitment, his devotion to the school, its welfare and its progress, there can be no doubt. His friend the eminent Professor Long wrote 'I have never known anyone who had a more genuine love of the best writers of antiquity, or a juster judgement in duly appreciating them'. Joseph Newton, appointed to the staff by Macleane and, from 1857 to 1888, Vice Principal, testified that the school 'owes a very great deal to him for the way he nursed it in its infancy, and impressed upon it his own character.' While we need not doubt Newton's sincerity, those words were spoken in the charged atmosphere of a nostalgia-tinged Old Boys' dinner in 1881. Macleane was a difficult man to work with. Disputes were an almost permanent feature of his reign. During 1847, a series of disagreements developed between the Council and their Principal, some over trivial matters such as the date of the summer vacation, or regulations for academic dress. More serious was their difference over leaving scholarships tenable at the universities (very much the norm in pre-grant days; the way student funding is currently under attack, something schools should consider reviving). When on top of these disputes there developed a serious difference of opinion over staffing levels, the first cracks began to appear in their relationship.

The Rev. Joseph Newton, sketched by Walter McCowan (1881-86, Master 1911-30)

Macleane identified the fundamental problem as being 'the freedom of communication between the Council and Principal'. The latter never attended the former's meetings. Company rules did provide for the Council to invite the Principal to a free conference, but Macleane found the procedure 'to be inoperative'. From the tone of what is recorded, it seems that each party rarely communicated with the other except on paper–no wonder it was easy for misunderstandings to develop! As ever, Macleane spoke candidly, telling the Council that (as was inevitable) he found the resolutions which formed their replies 'curtly put and destitute of explanation'. This was no way to do business, yet the obvious solution–allowing the Principal to attend Council meetings, with or without a vote–was specifically rejected, thereby ensuring ongoing dissension.

Not everything can be blamed on Byzantine procedures. The troubles of 1847 reveal that Macleane was a man over-sensitive to criticism:

> For my own part all my thoughts are wrapped up in this College–it is my one idea–and on the strength of this, and of the obvious fact that in a new institution slight modifications of previous rules or previous understandings must be occasionally necessary, I must respectfully beg to be exempt from a hypercritical examination of my mode of carrying out the system of instruction which, as I myself devised it, none are more interested in carrying out in all its integrity than myself or more likely to do so.

Every one of these disputes was jurisdictional, concerning the power and authority of the Principal. Macleane was insecure. Soon after Easter 1849, there erupted a titanic and exceedingly public quarrel between the Principal and the Headmaster of the Lower Department, Rev.Frederick Metcalfe. From what can be reconstructed, it seems that these two had joined battle within six months of Lion House opening. In November of that year, Macleane, having decided that Metcalfe had 'no warm interest' in his position, urged his Headmaster 'to take advantage of any opening that may occur to vacate your office'. According to the account in *The Brighton Herald* (which took Metcalfe's side), Macleane's dissatisfaction stemmed from the Headmaster considering the offer of another post. *The Herald* reported that Macleane decided Metcalfe was not considering the question according to 'high spiritual considerations', but upon 'which salary might be the most lucrative of the two situations' (his Brighton salary was £300pa). The Headmaster was 'trifling with his office from considerations of private interest'. When Metcalfe did not take the Principal's hint to leave, Metcalfe's version has it that Macleane pursued him relentlessly, trying 'to reduce me to an almost servile position' and 'to lower me in the estimation of the Junior Masters'. The final straw for Metcalfe was the rejection of his claim for a pay rise. Presumably believing that the Council had been influenced against him by the Principal, he threatened publication in May 1849 of the sheaf of correspondence that had hurled between them, whereupon Macleane dismissed him on the spot. The Principal's version of events does not survive, but *The Brightonian* of December 1852 contains, again from the pen of young Holland, an astute summary of the contest:

> This had been brewing for a long time, the Headmaster asserting his independent authority over the Lower Department, and the Principal treating him only as one of the masters under him; the papers were filled with statements of Mr. Metcalfe's grievances, parallel columns contrasting the Principal's words and acts, etc., and in person he canvassed among the proprietors. Macleane dismissed him and he managed to get a [special] general meeting of the proprietors called to consider his case and

take away the power of arbitrary dismission from Macleane but there not making a clear case the meeting was adjourned sine die. So ended the affair, but the discussion of the Principal's conduct, etc., gave the College a blow which it took long to recover from. On Mr. Metcalfe's dismission, Mr. Swayne also resigned... The office of Headmaster of the Lower Department was abolished.

What are we to make of this extraordinary breach? Belcher's *History* (*Brightonian* 1948) never mentioned it, but accepted that Macleane 'perhaps was a difficult man to work with'. Burstow's 1957 *History* ducked the question, noting only that, while Metcalfe 'apparently took an exaggerated view of his own powers and rights', Macleane's 'relations with his colleagues were not always happy'. Before we can come to any judgment, the enquiry must be broadened. Holland reported another master as resigning in protest or in solidarity. He was Rev. George Swayne, Fellow of Corpus Christi College Oxford and later a master at Harrow. Swayne's thinking remains unknown, but back in 1846 he had applied to be Vice Principal of Brighton College and (whether he knew it or not) had reached the final shortlist. When to that curious detail is added the even more singular fact that Metcalfe had also been a candidate, not only for that place but for the Principal's as well, the potential for mischief becomes an obvious possibility. Equally, one has to question Macleane's wisdom in appointing these gentlemen as assistants under him. In fact, he actually appointed another of the unsuccessful candidates for the Vice Principalship (Walter Awdry), which meant that half the body of assistant masters during the period 1847-9 had bid for high office within the school. What was the man about?

In as much as they passed any judgment, Belcher and Burstow were critical of Macleane while saying nothing of Metcalfe. The latter was eight years younger than the Principal, a Fellow of Lincoln College Oxford and had been a schoolmaster for four years, at the Wesleyan Proprietary School and then The City of London School. If we know nothing of his character before Macleane sacked him, there is plenty to tell of his subsequent years at Lincoln College and in their parish of St Michael's Oxford, where he was vicar (1849-85). As an academic, he became known for works on Scandinavian and Icelandic sagas; he tried unsuccessfully for the Rawlinson Chair of Anglo-Saxon. But within the College and parish, he exhibited patterns of behaviour all too reminiscent of what had happened at Brighton. He figures frequently in the pages of V.H.H. Green's *Commonwealth of Lincoln College* (1979) 'often at loggerheads with his colleagues'. The fellows found him 'irascible and tiresome ... an ardent and litigious upholder of his rights'. At one point when College Bursar, he refused to pay any salaries. Green describes him as 'crabbed', states that at St Michael's he 'created almost as much dissention in the parish as he did in the College', and reports Lincoln rumour 'that he had once killed a man in a fight'.

Macleane was difficult, but Metcalfe was impossible. No wonder the Principal wanted to get rid of him. Possessed of an overweening sense of his own significance, Metcalfe was bellicose, vindictive and shameless; he even applied to the Council in 1851 for a testimonial. When such a man had aspired to the Principal's chair and been rejected, he should never have accepted (or been offered) an appointment under his vanquisher. Once together, such temperaments would convulse the infant College. Their animus could bring only ruin, to themselves and to the school. Metcalfe was a muse of fire.

His appeal to the shareholders raised the temperature as much as his publication of the correspondence with Macleane. The shareholders probably knew next to nothing of this trial of strength, but at the very least a significant number felt that there was a case to be answered. Under Rule 17, a special general meeting could be summoned at the written request of 12 shareholders. Within three weeks of his dismissal, Metcalfe presented the College with the signatures of 37 proprietors, almost one quarter of the total. Among the names subscribed were Soames the founder, the Clerk to Brighton's Commissioners (Thomas Attree), the Clerk to the Brighton Vestry (Somers Clarke), the High Constable of Brighton (H.P. Tamplin) and four future College governors (Charles Carpenter, Rev. Thomas Holland, Dr. W. Kebbell and Rev. R.C. Hales). Metcalfe failed, however, to make his case before them. The meeting, held at the College on 16 June, was attended by 77 proprietors. A detailed report of the proceedings does not survive, but tempers do not seem to have flared and, on the proposal of Somers Clarke, a motion to 'adjourn *sine die*' was carried without opposition.

In the contest between Principal and Headmaster, the Council upheld their Principal throughout. We may guess, however, that this protracted affair sowed seeds of doubt in the minds of the governing body. Within eight months, they were locked into new and serious wrangles. This time, Macleane would not survive. To the boys writing *The Brightonian* of November 1852, it seemed that, throughout 1850, Macleane 'was always quarrelling with the Council'. Their perception shows us just how perilous the situation had become. Discontented with the College's situation, Macleane began pushing for fundamental changes. In an attack on 'the proprietary form of government' as an 'obstacle to the progress of the College', he observed that most parents did not buy a share, opting either for the £10 annual premium or seeking presentation via another shareholder. Of the 69 admissions of 1849, only seven had been presented on newly-purchased shares. Not only did that 'deny the very purpose of the shares which is to raise a capital fund for building'. The very share system, he argued, was seen as 'a fine upon entrance and many who would give it as a subscription in a good cause would not pay it to become a Proprietor'. In this outburst, he revealed more of himself than perhaps he realised.

> The Proprietary Constitution does not offer much hope of stability, but rather leads to the expectation of disturbances very damaging to the respectability of a school and public confidence in it ... That Proprietary form [should] be set aside and a small body of permanent Trustees and a Visitor be appointed.

Macleane's opinion surely reflects his experience at the hands of Metcalfe who had used the proprietary constitution to summon a shareholders' meeting in the hope that it would censure the Principal. The Council, however, were not prepared to entertain a proposal 'which goes utterly to dissolve the Constitution of the College'. Macleane had come to see the shareholders as a danger to his own position. Metcalfe might have failed to mobilize them against him, but others? Prickly from the start, the Principal had emerged from the Metcalfe business seemingly paranoid about his authority.

But Macleane had wider concerns. He presented the Council with an examination of 'those drawbacks which in the eyes of the parents act against the College'. Chief among those were its lack of buildings and 'the danger that arises from the temptations of the Town'. Founded at the start of a quarter century of economic development and social stability, the College should have been overwhelmed by parental demand. Yet that was not happening. Given the social base from which the school was prepared to draw, Macleane was correct in concluding that 'it is perfectly clear the town cannot support a College ... The great mass of the intended 600 boys must come from places other than Brighton'. In 1850, dayboys made up only 29 per cent of the College. The College roll had stopped growing and was beginning to drop back:

Numbers in College

	maximum number	total entrants	dayboy entrants	boarder entrants	leavers
1847	105	112	52	60	17
1848	153	78	35	43	37
1849	166	69	19	50	55
1850	147	57	18	39	82
1851	112	27	9	18	43

Admissions of dayboys and boarders were falling. The Metcalfe case, spread with tabloid-style relish across Brighton, wrought havoc with the College's local reputation. But a weakness in local recruitment was already present before Metcalfe's storm broke. While the restoration of the College's name in the town must be set in hand, Macleane had come to see the future as lying with boarders:

> I do not believe from experience that the Town of Brighton does or ever will contain the materials for a College of any importance, certainly not without the introduction of popular elements ... which would greatly lower the character.

His first priority was thus to tackle the College 'in its naked and incomplete condition' by building 'accommodation for the Principal and Masters and about 150 boarders, together with a Chapel and Schoolroom, according to the Original Plans'. As things stood in 1850,

> it would have been better to have kept the money for other purposes and remained in the private residence that served us for the same uses to which the new Building is devoted. That house, if it did not attract attention from its beauty, did not draw invidious notice upon the financial state of the College.

He had a point.

Of course, the Council wanted to push forwards too. But they did not agree that 'to stand still at this stage of our Existence is only to prepare for a retrograde movement'. They met with the Principal, discussed his proposals and set up a sub-committee. But eventually the full Council decided 'that it is not within their power, nor if it was that it would be expedient to enter upon such a scheme as that proposed by the Principal; or to recommend it for the consideration of the Proprietors'.

With a rectitude for finance of which Gladstone would have been proud, the Council refused to authorise further capital outlay given the state of the College roll and balance sheet. Indeed, one assistant master was made redundant and salaries over £200 per annum were cut by one-seventh.

The College as originally built, 1848-49

	income from		expenditure on		
	shares	*fees*	*buildings*	*salaries*	*other*
1846-50	£8,279	£12,437	£7,255	£10,767	£2,977

Undeterred, the Principal returned with a proposal to build one boarding house 'on the ground belonging to the College at his own cost and risk, provided the Council give him a guarantee for the purchase within a fixed time'. Again, he was turned down. Were the Council right in seeing any development as out of the question? When the College did not own the freehold to Bakers Bottom, their refusal to contemplate a mortgage was quite proper. So too was their determination that the company's first priority must be 'the absolute ownership of the land'–which they duly purchased the next year for £2,082 0s. 6d., plus fees. An appeal was also out of the question. Proprietary schools did not make appeals. In forming a company and offering shares, they had already made an appeal for support and to do so again was thought to admit weakness or even failure in the company. By contrast, Woodard's private schools depended entirely on donations and in his first year raised £27,000 (over two-thirds as much as Brighton generated from its shares). For all the differences, and these should not be underestimated, a proprietary school limiting even enthusiastic supporters to the purchase of a maximum of four shares (i.e. £100) cut itself off from the financial aid of well-wishers. The behaviour of the Bishop of Chichester illustrates this clearly. He was the diocesan for both Soames' and Woodard's schools. Of Brighton College he was the Patron, of Lancing and Hurstpierpoint the Visitor. Yet while he gave £25 towards building the Chapel and never bought a single Brighton share, he gave Woodard £100 a year for four years.

Two other routes were, however, open to a proprietary company wishing to raise additional capital. The maximum capital available to a proprietary school from its ordinary shares could never be enough to buy land and erect even the basic buildings required by a Victorian public school. If Brighton had sold all 600 shares by 1850, a capital of £15,000 would have been raised. Including interest, the sum actually collected was £8,279 (£11,943 had every pupil's parent purchased a share). Cheltenham fared slightly better, raising £9,500. But it did not then stand still. Rather, the company proceeded to bring in another £4,700 by issuing 4 per cent debentures on the school, sold to wealthy well-wishers. Malvern pursued a different but even more successful course. The proprietary company established a separate building company with 150 shares of £100 each. Within a year, all were sold and the building company proceeded to buy land and erect five boarding houses, which they rented to the school (at 6 per cent per annum) until, gradually, it could afford to buy out the building company and dissolve it.

Receipt for investing some of the share capital, 1846

Could Brighton College have done the same? Without doubt, the school had more than enough wealthy friends for us to feel certain that the answer must be 'yes'. Instead, Brighton College struggled on, stunted by chronic underfunding.

Each of these wrangles was a symptom of a creeping malaise brought on by the failure of initial hopes for the triumph of Brighton College. Now four years old, everyone recognised that all was far from well. Although they could not see it, the failure in dayboy demand stemmed from the social crisis which hit Brighton in the 1840s, with royal withdrawal and the arrival of excursion trains from London. The market from which the College was prepared to draw had certainly stopped growing, and had probably started to contract. Macleane put his finger on one fundamental:

> The College occupies no distinctive ground and appeals to no distinctive Interest or Classes but those to which Eton, Harrow, Rugby, Winchester, Westminster appeal. It has therefore to compete with those long established schools upon their own ground'. Ten years earlier, that would have been relatively easy, but reform was changing the landscape of the old public schools too, 'in favour of which a strong reaction has of late taken place owing among other causes to the great improvement in their moral tone and discipline.

Another factor was surely the foundation of rival new schools, locally at Lancing, nationally at Bradfield, Radley and Taunton. When Soames had rallied and recruited in 1845-6, Brighton College had enjoyed a Sussex monopoly. One further factor, which nobody seems to have spotted, was the high level of College fees in that increasingly competitive market. Tuition fees were £5 per annum higher in the Senior Department at Brighton than at Cheltenham, the proprietary college which most exactly matched the aims and aspirations. As for boarding fees, the maximum Cheltenham charged was £37 10s. 0d., whereas the minimum Brighton charge was £45 (£65 if a boy lodged with the Principal). No wonder Cheltenham's roll rose and rose, at Brighton's expense. Burstow printed an undated and unsigned memorandum from these troubled days. The document is in the hand of Lt. Michael Turner R.N., appointed Secretary to the College that year.

> Reasons which appear to me to be operating against the College:
> The state of the shares being two classes and £40 too much.
> The certainty of underselling in Market operates by depreciating the Character of the College.
> The necessity of obtaining a Presentation or paying too high for Council nomination.
> The want of more general and practical education, particularly English Literature, Writing and Sciences.
> The fear of dismissal and a want of Discipline.
> The private tuition fees.
> The unfinished state of the ground and buildings operates prejudicially in boys and public.
> The unpopularity of the [ ].
> The unsatisfactory conclusion of Mr. M's case.
> The application for Rugby.
> The want of discipline and the mode of teaching in the Lower Department especially.
> Too high rates in some Masters and want of discipline in other Masters. A want of unity in all.
> The absence of the power to use the Rod.

While several items are now beyond interpretation, this paper by the new Secretary shows that Macleane was right to be worried, and endorses his belief in the need for swift action. But he took the Council's rejection of all his proposed solutions as a slap in the face. In December 1850, he issued them a direct challenge: 'whether their confidence expressed to him very strongly about eighteen months ago has been shaken, and if so by what cause?' Their considered response was brief, but devastating: 'The Confidence of the Council in the Principal has been shaken'. Subsequently they clarified this brusque statement, explaining that 'it is in no way attributable to any defect affecting his Moral Character or the professional abilities and zeal with which his duties have been conducted and of which they continue to entertain a very high estimate'. But equally they made it plain that, in their view, 'the Principal was neither disposed nor perhaps able to carry on this Institution with efficiency and success without such organic changes in its Constitution as they are not prepared to recommend'. They were right. Macleane had called their bluff, and lost. No course was open to him but resignation, which he offered on 31 December. We should note, however, that the parting was without lingering bitterness, on either side. In 1853, Macleane returned to conduct the examinations and in 1855 the College made him a (belated) presentation. The Council must also have provided him with a good testimonial for, straight away, he became Principal of Sheffield Collegiate School (where he succeeded George Jacob, runner-up at Brighton in 1846), and two years later of King Edward's School, Bath. That final move proved tragic. In the words of Bath's headmaster in 1951, he

came here, it is thought, in ignorance of a very considerable change that had just taken place in the scheme of government for the School, and this new scheme adversely affected [financially] the Headmaster to such a degree that, as far as we can see, it virtually killed Mr. Macleane ... It is said that he came here as a man of sprightly temperament and with ardent ambition, but before he had long grappled with his difficulties in Bath despair seized him and never left him. He was never known to smile. His health broke down and he died at Charlecombe on 14th May 1858.

Did anything ever go right for the poor man?

Three

1851-1880

The dawn leads on another day

Macleane's resignation brought down salvation and saved the young school. The virtual impasse between Council and Principal had made his continued presence the paramount factor working against Brighton College. There could not be a new governing body, so there must be a new Principal. His departure would force the Council to act. Weaknesses in the original scheme must now be put right. Problems which had developed since the College opened must now be addressed. Fortunately, remedies were to hand. Plans of action proposed by Macleane, and dismissed two or three years earlier as impossible, were now dusted off and implemented. His assessments were now largely accepted, his solutions largely acted upon. Everyone had needed to stare over the brink before anything happened. But it did. Reassessment and reorganisation reshaped Brighton College in the early 1850s. The Council had changed.

No advertisements were placed to find a new Principal. The Council decided to appoint the current Vice Principal in his place. He was Rev. Henry Cotterill, formerly Fellow of St John's College Cambridge and not simply a double first but the very best classicist and mathematician of his year (1836). A glittering career beckoned, yet he had thrown up everything under the influence of the perpetual curate of Holy Trinity Cambridge, Charles Simeon, the foremost church evangelical of his day and a founder of the Church Missionary Society. Simeon's magnetism gathered many disciples. The young Cotterill was one of his stars and in 1837 he accepted an East India Company chaplaincy, in Madras. Driven back by malaria, he had come to Brighton College in 1846 at the invitation of Macleane whom he had befriended in India. Cotterill would be Principal but six years. Yet his short reign must be

Rev. Henry Cotterill

accorded a signal place in the College's annals. His energy, his resolution in pushing forward with his old friend's schemes, brought the school back from the abyss—because he was possessed of a sensitivity quite missing from Macleane, and because the Council was now taken with a spirit of realism. The reformation of structure, the rebuilding of morale and the recovery of reputation had to be a joint effort.

The Secretary's memorandum of 1851 had picked out disciplinary problems with the boys and difficulties in the share system as the most important structural defects. Turner rooted the first in the absence of flogging. The College's Deed of Foundation, dated 11 September 1848, was explicit:

> Rule 49. That no corporal punishment shall be allowed. In the event of any flagrant misconduct, the Principal shall be authorised to suspend the offender, or if he think proper, to report the offence to the Council who if they see fit may inflict the punishment of expulsion.

Beyond noting that the Principal could not himself expel a boy, such a régime was most exceptional, but not unique. University College School, founded in 1830, similarly forbade the rod. So too did the National Schools movement which from 1811 ran free schools for the poor. Others would campaign against it, notably *The Saturday Review* in the 1860s. But against such progressive thinking stood the bulk of opinion, agreeing wholeheartedly with Edward Thring, Headmaster of Uppingham, who in 1856 wrote that: 'caning or flogging is an absolute necessity for working the ordinary discipline of the school'.

Alas we have no knowledge of the reasons which prompted Soames and his coterie to adopt so atypical a view. As businessmen and clerics, none were likely disciples of Rousseau. Whatever their original reasoning, they had now to deal with the common belief that the absence of the rod had produced a disorderly school. Sir Thomas Jackson's *Recollections* bear out the charge. The Principal, he states, 'was somewhat at a disadvantage in being deprived of the *ultima ratio* of a schoolmaster, corporal punishment not being allowed. The consequence was that expulsions became so common for want of an alternative that the School suffered'. A glimpse of early discipline was also recorded at the Old Boys' dinner of 1897. College punishments, we are told, included copying five hundred lines of Vergil and 'confining boys during the dinner hour'. Whereas the sheer tedium of protracted lines meant 'the effort was excellent', detention (in Lion House at least) proved somewhat enjoyable for 'the room overlooked the garden of a retired sea captain, named Magan, who, pitying their misfortune, used to supply them, with the aid of a string, not only with necessaries, but also with luxuries, so that they used to look forward with pleasure to their incarceration'. Supervision would, of course, have remedied that situation—but, then, there were no prefects either.

The College's bad name resulted from frequent suspensions. The Register shows 16 boys as having been expelled, suspended or asked to leave in the period 1847 to 1851. Usually, the only information recorded is the solitary word 'misconduct' (twice, 'gross misconduct'). But occasionally, a little more detail was noted down. Three were guilty of theft, one of 'intoxication', one was 'an unfit subject for our discipline' and one was 'very depraved', the usual code for homosexuality. Interestingly, there is little sign here of that perennial Brighton College problem: the right relationship between the school and the town. Presumably, the boys hoodwinked the authorities about their betting on the turf or their frequenting of billiard halls. Perhaps a new school, lacking traditions, was liable to some unruliness. Not everyone thought the régime too lax or too weak. The parents of Philip Hammond (1849-51) removed him because 'not sufficient liberty is allowed'. But they were the exception. What really mattered was not the mode of punishment employed but the perception spread in the town by a school which had to expel 4.7 per cent of its pupils. As Rev. Henry Venn Elliott had noted dryly in 1848, 'Ah, like the French, they never flog, and therefore shoot'. A vigorous, well established school might have been able to ride out such a ferment. Weak, insecure Brighton College could not.

The cane had to come in (the College seems never to have used that more fearsome weapon, the birch). Cotterill proposed its introduction in November 1851 and the Council agreed. From the controls they sought to impose, we may perhaps deduce reluctant aquiescence on their part. Every case would have to be reported to the Council and only the Principal could authorise its execution. Such a change required an amendment of company rules, and that needed the consent of the share-holders at the A.G.M. (February 1852). By November 1852, *The Brightonian* could report, under 'College News':

> College orders... when making a noise in our bedrooms, the master comes and tells us to go up to his desk the next morning to get a flogging.
> That desk we boys do fear I wean
> For in't the master kept his cane,
> When boys approached one tear was seen,
> When they came down you could see twain.

The pupil journalist then commented that the Reverend Principal 'is so very fond of putting orders on the College board that he ought to keep the students in first rate order' and proceeded to print a recent example:

> 7th October 'The Day Scholars and Day Boarders are cautioned against purchasing any articles in the town for the boarders. Any scholar procuring or assisting another to procure by this method any articles forbidden by the regulations will render himself liable to the severest punishment'.

For the sake of the College's reputation in Brighton, Cotterill had instigated a crack-down. Are we really to believe that, in the first extract, masters in boarding houses sought out the Principal's permission on each and every occasion? The alternative is that Cotterill would automatically endorse whatever had been imposed by an assistant master. Regardless of the official rule, surely the Principal had issued his assistants with canes and authorised them to be used at their own discretion, even if that contravened company rules. Ill repute was to be beaten out of the College.

What of the other great problem raised by the Secretary: share price and the cost of nomination? Shares in the company had been issued at £25 each in confident expectation that, as at Cheltenham, the entire issue would be snapped up. On the opening of the College, the Council raised the share price to £40. Theoretically, the value of a proprietary school's shares should rise with its development, bringing additional capital for further building. Cheltenham College, the great success among the proprietary schools, saw the price of its shares rise from £20 to 130 guineas in its first 20 years. But Brighton College's price rise of 1847 was wholly artificial and naturally proved disastrous. The shares had not been snapped up. Just 241 of the 600 shares (40 per cent) had been sold at the original £25. Only 99 more (16.5 per cent) were sold during the next 24 years, leaving 330 unsold. While there is record in June

1848 of a £25 share changing hands for £40, supply always exceeded demand. Re-sale values rarely topped £20.

From February 1850, the Council struggled to extract itself from this mess of its own making. The deal they offered was a return to the original price of £25, the reduction of the gross shareholding by half and a plea to the £40 shareholders to pay an additional £10 so that they would then possess two shares. Not surprisingly, those owning £40 shares were not enamoured with this proposition. Negotiations dragged on with some shareholders for years and a new drive to equalize was launched in 1857, but only 13 of the 47 £40 shares were ever upgraded, the last in 1860. Occa-sionally, new shares were sold at £25–17 between 1867 and 1893–but the College Secretary in 1877 judged their market value to be around £12. When three years later the local booksellers Messrs. Treacher and the solicitors Hill, Fitzhugh and Co. were found to be acting as brokers for College shares at just £10 each, the Council knew they were beaten. From that moment, no new shares were sold, except to Council members or other known well-wishers effectively making a donation. Thus was regu-larised what had been true for all but the first two or three years–the proprietary basis of the school was a great sham. While the story of Cheltenham College shows the proprietary principle could work, the experience of Brighton College illustrates the pitfalls of a financial structure inappropriate to the realities of running a school. Cheltenham was very much the exception.

If shares proved intractable, what of boarding facilities? Within a month of appointment, Cotterill was pressing the need for Houses within the College grounds, as envisaged in the original plan. The problem would be how to finance any building. The company had no capital and a mortgage was out of the question because, at that very moment, a loan from their good friend Lord Alfred Hervey and from the Royal Sussex County Hospital had just been negotiated (for £2,945, at 4 per cent) 'to acquire the fee simple of the land forming the College estate, to enclose the larger part with substantial walls, and considerably to reduce the outstanding liabilities'. Cotterill's solution was not too dissimilar from Macleane's the previous September. If the Coun-cil would lease him (for 42 years at a rent of £200 per annum) the eastern side of the College, he would at his own expense build a residence for the Principal, with a boarding house attached. In the new atmosphere, the Council overturned its veto of six months previously and accepted Cotterill's proposal, with fulsome thanks. If they wanted the College to prosper, they had no choice.

Built in 1852-3 (not 1853-4 as Burstow and my *Short History* state), it cost £5,000. Scott did Cotterill proud, putting up a lively and imposing house which much en-hances the Quad. That the architectural detail is so much more elaborate than the Main Building should be put down less to a need to mark out the residence of the Principal than to the fact that Cotterill was paying for everything himself. As well as boarding quarters, he was building a family home for his wife and six children. Cotterill was delighted and his successors have found it more than agreeable to live there. No wonder then that its first occupant subsequently commissioned Scott to alter Grahamstown Cathedral in 1860 and favoured his (successful) submission to build the new St Mary's Cathedral in Edinburgh in 1872. As for the house in Brighton, it remained Cotterill's property when he left in 1856 and, while he continued to pay £200 ground rent to the College, successive Principals rented house and land from him for £250 per annum.

The Principal's House, which illustrates Gilbert Scott's use of picturesque asymmetry at its very best

Despite the church basis of the foundation, a growing fear that agnosticism was a rising problem and an awareness that Anglicanism was weaker in Brighton than in other spa towns like Bath and Cheltenham, the College yet possessed no chapel. In March 1848, the Council had turned down Macleane's scheme to raise contributions for a chapel. In another *volte-face*, they authorised Cotterill in December 1852 to do just that. Subscriptions came in exceedingly slowly. By Christmas 1854, the fund stood at around £350, of which £100 had come from the Marquis of Bristol, £50 from Soames and £25 from the Bishop of Chichester. Thereafter, the fund became stuck and it was left to Cotterill's successor to secure for the College a chapel.

Three small-scale projects changed the College's appearance. First came the building of boundary walls, funded from the 1851 mortgage and already referred to. Second, for that enclosed estate, now owned absolute, the President gave 150 elm trees in 1855, and a further unspecified number two years later. The third was the connecting of the College to the town gas main in 1855-6. All were symbols of improvement. All are difficult for us now to appreciate. What must the school have looked like when lit entirely by candles? Cotterill also undertook academic reform. In 1851-2 he revived Macleane's idea for 'occasional students'. Originally, they had been admitted to 'special courses of lectures in Classical Literature, Mathematics and Theology', attended also 'by the more advanced pupils'. Cotterill's fundamental change was to admit occasional students to ordinary College classes–first mathematical drawing and then mathematics, foreign languages, military drawing, surveying, 'civil drawing' and chemistry–at a charge of eight guineas for the first two courses and two guineas each for the others. The occasional students scheme may have helped, a little, but it added precious little to the school's finances. Throughout the 1850s, the Register records only 13; none at all after 1865.

With his own Indian background and Brighton's popularity as a residence for retired or invalided officers, civil and military, who had worked for the East India Company, Cotterill not surprisingly thought about promoting the College as an establishment to train those intending a career in the sub-continent. In 1852, therefore, he added to the curriculum 'instruction in Hindustani and other Oriental Languages', probably Sanskrit and Persian. If to us such languages seem highly exotic, to Cotterill's world they were very practical. Alas, we do not know how long such classes were on offer. Very possibly they did not even last the decade. The other area we know he tackled was the provision of science in the College. Demand for science teaching had been a core theme of educational reform since the late 18th century and was a major feature of the proprietary school movement. Yet Brighton College had been founded without any science teaching at all–a curious discrepancy discussed in Chapter Seven. Ten months into his Principalship, Cotterill launched a successful subscription for over £200 to buy and install a sizeable telescope in the College grounds. A year later, the large ground-floor classroom at the east end of the Main Building was converted into a laboratory where astronomy, chemistry and physics were studied by at least some pupils. Thus began one of the most distinctive features of Brighton College before 1914.

What else Cotterill planned we will never know, for in September 1856 he was nominated, on the recommendation of the great Earl of Shaftesbury and Archbishop Sumner of Canterbury, as Bishop of Grahamstown in the Cape Colony. The following month he wrote to the Council tendering his resignation at Christmas. Only the elite of Victorian headmasters were translated to episcopal thrones, even if in the colonies. After 15 years, he was elected coadjutor Bishop of Edinburgh (diocesan from 1872), where he remained until his death in 1886, aged seventy-four. Cotterill the man remains lost in the shadows. Of his character, his personality and his interests we know virtually nothing and can speak only of his energy in promoting the College. After the rancour of Macleane's era, everyone was overjoyed by what one of the Council termed 'the harmonious working of the machinery'. There was one more public feud, waged this time by the French master, M. Direy, in 1855 through *The Brighton Herald.* For all the exchange of letters, its subject remains wholly obscure. Direy was sacked. The magnificently named Algernon Foggo resigned in protest and everthing settled down rapidly. Not before time, Council and Principal and staff were working together with marked cordiality. Cotterill himself paid special tribute to the contribution of Rev. Joseph Newton 'whose judicious, able and self-denying assistance has alone enabled me to bring the discipline of the College to its present satisfactory state'. Self-denial was needed on all sides.

Numbers in College

	maximum	total number	dayboy entrants	boarder entrants	leavers entrants
1849	166	69	19	50	55
1850	147	57	18	39	82
1851	118	27	9	18	43
1852	118	39	15	24	30
1853	109	47	16	31	45
1854	113	33	15	18	57
1855	95	61	33	28	33
1856	120	46	22	24	51
1857	137	72	31	41	44
1858	162	72	34	38	33

The fall had been stopped almost straight away. The fight back took longer. Despite an upturn from 1855, it was not until 1859 that the College pushed beyond the high mark of 1849, with 172 boys. Across Cotterill's years, the roll increased by less than 2 per cent, and then only at the very end. But that is not the point. The slide had been halted. Within his tenure, numbers were pushed back up 26 per cent and it was upon that platfrom his successor built. Dayboy admissions during 1856-60 increased by 67 per cent over those of 1851-5, boarding by 41 per cent. Further, this growth was achieved despite the financial crash of the winter of 1857-8 which brought down half the banks of England.

College fortunes had been turned around. The roll edged forward, peaking at 207 in 1864 (a level not reached again for 20 years). The secret lay not simply in increasing admissions, but in reducing the proportion of leavers—which before the days of compulsory schooling and minimum leaving ages was a perpetual headache. The gain in pupils per year was better than at virtually any other time before the outbreak of the First World War. Net increases of 28 in 1855 and 1857 were matched or exceeded in only five other years (1858, 1882, 1886, 1906, 1914).

'Indefatigable zeal and Christian deportment' marked, in the Council's view, Henry Cotterill's tenure and his going was 'a source of genuine regret'. What exercised everyone's mind that autumn was the question of his successor. Most governors remembered first-hand 1849-51. Again, the College seemed to hang in the balance. According to his speech at the Old Boys' dinner of 1885, Cotterill had himself confessed to a member of the Council 'despair as to the future'. He was thinking seriously of refusing the splendid opportunity, even though it offered the prospect of further missionary work. He then turned to his companion, he tells us, and asked 'Would it not be possible for you to become my successor?' to which came the reply 'Well, I am not quite sure that it might not!' Cotterill's confidante was John Griffith, perpetual curate of Trinity Chapel, Ship Street, and a man prominent in Brighton life. He played a prime role in establishing the Volunteer movement from 1860. He was selected to be the inaugural chairman of the Brighton School Board, set up in 1870 under Forster's Education Act. Non-sectarian organisations were the ones to which he devoted his energy, like the YMCA and the Brighton Town Mission.

Rev. Dr. John Griffith

The Council seems to have accepted the idea without demur. There is no record of dissention or alternative candidates, and the post was formally offered to Griffith by the President at the extraordinarily low salary of £250 per annum, plus capitation fees (half the basic salary Macleane had been offered in 1846). Only then, three days later, did Cotterill put pen to paper and send in his formal resignation:

> I shall hope to retain the charge of the Principalship till the Christmas vacation. But as my other arrangements will occupy much of my time I have arranged with Mr. Griffith that he should take almost all the instruction of the classes which would otherwise devolve on myself ... I cannot sufficiently express my satisfaction at the conclusion to which the Council has been led, I trust by a higher direction than that of worldly wisdom, in the choice of the future Principal.

Griffith was the first Principal to enjoy a lengthy tenure. During his 15 years, he became known for a genial smile and, in those circumstances in which a schoolboy can find himself from time to time, a formidable frown. To his Vice Principal, he represented 'energy of character, the force of example, the earnestness of teaching'. To William Stewart (Headmaster 1950-63), he seemed a 'robust, unconventional type'. That was certainly how one of Griffith's pupils, the free-thinking writer Edward Carpenter (1855-6 & 1857-63), viewed him. Writing in later life, Carpenter offers us an intriguing pen portrait:

> [He was a] burly, headstrong, muddle-headed, perhaps rather good-natured man. As often as not he would arrive in the classroom late with his hair a-tumble, and looking as if he had not slept all night, would complain that some naughty boy in the Fourth Form was preoccupying his mind and would leave us again alone with our books. Then probably his study door would open and he would push the said boy into the room, saying, 'I wish one of you gentlemen would *cane* this boy', and throwing a cane in over the boy's head would close the door again. Once, drawing a handful of silver and gold out of his pocket he asked me to cane a boy for him, and afterwards I felt sorry I had not accepted the bargain. I think he must have been a little touched in the head.

Here was no tyrant prowling the corridors. The boys called him 'John' and, according to the schoolboy diary of the future Cornish banker and MP Charles Ross (1858-67), his chastisements often took a different form: '...caught out of bounds yesterday and sent to John. He made us sit down for half an hour and then jawed us for going out of bounds. I *will* try to do my duty. ... In the morning, John gave us a long lecture about the indecency of talking in the bogs'. Some, however, most certainly regarded him as more than a little touched in his theology. One College parent, Mr. Emilius Clayton, attempted to frustrate Griffith's appointment, firing off a series of despatches to the Council questioning the suitability of the Principal-elect:

It is currently reported and has been directly stated to myself, and others of my acquaintance upon authority... that Mr. Griffith does not consider the Ten Commandments as binding upon Christians, and that he manifests this Opinion by expressing a desire that places of public recreation should be open on Sunday, that he considers the sense but not the whole language of Scripture to be inspired, and also that Our Saviour did not bear the entire punishment for the Sins of the World.

Clayton trembled for the spiritual and moral safety of his sons and their schoolfellows. Had the staunch church evangelical foundation crumbled already? There is no reason to think so. The key Council figures of 1845-7 were still in place. Council meetings still began with prayer and their annual reports still ended by committing the College 'to the care of Him without whom nothing is strong, nothing is Holy' (1858). Yet the 'heresies' of which Griffith was accused were indeed his beliefs. He openly supported F.D. Maurice when sacked as a Professor at Kings College London for questioning the doctrine of endless punishment in hell. He did favour a shift away from strict sabbatarianism. In microcosm, this affair symbolised the battle then just beginning for the mind of the established church, and foreshadowed the storm which broke just three years later on the publication of *Essays and Reviews*. In theology as in politics, Griffith was a Liberal, broad of church and broad of mind.

Like those powerful Congregationalist ministers of Birmingham, John Griffith had discovered a faith with a cutting social edge. Support for good causes had turned to a belief in the need for good works. He campaigned for decent homes with proper sanitation for working families. According to his *Times* obituary, he was

a genuine man, of great force of character, always both in theology and in social politics somewhat in advance of his contemporaries, yet holding his views with a moderation and a consideration for others which enabled him to conciliate if not to convert his opponents.

Mr. Clayton aside, such views suited the town of Brighton very well in the 1850s and 1860s. It was known as a radical town, invariably returning two Liberal members to Parliament. Few Anglican clerics across the kingdom were Liberals. Even fewer endorsed the 1870 Education Act and its compulsory, free education funded from the rates–the most maligned piece of legislation from Gladstone's first ministry. Yet it was his wholehearted endorsement of that Act which led the largely non-conformist School Board to pick John Griffith as its first chairman: a remarkable testimonial, or a treacherous outrage, depending on your viewpoint. It is noteworthy that he was nominated to the Council in 1854 by Mr. Soames and proposed as Principal by Mr. Cotterill, both arch-evangelicals.

We need to remember that 'evangelical' is a vague term. The redoubtable Rev. Henry Venn Elliott, universally recognised as the leader of Brighton's church evangelicals, was deemed lax by some for driving by carriage to church on Sundays. We must conclude that, unlike some, the Brighton College group were not narrow of heart and mind. Cotterill's enthusiastic endorsement is particularly interesting for, seven years later, he would play a central rôle in judging his old Cambridge friend Bishop Colenso of Natal guilty of similar heretical propositions. As for Mr. Clayton, he withdrew his sons Arthur and Emilius that Christmas and sent them to another of the new schools, Bradfield College.

Dr. Griffith represented the new. In 1876, the College Debating Society carried by eight to five the motion 'that it is inexpedient that all places of public recreation should be closed on Sundays' (the audience agreed by 18 to 12). He was a thinking cleric, as formidable in energy as in girth. His Vice Principal went so far as to claim in the obituary he wrote in 1892, that 'a new era in the history of the College began with the new Headmaster ... [He gave] a fresh impetus to all life in the Institution.' In 1897, the same author asserted that Griffith 'made a great change in the position of the College ... The whole tone of the place acquired a higher pitch'. Certainly, his tenure was marked by growth in the College estate, its buildings and facilities. Numbers increased too, and thus also financial viability. But a new era? To say that is to ignore the earlier 1850s. The new era began in 1851. Cotterill saved the infant's life and, following Macleane's diagnosis, laid down the treatment needed for recovery. Griffith then took over the stabilised patient and nurtured it to the bloom of health. That would be the not inconsiderable achievement of Rev. Dr. John Griffith.

Finances were reordered by the Council in August 1859 when Lord Alfred Hervey called in his 1851 mortgage. This they paid off by taking out a new 10-year loan for £6,000 at 4.5 per cent from the County Hospital. With this sum they would also fulfil the Principal's plea for the building of a chapel and adjoining gymnasium-lecture hall. Gilbert Scott was summoned back, but Cotterill had built the Principal's house on the site originally earmarked, so the chapel had to be placed to the south-west of the Main Building, not the south-east. With only £600 collected in subscriptions, the Council ordered from Scott's now busy practice its cheapest country church pattern: a short single cell building. Even so, Scott's initial design of October 1858 was referred back, the Council asking for 'all the reductions he can possibly make'. The architect duly obliged, lopping £508 from the chapel and £448 from the Hall to give a total cost of £3,372. The Council sent it back again, specifying a maximum expenditure of £3,200. Scott's third version (December 1858) was estimated at exactly £3,000.

Some still demurred. Richard Carr Glyn (Council 1849-59) opposed the entire project on the grounds that the College could not bear any capital outlay. With some trepidation, the Council in January 1859 authorised work to commence on the chapel alone; the decision to build the 'West Wing' at a cost not exceeding £771 being taken only on 3 September. As originally erected, the chapel therefore had a minimum of carving and was totally without encaustic tiles, stained glass or coloured marbles. Council caution meant also that the adjacent hall would be considerably smaller than the 'Big Schoolroom' of Scott's 1848 plan (which was to have occupied virtually the same spot). Alas, it also meant

Ret. marked inversion here
14/6/58

Brighton College,

May 19th, 1858.

SIR,

A Special General Meeting of the Proprietors of Brighton College will be held at the College, on Tuesday the 1st day of June next, at One o'clock precisely.

To consider the following proposition, recommended by the Council:

That the College shall borrow a sum of money not exceeding £6000, at 4½ per cent. Interest per annum, for the purposes of

1st—Paying off the present Loan, which has been called in;

2nd—For Building a Chapel and the West Wing to the College, &c., &c.

I am, Sir,

Your obedient Servant,

Secretary.

the hall would not be raised on arches to create a vaulted wet-weather playground. Building took seven months and, £574 over budget, the new wing was opened on 27 September 1859 with a service of mattins followed by communion presided over by the Bishop of Chichester. After worship, the assembled company adjourned to the new hall–surely still incomplete since it was only three weeks since the Council had authorised its construction–where luncheon was served: 'The tables were covered with viands of the most *recherché* description, the wines were all that could be desired and the wants of the company well supplied by an efficient staff of waiters.'

Griffith also pressed for improvements to the grounds. In 1865, the land to the south of the College was laid out with paths and trees. The following year, the front wall was raised 'for keeping the public off' and 'lighting the front of the College with five gas lamps' was carried out. Three fives courts were built in 1865. An area was asphalted in 1866 to make what we would consider a playground. As for *the* Playground (which we call the Home Ground), Joseph Newton asserted 'it should not be forgotten that the possession of the playground is due almost entirely to the energy displayed by him [Griffith] in overcoming the

The Chapel in 1864, as originally built

difficulties of securing the land just at the right time'. Long and wearisome negotiations with its owner, the peppery William Percival Boxall of nearby Belle Vue Hall, dragged on for three years before he finally agreed to sell a substantial area immediately to the north of the College, for £3,000. Why Boxall was so difficult is unknown. He was a College shareholder and later (from 1864 to 1874) was one of its auditors. But it nearly did not happen. In 1862, Boxall threatened to sell all his land in Bakers Bottom to a developer, for housing. Had that happened, the College would have been trapped on an impossibly small site and that, in the opinion of the Council 20 years later, would have caused 'the extinction of the College'.

Like the chapel, which the Council helped to fund retrospectively by levying a compulsory annual charge for 'seating in the Chapel' (one guinea on all new boarders and half a guinea on all new dayboys), all pupils were charged one guinea per annum from 1865 as a 'Playground Fee'. This went towards paying the installments on a new mortgage, taken out to buy the Playground and surround it with a six-foot boundary wall. Other works Griffith paid for himself. He met the cost of entrance gates on Eastern Road. He funded at least three leaving exhibitions for individuals off to university whom he knew to be in need of assistance. He built a science laboratory. Had he not bought an organ for the new chapel, there would not have been one.

He also himself provided several loans and mortgages to fund projects which the Council could not yet afford: the levelling of the newly extended Playground (costing £1,034 in 1864); extensions to the Principal's house, first building a kitchen and scullery and digging out cellars under Walpole Road (1864); then a servants' hall, a dormitory block and adjoining hall (1865-6). All works on the Principal's House were by Gilbert Scott and cost £2,300. What a turnaround from the days of 1849-51 when the Council could afford nothing, would not raise a mortgage and refused building schemes involving subscriptions or advances from the Principal. Only when the Council had accepted that company share capital need not be the sole source of funding did College facilities develop apace. They had come to recognise that the school could not be treated as a mere trading enterprise.

New-found confidence enabled the Council to turn its eyes to the College neighbourhood. Growth had been hard won. Future prospects needed to be safeguarded and in the 1860s that meant the changes which were starting to overtake the approaches to the school. Building development between Queens Park and Kemp Town threatened to destroy the exclusivity so craved by the Council, but the Council could do little but watch, complain and despair. They were not totally powerless. In 1866, the College clashed with The South Eastern, London, Chatham & Dover Railway over the building of the Kemp Town branch line. Precisely where the Company originally intended the 1,000-yard tunnel from Elm Grove to come out is not clear, but they are described as 'proposing to tunnel across the front of the College ground'. In all probability, the Council did not want the railway at all, but the company already had its act of parliament so that was a vain hope. Nonetheless,

The College at the end of the first phase of building, *c.*1865

Gilbert Scott's Dining Hall, built originally for the exclusive use of School House, in 1896

they petitioned Parliament successfully and the tunnel was altered to emerge west of the College.

As for developments south of Eastern Road, the school was in rapid danger of being blocked off completely from the sea. In 1867, the Council therefore spent £800 on buying a 'beer shop' known as Burlington Cottage, on the sea front. This they then demolished 'in order that an open way be formed to the Marine Parade'. Obscure references in the 1880s talk of a carriageway down from the College to the sea front, but nothing is discernible from contemporary maps. Obviously the cottage came with a long belt of land running north-south, but where was it? When did the College sell the land again? Why couldn't they have kept it! Wishful thinking on our part is also in order for Dr. Griffith's offer on his retirement to sell the College the land he owned to the south of Eastern Road: the block bounded now by College Road, St George's Road and Montague Place. Alas, the proposal came six or seven years too late. With substantial liabilities secured against existing property, the Council would use available funds only to redeem existing pledges and free the original estate.

When in 1853 Cotterill told the Council 'I believe we suffer much from not being known', he reminded them of a reality they already knew. He himself believed that, 'if ever our numbers are to increase very large, it will probably be from London that we should be chiefly supplied'. The College began placing regular advertisements in the London papers. By 1858 they were also advertising in the Liverpool, Manchester and Newcastle press; from 1864 they added Birmingham and Leeds. As for the local market, the College hired a 'fly' in April 1860 sufficient to carry up to five boys and offered parents of Cliftonville and the area of Lansdowne Place, Brunswick Terrace and Adelaide Crescent transport to and from school at the subsidised rate of £1 per half. Dayboy numbers in Griffith's first six years rose by almost two-thirds as compared with the six years of Cotterill's tenure. Perhaps the third Principal's very considerable stature was itself a significant magnet.

Numbers in College

	maximum number	total entrants	dayboy entrants	boarder entrants	leavers
1856	120	46	22	24	51
1857	137	72	31	41	44
1858	162	72	34	38	33
1859	172	57	21	36	68
1860	173	68	39	29	51
1861	197	61	29	32	70
1862	183	63	26	37	56
1863	207	73	37	36	65
1864	207	67	22	45	67
1865	204	60	26	34	63
1866	203	66	29	37	64
1867	203	62	24	38	72
1868	200	49	23	26	73
1869	156	45	15	30	60
1870	149	52	20	32	51
1871	142	55	30	25	57

After the alarming collapse of 1851-55 when there had been an average of only 110 boys per year, applications for places pushed forward again from 1857. In two small surges, the roll crept higher and higher until, for the first time, it topped 200. As fee income (boosted a little by occasional share sales and more frequent share transfer fees) increased and a much tighter control was exercised over the salaries budget, a healthy annual surplus began to appear. Here was the cause of the sudden outburst of regular if modest capital projects. Brighton College had never been so full or so well off. There might not be enough money to pay cash for land and buildings, but three mortgages totalling £9,000 at 4.5 per cent or 5 per cent could be serviced with confidence.

Brighton College had come a long way since Macleane had resigned. The Council's annual report on 1865 expressed the new mood of confident satisfaction: 'The College is now passing its 20th year; may the same Providence, which has guided and fostered it hitherto, continue to maintain and increase its usefulness.' Seven fat years were, however, followed by five in the mid-1860s when the roll stubbornly refused to advance any further. Yet Griffith and the Council would gladly have swapped those doldrums for the abrupt fall in admissions from 1868. Within two years, the College population had been cut by one quarter and Griffith ended his tenure leaving a College barely larger than the one he had inherited from Cotterill. Boarding growth reversed and admissions in 1866-70 were 12 per cent lower than in 1861-65. Was this the result of stiffer competition? Fourteen new public schools were founded during the

1860s, including Clifton, Cranleigh and Malvern as well as nearby Eastbourne. Perhaps they were a factor, but the real loss was not to other boarding schools. Whatever was going wrong had happened in Brighton. The fall of 5 per cent in day entrants in 1861-65 became a torrent over the next five years as 26 per cent fewer local boys joined the College. Not even the opening of the Kemp Town branch line in August 1869 could in any way stop the haemorrhage. One contributory cause was probably the first increases in tuition fees: from £25 for seniors and £20 for juniors per annum to £28 and £23 respectively in 1865; and then up again to £31 10s. 0d. and £27 two years later. Imagine a world where fees stood still for 18 years!

England in 1866-7 was suffering severe economic depression, yet that was the moment Brighton College raised its fees. The new St Edward's Oxford charged a senior £22 10s. 0d. per annum for tuition and Malvern £25 per annum. Cotterill had argued (unsuccessfully) that the Junior Department fees should be cut by £5 per annum. In his opinion they were 'high in comparison with many schools... for the commencement of an elementary education'. That was serious because the juniors 'are much the most important as regards our material prosperity'.

Whatever drove numbers down, we certainly have to accept that Brighton College was a weakling. It had taken the College 16 years to reach 200 boys. Malvern achieved the same target in ten, Rossall in three. Cheltenham exceeded 300 in only four years. Marlborough made 400 in just two. In the time taken by Brighton to reach 200, Clifton managed 680.

The Masters, 1871

By 1871, Griffith had completed 14 years as Principal. Numbers were falling. The mortgages were becoming difficult to sustain. Cuts and redundancies seemed to have become permanent features of his work. Was he tired? Certainly he was confused and he knew that changes were needed. So he wrote to the Council on 1 May:

> Though I could work on for some years hopefully and much as I have been used to do, yet as it seems most desirable that the Council may consult on the future of the College with as little reference as may be to personal interests, I wish to place in your hands my resignation ... This I consider necessary to my own self-respect and to the perfect freedom of your consultation.

They tried to persuade him to withdraw his resignation, but Dr. Griffith was not to be moved and he accepted the vicarage of Sandridge, Hertfordshire, from Gladstone's sterling Irish Secretary of State, the fifth Earl Spencer. There he restored the church, rebuilt the village with model cottages and remained until two years before his death in July 1892. On his departure from Brighton, the *Sussex Daily News* wrote that:

> He did wonders for Brighton College. One who knew him well has stated that he was a man whose very presence was a tacit protest against all that was base and unmanly; and a Headmaster of that stamp could hardly fail to be popular with young men.

He had been a fount of ideas, a well of inspiration. *Pace* Mr. Clayton, 'John' was infused with a fortitude from heaven.

Twice now the Council had looked within the institution to find a new Principal. Not so in 1871. Advertisements were placed, as 25 years before, inviting applications from those 'in holy orders and a graduate of the universities of Oxford, Cambridge, Durham or Dublin'. This time the Council offered the much improved salary of £400 per annum and a capitation fee of £5 for every boy between 100 and 200 (Percival at Clifton was then being paid £800 per annum plus £2 per boy over 200; Faber at Malvern £800 per annum plus £3 per head over 200). On top of all these sums must also be added the profits of running the Principal's boarding House, which meant that, if 50 out of 200 College boys were in the Principal's House, the new man's gross salary would be £2,350. There were only 11 applicants, which does not speak well for the name of Brighton College. Rejected were the headmasters of Loughborough Grammar School and Richmond School York. So too was Charles McDowall who was later Headmaster of Highgate.

Instead, the Council chose Charles Bigg, Second Classical Master and Vice Principal at Cheltenham College. He had a double first in *literae humaniores*. He had also collected various university prizes, including the renowned Ireland, and he

Rev. Dr. Charles Bigg

had won in open competition (then very rare) a Senior Studentship at Christ Church. His paper qualifications were impeccable and obviously the Council was dazzled. Perhaps the Council were actually looking for a scholar because they wanted to base the College's recovery on a first-rate academic reputation. More than likely, they hoped a senior man from the most successful of the proprietary colleges would bring the missing secret to Brighton. They may also have been looking for something different. Burstow's *History* draws the wrong inference when noting that he 'must have been a striking contrast to his robust predecessor'. The contrast was very real and invites comparison. Both men were of considerable energy, but they channelled it in very different ways. They represented very different styles of headmastering. Burstow goes on, however, to quote Belcher's *History*, 'We may picture him as a charming personality, as a brilliant scholar and lecturer in Classics and Theology, but more at home perhaps as a don than in the hurly-burly of school life'. Belcher took his cue from Bigg's *Times* obituary which would say, 'It is no injustice to a charming person-ality that his work as a schoolmaster was less congenial and less successful than other occupations which fell to his lot'. Of his personality there can be no doubt. He was loved wherever he went. 'Less congenial' than Oxford seems spot on, naturally. Where could be more congenial than Oxford? 'Less successful' cannot go unchal-lenged; neither can Belcher's aspersions against his suitability for schoolmastering. The first indicates ignorance, the second betrays prejudice.

   Bigg's scholarship is not in question. His headmaster at Cheltenham, Thomas Jex-Blake, wrote that 'the Head Masters of English schools who are Mr. Bigg's superiors in scholarship must certainly be few or none'. The High Master of Manchester Gram-mar School, the almost legendary Frederick Walker, stated categorically: 'It is not too much to say ... that of all the scholars who have proceeded from Oxford during the last ten years, Mr. Bigg stands at the head.' Neither is his work in the classroom at dispute. His own Vice Principal testified that Bigg 'was a classical teacher not easily surpassed'. One of his pupils, Cyril Starkey (1872-81), when himself Headmaster of Edinburgh Collegiate School, rated his old master 'a keen, stimulating teacher'. Charles Bigg must be assessed on the rest of his record—and for Brighton College that means first and foremost the health of the roll:

Numbers in College

	maximum number	total entrants	dayboy entrants	boarder entrants	leavers
1869	156	45	15	30	60
1870	149	52	20	32	51
1871	142	55	30	25	57
1872	138	48	23	25	49
1873	155	62	21	41	56
1874	156	48	24	24	46
1875	178	76	27	49	52
1876	185	58	22	36	71
1877	173	42	15	27	61
1878	166	69	28	41	63
1879	159	41	17	24	58
1880	144	58	18	40	58
1881	150	38	14	24	82

The slide of the late 1860s proved less serious than the collapse of the late 1840s. Numbers fell neither as fast nor as far before the upturn began. While it is surely true that, rid of Metcalfe's septic legacy and possessed of better facilities, Bigg's task was easier than that of Cotterill and Griffith, it is equally the case that recovery was not to be guaranteed. Griffith had not been able to stop the very considerable decay of his last four years. Bigg turned that around within one and then pushed onwards to 185 boys, a level well in excess of anything known under Macleane or Cotterill, and a position bettered in only half of Griffith's era. Recovery was due entirely to local demand. After weakening across the 1860s, the years 1871-5 saw dayboy admissions rise by 12 per cent. Boarding demand remained totally static.

In his turn, however, Bigg suffered the cycle of bust after boom. Demand slumped and in four years the College shrank by almost one quarter to 144 boys. This decline he attributed to a combination of 'the change in two of our boarding houses' and 'the depression of trade—which has certainly caused the withdrawal of many boys'. Cereal prices collapsed in the mid 1870s, causing a sharp fall in income for all dependant on land revenues. But few among the middle classes should have been affected. Perhaps well-publicised outbreaks of scarlet fever in Brighton and ongoing scares relating to the town's defective sewage system were more to blame. Certainly the chairman of the London, Brighton and South Coast Railway claimed in 1869 that reports that the town was unhealthy had cut passenger demand. But all of this only takes us so far. Again, perhaps, we have to see such capricious fluctuations as unconnected to any specific cause. A school without a great name was exceedingly vulnerable to the whims of a competitive and unpredictable market.

Bigg did not stand by and wring his hands. Before decline set in, he had in 1872 led the Council to fund the College's very first entrance scholarships. Soon, there were eight one-year competitive awards (termed Council Scholarships), three for boys already in College and five for outsiders, varying in value from £10 to £25 per annum (when tuition fees for a boy aged 10-15 were £27 per annum). In 1875 he

> **B** R I G H T O N   C O L L E G E.
> Principal, the Rev. Charles Bigg. M.A., late Senior Student and Tutor of Christ Church, Oxford.
> Vice-Principal, the Rev. Joseph Newton, M.A.
> There are two divisions—the Classical and the Modern.
> There is a good Laboratory and a well-fitted Carpenter's Shop.
> The College is situated in the healthiest part of Brighton.
> The climate is peculiarly favourable to boys of a delicate constitution.
> The College is endowed with fifteen Scholarships.
> Terms—For Boarders, 80 gs. to 90 gs. per annum, according to age; or, for the Sons of Clergymen, 60 gs. to 70 gs.; for non-Boarders, £22 10s. to £31 10s. per annum.
> For further particulars, address the Secretary.

From *The Illustrated London News,* July 1875

extended advertising every term to the great national press. But there would be no special effort to attract extra dayboys. In April 1876, the Council endorsed his wish 'not to advertise the College in any local papers', thereby ending a significant feature of the College's marketing strategy of the previous 20 years. When dayboys had been the sole cause of expansion in the early 1870s, that was an extraordinary decision. It was a calculated decision. Bigg's proposal was taken because of recent experience. Dayboy growth threatened Brighton College's position as a public school. As a species dayboys would be tolerated, but not encouraged—a stance which, apart from the reign of Arthur Titherington (1895-1906) and the desperate days of the Depression and World War II, was maintained until 1963. Bigg's view was no whim. The school he had taught at previously (Cheltenham) kept its 'homeboys' at around one quarter of the whole College; town schools could not but have some day pupils. Brighton College was, however, out of step now with public school and middle-class fashion. The bias towards day scholars of the 1820s-1840s, in which spirit the College had been founded, was no more. Aided by an expanding railway network, the ideal of the boarding school had caught on. Now almost everyone believed that such institutions were the best place to turn out, as Squire Brown tells himself before sending Tom to Rugby, 'a brave, helpful, truth-telling Englishman, and a gentleman, and a Christian'. The influences of home, mother and sisters must be removed. In the words of George Bradley, Headmaster of Marlborough, in 1869, it was only by 'the practice of a plain life, in common ... under the guidance of public-spirited masters ... that boys could be turned from the foul nakedness of human nature'.

Bigg did, however, forge links with a local boarding preparatory school, run by Mr. Joshua Fayle at 18 Eaton Place. From 1879, its boys came up to use the Playground, and from 1880 it advertised within the College prospectus. By the end of that year, 13 of Fayle's boys had come on to Brighton College. Despite all the advertisements, however, the battle for boarders was a disaster. The College probably conveyed the wrong message by maintaining a Council composed almost entirely of Brighton men; the others came from Sussex. Static in the early 1870s, boarding admissions rose by just 2 per cent between 1876 and 1880. Meanwhile, the message had got out. Why should local parents send their son to a school where they would not be valued? A 12 per cent increase in dayboy numbers was turned during 1876-80 into a 25 per cent decrease. Slump from 1876 might well have been unavoidable, but it need not have been so severe. To be a dedicated follower of fashion, regardless of the circumstances, is to tempt providence. The fall from 185 to 144 was a self-inflicted wound.

Bigg's era has looked like an interregnum because, unlike the 1850s-60s or the 1880s, there were no great building projects. That was not his fault. As Burstow put it, quoting Belcher almost word for word, 'the Council had pledged its credit beyond its resources and was compelled to tighten its purse strings'. All of the new schools, except it seems Cheltenham, were financially precarious. Marlborough and Malvern almost collapsed under their debts. Bradfield went bankrupt. We need, however, to look twice at the capital accounts, for what Burstow states does not fit the facts.

As early as 1873, a four-year mortgage of £1,100 at 4 per cent was taken from the new Principal. Together with £1,200 accumulated for the purpose from the revenue account, Dr. Griffith was paid back for the extensions he had built to School House. Also in 1873, a fifth mortgage was taken, this time for £2,000 at 4.5 per cent, to buy back from Bishop Cotterill the house and land sold to him in 1852. This last move they could afford only by adding in the £3,000 capital just

DEATH OF W. A. SOAMES, ESQ.

We announce with regret the loss of a well-known and highly respected inhabitant of Brighton, W. A. Soames, Esq. The above gentleman who had only been ailing a short time, died at his residence, Tramore Lodge, at the advanced age of eighty-four. Few have given such valuable help to all our charitable institutions, for not only did he assist largely by contributing to their funds, but he gave, for nearly thirty years, what is more difficult to obtain, personal attendance to their management in committee, where he was always distinguished by exact regularity in attendance, sterling good sense, and a knowledge of business.

The Hospital was one of the many charities benefited by his assistance, and the very last that he continued to visit, when his failing strength and advanced age obliged him gradually to withdraw from others. He was at the Board even so late as Wednesday, September 20th, only a few days before his death.

In the erection of the Brighton College, the most important of our educational establishments, an institution which he originated and carried out, obtaining the valuable co-operation more especially of the late Sir T. Blomefield, Rev. H. V. Elliott, and E. Cornford, Esq.; he leaves a permanent memorial in Brighton.

Obituary of William Aldwin Soames, *The Brighton Gazette*, 28 September 1871

donated by the Soames family to fund leaving scholarships in memory of the founder (to which appropriation Mrs. Soames and her children gave their consent). The Council promised to fund the scholarships from the rent they would now be charging the Principal.

Whereas the loans of Dr. Griffith's era were mostly taken out against a falling roll, these new mortgages were planned when fee and share incomes were rising again. To borrow against fee income was risky when the roll could be so capricious, and the Council knew it. They thus rejected Bigg's proposal in 1874 to build a cricket pavilion, arguing that the £700-1,000 it would have cost could not be afforded. Funds were available, but were allocated to other capital projects. Drains came before cricket. From the start, the octagon, as the lavatories behind the Main Building were called, used water rather than earth closets; the water being supplied by an artesian well sunk below the building. For some time, however, the health hazard from the College's two cesspools had been a real worry. So too had the smell for, until 1863, they were open! In that year, the soilmen were brought in, the pools dug out and then covered over. By 1874 they needed emptying again, but digging them out was no longer an option. Public health stood high in the public mind after the Royal Commission on Sanitary Laws (1871), two Public Health Acts (1868 & 1872) and the sanitary provisions of two

Soames and his family. All of his sons attended the College. Two of his daughters married old boys. One of his sons married the sister of an old boy.

Artisans Dwelling Acts (1868 & 1875). All had made clear the inter-relationship between inadequate drains, contaminated water and the outbreak of fevers; it was only in 1861 that Prince Albert had died of typhoid. In Brighton itself, sewage disposal became an issue which, from the late 1850s, convulsed the town, especially after a damning report in *The Lancet* in 1862. From 1871 to 1874, the town built a great intercepting sewer and Bigg lobbied for the College to be joined to it. Both as a necessary project and as a smart marketing move by an institution trying hard to become a prominent boarding school, an entirely new drainage system was laid in the College in 1875, at a cost of £339. Good drains were as necessary to the success of a school as to the success of a town. A second development essential to the safety of a boarding school which Bigg brought about was the purchase, in 1876, of the College's first fire-fighting equipment: a long hose, two large ladders and 12 buckets. Another project of that era whose significance is easily missed was the incorporation of the proprietary company. Legal difficulties had been encountered in pursuing parents who defaulted on the fees. Because the College was not itself a single legal entity, that meant that an incorrigible debtor could force each of the governors to sue him individually for unpaid fees. Limited liability joint-stock companies, the standard bearers of capitalist enterprise, had become possible in 1855, but initially the Council rejected incorporation as incompatible with a non-profit making company. But the 1862 and 1867 Companies Acts had created a new class of 'associations not for profit' which allowed them limited liability without having to display 'Ltd' after their name. Brighton College became a limited company under these provisions in September 1873. The following year, the Privy Council granted the Council 'a licence to hold lands'. What were they up to? The College solicitor was tying up legal loose ends, but these were also preparatory steps to obtaining the prestige and tax exemptions accompanying incorporation by royal charter or act of parliament. Bigg was always on the look-out for improvements. In 1874 he obtained Council approval to introduce a significant alteration in the fee structure by offering a one-third reduction in tuition fees, and a 10 per cent discount on boarding fees, for sons of the Anglican clergy. Why? Schools like Brighton College linked themselves closely to the Church of England and its clergy still automatically carried the status of gentlemen. But many parishes provided, by respectable middle-class standards, an inadequate living: the average income in 1840 was £300 per annum and while nearly 1,500 parishes paid over £500 per annum, almost 5,000 offered under £200 per annum. Thirty-five years later, nothing had changed and it is only surprising that Brighton did not make such an offer before Bigg's day. It was an instant success. In two years, the number of clergy sons almost doubled from 16 to 34, averaging 30 over the next five years. But the Council stuck strictly to their Anglican allegiance. While in 1875 they agreed to admit totally free of charge Henry Satchell (1875-9), one of the sons of an impoverished cleric with nine children, they refused to grant the clerical reduction to sons of 'Mr. H.J. Lawson, Dissenting Minister' (1877) or 'Rev. A. Gonin, pastor of the French Reformed Church in Brighton' (1880).

When the roll began sliding in 1876, the clerical group paying two-thirds fees served to guarantee income and buoy up an otherwise dire situation. Without that lifebelt, numbers would in all probability have sunk below 120, returning the College to the calamitous days of 1851-5. The sons of the clergy were attractive, however, for another reason. They were thought especially likely to enter the learned professions themselves, which meant the need for a university education and, therefore, the preparation of a classical curriculum. Favourable terms for clergy sons helped to sustain Latin, Greek and university scholarships–the qualifications needed by the new schools to claim public school status alongside Winchester and Shrewsbury.

The Principal of Kings College London described Charles Bigg in his testimonial of 1871 as possessing 'a power to originate'. His prime objective from 1875 was the building of two boarding houses on College ground. Cotterill's House, known from its foundation as School House, had opened 22 years before, since when the subject of additions had never been discussed formally by the Council. Rightly, Bigg considered further houses more than long overdue. It was now fundamental to any College progress. Educational opinion had shifted since the 1840s. None of the second generation public schools founded in the 1860s, like Clifton and Malvern, employed the system of boarding out, even in the private homes of the masters. Boys must be supervised properly at all times. The same rules must apply to all. They must be available at all times to take part in collective activities, whether in debating or competing for the fives cup. A school must be thoroughly one. The House system as we know it was being born.

As we have seen, Bigg was aiming to make the College an essentially boarding school, in line with another new fashion. He was, therefore, correct when arguing that, if Brighton did not change its practice, it ran the serious risk of losing substantial custom: 'Arrangements such as ours, which twenty or thirty years ago were not exceptional, are now almost unknown.' Naturally he linked this College deficiency to the falling roll of the later 1870s. He went further, arguing that because fewer pupils came and most who did stayed under three years, the lack of on-campus boarding houses explained the stunted growth of Brighton College. He was wanting no more than other public school heads were then busily engaged upon; this was the 1860s-1870s equivalent of the building of sports halls a century later. But Bigg overstated his case. Boarding admissions remained remarkably constant across the years 1856-1880. If the Principal was right, the isolated jump to 184 admissions during 1861-5 should not have happened and demand should have been waning across the 1860s and 1870s as parents turned instead to schools which did meet the new requirements. The Council did not, however, consider College-funded building of even one boarding house to be possible in the forseeable future. When the school was already mortgaged to the tune of £11,100, they refused to increase indebtedness. Yet when Bigg came back proposing to fund building a house 'through himself or others' for £5,000, charging the College 4.5 per cent (£225) per annum, that too was rejected. While no details are recorded of their objections, their decision does not make sense. Bigg's scheme differed in no material details from that sanctioned in 1852 to enable Cotterill to build School House. Undeterred, Bigg returned in 1877 suggesting the foundation of a

The Front Quad, *c.*1870

separate building company whose share capital would buy land then for sale immediately to the east of the College, and there build one or two houses. Building companies had been enormously successful at schools like Malvern and Cheltenham,
selling a limited number of expensive shares to known well-wishers. Brighton most
certainly had such supporters and the Council, having inspected the site, declared 'no
objection to the scheme'. There, however, the trail ends with a quenching silence in
the sources. Certainly no company was ever set up.

The next we hear of boarding houses is two years later when Bigg, resilient as
ever, asked the Council whether they would raise £7,000 to build a house 'on the plot
of ground before the Chapel'. The idea was investigated. Finances were considered.
The Principal consulted the local architect Somers Clarke junior, who drew up plans.
Again, we know that nothing came of this, but even its rejection went unrecorded, let
alone any reasons. In all probability, uncertainty as to the future and the parlous state
of College finances in 1879-80, both caused by a 19 per cent fall in the roll and a 21
per cent fall in fee income in four years, put paid to Bigg's third initiative. Between
1876 and 1881, the salary bill had to be cut by 17 per cent. In 1880, the Council
contemplated extinguishing all scholarships. In such a climate, the building of a boarding
house stood no chance of authorisation, especially when the Council was simultaneously rearranging its mortgages to develop the Playground. Negotiations with William
Boxall to purchase further land in Bakers Bottom had, after 26 years, still not been
concluded. But in 1880 he did finally agree to sell to the College the many restrictive
covenants he still held over the freehold of the existing Playground, for £1,000. Of
these, the most critical was a right of way for shepherds to take their flocks to and
from the Downs—which caused interesting chaos during cricket matches.

Further proof that Bigg was trying to modernise the College can be found in the
change he made to the prefectorial system in 1875. Until then, senior boys were
picked by the Principal and appointed 'praepositors'. But they had no formal training for office so he introduced a junior grade of apprentice prefects, termed 'proba-
tioners'. Eight in number, they assisted in the maintenance of discipline, but enjoyed
none of the praepositors' perks. Significantly, however, he did not touch the now
time-hallowed tradition under which the entire pupil body elected the captain of the
school.

Like all heads, Bigg had his disagreements with his governors. The first we know
of occurred in 1874 over his 'right' to determine the dates of the College holidays—
an issue over which Macleane and his governors had also fallen out. Both Principals
lost. In itself the issue was trivial, but the fact that Bigg resorted to publishing a printed
circular on the subject was a bad omen. More serious tensions developed in 1875 as
the Principal sought to exercise day-to-day control over College expenses, minor
building alterations and repairs. This initiative both Secretary and Council stoutly
resisted as encroaching upon their jurisdictions. But Bigg would not let go. In 1877,
he proposed 'that the office of Bursar should be revived and given to the Principal'.
The two halves of College administration were drifting apart. Under Dr. Griffith, of
course, the relationship had been highly unusual. He had been a member of the
governing body and knew all the Council as friends and colleagues. Those days were
now gone and the old troubled relationship returned, suggesting that the separation
of powers enshrined in the College's constitution was too severe. When Principals
were so dependant on the Council for permission to act in areas over which they

needed some executive authority, frustration and dispute were inevitable. The rules of the proprietary company allowed insufficient integrity of command to the Principal.

By 1880 the fall in numbers invited, in the Council's own words, 'grave consideration [on] the state of the College'. Inevitably, that meant that the talents of Charles Bigg were under the microscope. Precisely what happened is obscured by the blandness of the relevant Council Minutes, but under April 1881 there is reference to letters exchanged between the Principal and the Chairman. The subject is never mentioned. All we are told is that the Council desired to explain 'emphatically that in no respect have they meant to cast a slur upon his [Bigg's] word'. We have here only the end of the affair. The Principal had sent in his resignation on 25th and the Council, that very day went on to declare 'that for other reasons they feel that they have no alternative, but that of accepting his resignation'. An intriguing twist is then added to this mystery with a series of public, printed letters which passed between the masters and the Principal. The staff sent Bigg 'a testimonial of our regard and esteem', paying fulsome tribute to his scholarship, dedication and achievements, ending 'we lose a Head whose kindness and good feeling have been manifest in the general harmony of our mutual relations'. In themselves, these sentiments are no more and no less than the kind of statements made by any Common Room saying farewell to a Head they have liked and admired. But it is what happened next that is so suggestive. When Bigg returned his thanks, he asked them specifically,

perhaps there is a further meaning in what you have so generously said. It may have come to your knowledge that the reason for my resignation was that the council appeared to have made themselves the mouth-piece of what I could only regard as an impudent fabrication, to the effect that there was ill feeling between the Principal and the other Masters. Am I right in supposing that your letter is intended as a direct denial of this? And do you wish me to lay it before the Council in that sense, and invite them to withdraw the damaging insinuation?

The masters' reply was all Bigg could have hoped for:

21th May, 1881
My dear Principal, In answer to your letter I beg to say that we should most certainly, in any case, have expressed to you our feelings on your leaving in some such letter as we have sent you; but the reason why we have taken an early opportunity of doing it is that we wished to satisfy your mind that the impression under which we heard the Council was labouring, that there was a want of cordiality between us and you, was unfounded, and the letter was meant to show you this distinctly. With regard to the use to be made of the letter we wish to leave it entirely in your hands to do what you think best for your own satisfaction.

Newly armed, the Principal wrote again to the Council:

25th May, 1881
Gentlemen, Twice I have appealed to you in vain to withdraw the accusation which the above letters prove to be false. And now for the third and last time, in the name of your own reputation, I call upon you to do what justice and honour demand. I am unwilling to believe that you can consent to appear in the position of men, who, having made use of calumny for a purpose, and having effected that purpose, no longer care either to justify or to retract it.

If Bigg hoped for vindication he was to be sadly disappointed. In reply, the Council 'received with regret the letter ... [and] cannot admit the construction which he has put on the facts before them'. If less protracted than the dispute with Macleane, that with Bigg was no less bitter and (to us) even more impenetrable for we understand even less what had occurred. Neither side offered an olive branch. No call came for the Principal to reconsider his position. The Council wanted him gone so much that they did not even pay the man any tribute in their official report on the year 1881. His bitterness is evident from his final letter to the Secretary, dated 14 June 1881:

> I have received the Copy of the Minute and will inform my colleagues that the Council do not dispute the truth of their statements. It was sanguine perhaps to look for an acknowledgement of error from the Council. All they regret apparently is the receipt of the letter which made it impossible for them to cling to mischievous calumny any longer. I may be allowed myself to regret that their confession did not precede conviction.

Shortly before Bigg departed, the boys presented him with a silver salver and claret jug 'of Etruscan shape, elegantly embossed with classic figures representing one of Flaxman's illustrations to the *Iliad'*. In the report of his speech of thanks and farewell, he revealed a weariness more than understandable after his recent ordeal:

> the life of a headmaster was full of many cares and troubles and anxieties. It was by no means a bed of roses. Notwithstanding that, in looking back upon the past ten years, he could say that it had been a happy time, and that for two reasons–first he was sure they had all co-operated in doing good and useful work, which he trusted would endure; and secondly, because he always felt certain he could rely on the affection and loyalty of the boys. He was going away from amongst them, going to a life of greater leisure, and greater opportunities for study–a life for which, by nature, he was fitted in many ways.

Too much has been read into his evident enthusiasm for pastures new. Very probably Oxford was, as Belcher put it, 'his spiritual home'. During his days after 1881, many of them in Oxford, 'greater leisure and greater opportunity for study' saw him mature to eminence as an historian of the early church.

But Bigg was one of those brilliant characters prone to fits of depression. He was melancholy in the summer of 1881. Yet for three years he had taught undergraduates at Christ Church and, for six, schoolboys at Cheltenham. In both he had tested his vocation, finding enjoyment as well as success. As a teacher he was peerless. As a master he was beloved and respected, not feared. As a headmaster, he enjoyed the confidence of his staff, was a fund of ideas for developing the school and a tireless worker on its behalf. Belcher's *History*, followed by Burstow's, judged him less at home 'in the hurly-burly of school life'–an opinion for which there is not the slightest evidence. What they meant was that Charles Bigg was no athlete. He might have won a double first, the Ireland and a Christ Church studentship, but not a blue. Under Bigg, the College gained a reputation for scholarship, but not for cricket. Belcher and Burstow belonged to a different world. Between the 1860s and the 1880s, the public schools underwent several fundamental transformations in character. Henceforth they would preach the absolute virtues of boarding; Bigg himself was an early champion of that movement. They also discovered games, not as a pastime, but as a team activity to develop manliness. 'Athleticism' as it is now termed still held absolute sway when Burstow wrote in the 1950s. In his attitude to the activities of the Playground, however, Bigg belonged to the past. No matter that the editorial magazine recording his leaving could declare 'how much he has improved the general tone of the place'. To eyes schooled under a very different ethos, he was not a proper schoolmaster. He was not 'robust'. He did not join in a game of football.

In the twinkling of an eye he was gone. Five years later he delivered an important
set of Bampton Lectures. Twenty years later, he was appointed Regius Professor of
Ecclesiastical History in Oxford. The two outer lights of our chapel's great east window were filled by subscription on his death in 1908 as his memorial. Someone who
knew him well was Dean Liddell, of Greek *Lexicon* and Alice fame. He concluded his
testimonial for Charles Bigg in 1871: 'I can only say, I think you will be fortunate in
securing Mr. Bigg's services'.

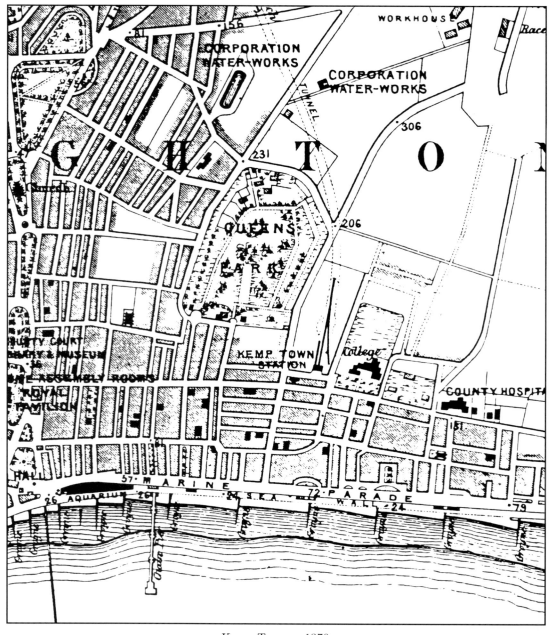

Kemp Town, *c.*1870

Part II

Principals and Headmasters

Thomas Belcher	September 1881
Robert Chambers	September 1892
Arthur Titherington	September 1895

The title was changed in December 1885, 'in accordance with the almost universal practice of English public schools'.

[Photo: David Holinshead]

BRIGHTON
COLLEGE
new gateway &
boarding house
J.G. Jackson
Architect

J.G. Jackson fec
May 31 1884

Four

1881-1887

A great and mighty wonder

Expectation sat in the air as the Council gathered to consider the appointment of their fifth Principal. The school had done quite well as a small provincial college. But they were not satisfied. Brighton College must be a large school of imperial renown. If the endeavours of successive governors and Principals had thus far failed to establish Brighton in the first division, hope's perpetual breadth kept the dream alive. Thirty-six men applied for the post, three times the number in 1871, even though offering the same salary and 'head money', and the field had been limited to those 'in priests orders, of the degree of Master of Arts at least of one of the Universities of Oxford or Cambridge'. From a short-list of five, the Headmaster of Taunton College, two wranglers and (despite the advert) a Trinity Dublin graduate, were all rejected. Instead, the Council for the first time called a candidate to interview before offering him the post: Rev. Thomas Hayes Belcher, aged 34, then Second Classical Master at Malvern College.

As against Bigg's double first, Belcher had a good second in classics. Testimonials spoke of his vigour and energy, his powers of organisation, 'his value in the classroom'. As a boarding housemaster, he was said to display 'great kindness and goodness to the boys under his care'. 'The conciliatory manner in which he dealt with parents' was also noted. His headmaster described him as 'sober-minded, straightforward and practical ... His temper is most equable, and his self command unfailing'. Doubtless, Brighton College's governors were reassured to read that his sermons 'were moderate in their Churchmanship' and that he was 'quite free from any ritualistic proclivities'.

THE "BRIGHTONIAN" CARTOON No. 69.

SATURDAY, JUNE 30TH, 1883.

"BRIGHTON COLLEGE."

Rev. Thomas Hayes Belcher

In Thomas Belcher, we meet a new tone in English education. Until a few years earlier, no one would have thought it relevant to testify to a candidate's 'influence out of school hours ... whether in the Chapel, the Boarding House, or the Playground'. But the day had now come when teachers had become schoolmasters, organising the boys outside as well as inside the classroom—and participating with the boys in those many activities. Belcher could not offer outstanding scholarship, but that was not what was now required. The qualities which picked him out were those of the all-round schoolmaster, among which his cricket blue (1870) counted for much. As with the turn towards boarding, so now with the promotion of games, Brighton College was, if a little belatedly, moving with the times. Belcher brought in new young masters who had played in their College XI or XV, and gave the Playground a semi-official status never seen before. Macleane and Cotterill would not have understood. But we do for, shorn of a certain excess, it is an ethos still powerful in the world of independent schools. According to an unnamed master of the 1880s, Belcher 'somehow or other always managed to find someone who would do the particular work he wanted done, and who would do it well'. The schoolmaster who would turn his hand to anything is the authentic voice of the new style. After all, this was the heyday of that perverse English cult of the amateur.

The Masters, 1892

In the early days, scholarship remained of real concern. Intellectual attainment remained genuinely cherished. But the balance was lost in most schools before 1914. Games became an end in themselves and the public schools of the inter-war years were a near academic desert. In the days of Mr. Belcher, however, games were still a means to an end: character formation. They would be a powerful agent in working the miraculous transformation of boy into gentleman. Preparation foreshadowed performance. The missionary ambition of these schools had not changed since their inception forty years earlier, but the message they preached had altered. The essential concern of the 1830s-1840s, with turning out *christian* gentlemen, had now evaporated. Moral earnestness had given way to manliness as the new tune. The newer definition was rooted in a vaguer creed, more sentimentality than morality, which emphasised bravery, honesty and loyalty. A footballer played not so that he could score goals and attain personal glory, but so that his side could win. No longer were football and cricket mere amusements for leisure hours. Along with discipline, reliance on one another and the subordination of the individual to the group were now judged the character-moulding lessons for life. These new virtues the public schools proceeded to promote. This was 'muscular christianity', an ethos deriving not from Dr. Arnold (who himself took virtually no interest in athletic activities) but from Rev. Charles Kingsley, the author of *Westward Ho!* and *The Water Babies*.

An easy gospel to preach and teach, 'team spirit' won for Belcher not simply a great reputation among his boys, but a lasting reputation in the annals of the College. In the words of his son's 1947 *History*, 'it was he who first brought Brighton really into the ranks of the Public Schools'. What he meant was that Brighton College was starting to shake off the world of the 1840s. Only from the 1880s could later Brighton College schoolmasters see an institution which they recognised as (apparently) the same as the one they worked in during the 1920s or 1950s, a games-playing boarding school.

The years of Thomas Hayes Belcher began in hope, matured into glittering success, and ended on the edge of catastrophe. Not that it was his fault. Burstow is quite wrong in saying that he 'carried the Council with him' in a grand scheme for building development which brought ruin and, very nearly, total extinction. He did separate the Juniors into a distinct department with their own boarding house, and he was responsible for the building of a cricket pavilion and a sanatorium. But that was all. The expansionist policy of the 1880s was not his but that of the Council which employed him. They set, funded and directed this agenda. Public school headmasters are often presumed to reign as autocrats (over boys, masters and governors) like some Ruritanian duchy. Always a caricature, it could come close to the truth, but not at Brighton before Canon Dawson. Belcher was indeed the strong and just captain required in the new creed. At no point in the 19th century, however, did the Principal attend Council meetings or have any control over financial affairs. The Principal was very much the servant of the Council. Does that take us to the heart of the problems with Macleane and Bigg? Were their suggestions for structural changes regarded as misplaced, even intrusive encroachments on the Council's sovereignty?

Hitherto, capital development had been very piecemeal and painfully slow. Fiscal reality had deflated every grand design. Now, caution was thrown to the wind, as Burstow's *History* explains:

Although, superficially, the eighties were for the College a period of prosperity and expansion, those advantages were purchased at a high price so that the next decade presents a very different story. Indeed it is hard at first sight to reconcile the depression and humiliation evident in every page of the minute books during the next two headmasterships with the buoyant self-confidence, sometimes bordering on recklessness, of the Belcher era. Yet the broad lines of the story are simple enough. It was a matter of over-bold expenditure on projects which could not be expected to yield returns quickly enough to keep the School creditors in a co-operative mood.

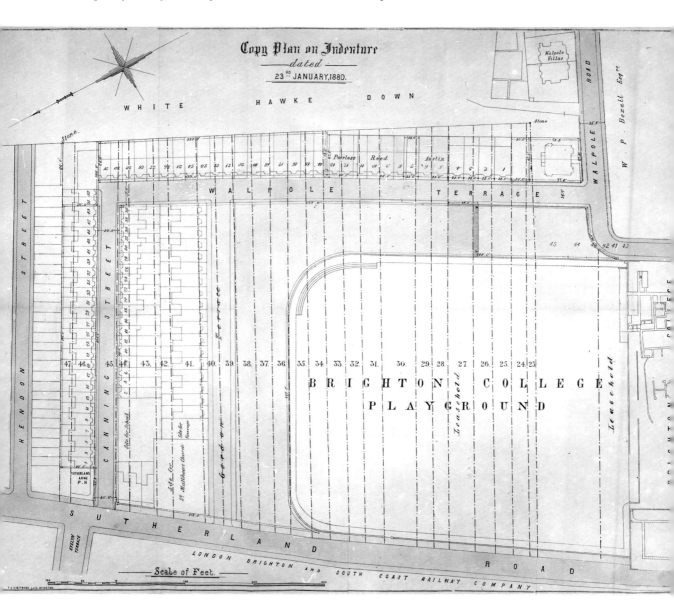

The College site showing the complex arrangement of paulpieces which made buying the land so difficult, so expensive and so long to achieve

The roots of this policy lie almost certainly in the pressures exerted by Dr. Bigg in the late 1870s. Most certainly it was his bringing to Brighton of the new public school spirit which, in the words of an unnamed governor of 1888, began the push 'for Brighton College to take its place among the great Public Schools of the country'. But, as with the story of Arthur Macleane, the Council would not then be told what to do, and dug its heels in against sound advice, converting from resistance to enthusiasm only on the resignation of the Principal. The driving force of this new vaulting ambition was Henry Griffith (1859-68), son of the third Principal and in 1881 both College solicitor and a governor. At Speech Day 1886, the Headmaster declared him to be 'the moving spirit of the whole', adding 'I do not hesitate to assert that when the College is completed, his name will go down to future generations as the second founder of Brighton College'.

What marks out developments in the 1880s from all earlier outbursts is the sheer scale and speed of capital projects planned: buying more land to extend the Playground and then levelling it, building four boarding houses, a sanatorium, a 'Big School' and a new chapel. There was also to be major expansion in scholarship provision. The new temper is well caught in a letter written in 1883 by one of the Council, Rev. Henry Latham (1881-99):

> At present the great competition between schools is in appliances, such as boarding houses built for the purpose, with every convenience and perfect drainage–Sanatorium and ample space for games. Parents think much of these things. They see them at one place and expect them everywhere ... Extent of ground is of the first importance–it ensures not only playground, but air ... I see that all schools to get boarders must be on a grand scale–small concerns cannot hold their own.

Expansion in facilities and in numbers had come to be seen as inseparable. The local solicitor, old boy and recent governor Arthur FitzHugh (1849-51, Council 1877-81) put it thus, 'Is it not clear that the College must either be enlarged and improved, or abandoned?' Between 1883 and 1887, the Council proceeded to lay out £33,000 (£5,000 more than their predecessors had scraped together and spent in the previous 37 years). On top of that, their plans involved expenditure of another £60,000 (two-thirds of which would go on building and the remainder on paying off all mortgages). Yet financial circumstances had altered hardly at all. Clearly, the decision was taken on a question of principle. Brighton College could delay such developments no longer, as another letter of 1883, this one from the old boy Henry Nicolls (1848-54), made brutally clear:

I wish I could see my way as an Old Member of the College to give it more support and send

Henry Griffith, originator of the grand design, old boy, governor and College solicitor. After the College declared itself bankrupt, the Phoenix Insurance Company suspected him of having embezzled £5,000

MAJOR GENERAL SIR HERBERT STEWART K.C.B.

Mortally wounded at the Battle of Abu-Klea, 1885, he was buried in St Paul's Cathedral. Sir Herbert was the first old boy to be knighted.

some of my sons there, but as compared with Winchester where my two eldest sons have been for four years, it seems to me in all points so distinctly and hopelessly in arrear that I really cannot do so.

When forwarding this communication to the Council, Belcher appended the note 'It seems to me that this letter very fairly represents the sort of feeling that may be supposed to exist in the minds of many sensible men with regard to the College; a feeling for which there is much justification'.

As their architect for these works, the Council turned to another old boy, and one-time pupil of George Gilbert Scott (d.1877), Thomas Graham Jackson (1850-3). He had shot to fame in 1876 by winning the competition to build at Oxford new Examination Schools. Since then, commissions had begun to flood in from Oxford colleges and public schools—so much so that he came to be regarded primarily as an educational architect. First came a long-desired cricket pavilion, built in 1882 and funded by subscription among the Old Boys whose Association was being formed that very year. In fact, £500 of the approximately £900 it cost was given by Henry Griffith. At the same time, £7,000 was spent buying six acres to the north and east 20th century. In 1884, that enlarged Playground was then levelled and enclosed. Here the moving spirits were Henry Griffith and two other members of Council, Edward Easton (1884-c.1900) and Richard Bevan (Treasurer 1860-1918), joined by Arthur FitzHugh. They had combined as a property development syndicate in various parts of the town, and bought out the awkward William Boxall, removing thereby his malign influence stunting the College. Some questioned the £7,000 they charged the school, accusing the syndicate of profiteering, but it is a charge which they hotly denied and which today is beyond investigation.

The year 1884 also saw the Principal spending £2,300 of his own money to buy numbers 1 and 2 Walpole Road which, the following year, he rented to the College to house the recently separated Junior Department. The corrugated iron sanatorium for 20 patients erected in 1887 at a cost of £900 was funded by all the boarding housemasters and similarly rented to the school. Meanwhile, Jackson's first on-campus boarding house, initially called 'House A' (from 1887 named 'Chichester' in honour of the College's first President, who had died the previous year) and designed to house 40 boys, was opened and a second started. Together, these Houses would form the western half of a group of four, arranged symmetrically either side of a grand

The Pavilion, designed by Sir Thomas Jackson, 1882

entrance tower and gateway. Brighton College was set to become an enclosed quadrangle, as opposed to the founder's instructions to lay out the buildings around a court open to the south.

Belcher's relentless pressure for a sanatorium needs special explanation. One of the now uncrossable gulfs between our world and his has been created by the development of effective treatments for, or innoculations against, all those illnesses which we can ignore but which he knew could kill: meningitis, measles, diphtheria, scarlet fever, 'the white plague' tuberculosis. In a Victorian boarding school, any one of these brought teaching to a halt and often caused the dispersal of the boys. Some would not come back and, when a school was labelled as unhealthy, its roll plummeted.

From the 1860s, the Principal's annual report made a regular point of declaring that the College had been free of all infectious diseases. Compared with some, Brighton College was very lucky. Beyond an outbreak of scarletina in 1863, when the school shut for three weeks, and another (on a smaller scale) in 1885, there was no epidemic until measles struck in 1907. As the story of the drains has already revealed, this was an era which took public health most seriously. Without a sanatorium and a qualified nurse, Brighton College could no longer be trusted. Thus in 1885, Belcher took a lease on a good size double-fronted villa close to the school, 1 Evelyn Terrace. 'The parents,' he told the Council, 'were exceedingly pleased.' Not so the local residents, for whom the presence of a school sanatorium 'caused such a scare ... that in the interests of peace and to avoid most injurious publicity, I have felt obliged to give up the house at the end of this term. In my opinion, the only way out of the difficulty is to build a Sanatorium at once'. How had the Council raised £33,000

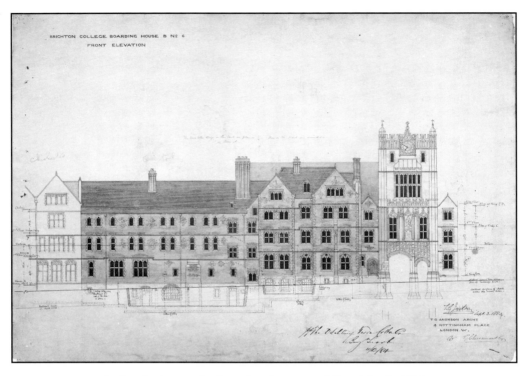

Jackson's designs for boarding houses and Big School, 1885

when on all previous occasions even one quarter of that sum had proved the maximum the College could manage? The crucial year was 1884. First, an attempt was made to sell the remaining 240 shares. On top of the old ordinary shares of £25, which would now carry a reduction of £3 per annum on tuition fees, a new class of presentation was created whereby, upon payment of multiples of £500, boys could be nominated free of all tuition fees. Second, College mortgages were entirely restructured, the old being paid off by four new loans which together extended borrowings from £13,000 to £27,000. In 1885, the Council next launched the school's very first appeal, for £40,000. Addressed to 'old students of Brighton College ... [and] a number of noblemen and gentlemen connected with the

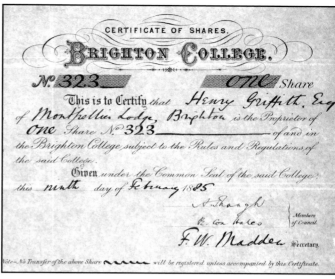

A new-style share, owned by the originator of the grand design

County', it pointed out the way in which 'the Buildings erected still fall short in many respects of the original design' and illustrated the plans to rectify those deficiencies. The Earl of Chichester spoke of the intention to place Brighton College 'more distinctly than ever in the position of the leading school in the County', and thereby secure nationally its 'due position as a *First Rate Public School*'. Half was to be collected by linking donations to 'privileges'. Every donor of £100 was offered the right of presentation at a reduced tuition fee of £2 per annum; donors of £500

received £12 10s. 0d. off the fees while those giving £1,000 'will have the perpetual right of nominating a pupil to be educated free of College fees'. The other £20,000 would be generated via debentures of £100 each, paying 4 per cent per annum. These monies would pay off all College mortgages, build a Great Hall ('the Big Schoolroom') and two further boarding houses.

How successful were these various fund-raising schemes? Scholarships received significant boosts from various anonymous donors. Some £900 was given to finance two Chichester Scholarships, open to the sons of noblemen and gentlemen of Sussex. Another £500 was forthcoming for a Hampden Scholarship. Both were named in honour of the leading lights in the appeal campaign. A further £500

BRIGHTON   **COLLEGE**

ADMIT _____

to the Royal Pavilion Brighton on the 8th day of April 1885 the occasion of the meeting for the completion of Brighton College.

(Signed)   CHICHESTER

President.

Luncheon at 2.0 punctually.

This Card must be presented on entering the Pavilion.

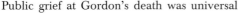

Public grief at Gordon's death was universal   Rev. James Vaughan

came in to endow a Griffith Scholarship commemorating the third Principal, while a third £500 was given to establish a Gordon Memorial Scholarship. Finally, £1,800 was subscribed by the parishioners of Christ Church Montpelier Road for a Vaughan Scholarship to benefit 'the sons of clergymen in the County of Sussex' as a way of marking the retirement of Rev. James Vaughan after 48 years as their incumbent (Council 1845-54). This injection of £4,200 doubled the College's scholarship endowments and, at last, gave the school something reasonable to offer. Quite scandalously, these and all other names were dumped in the 1950s when the scholarship trustees sensibly pooled the many individual endowments. Insensitive and myopic, such was typical of the rape of the College's heritage during the 1950s. When will those ancient names be restored?

What of the appeal? The magazine reported that it 'has awakened a warm expression of feeling throughout the County'. Despite the fact that the paying-off of mortgages was an unlikely cause to entice cash from the pockets of supporters, the Completion Fund raised £10,711 5s. 9d. in two years. Few details are available since the ledger and cash books are lost. The Earl of Chichester and Viscount Hampden, both of whom had refused to fund Lancing in 1881, made donations. At the reception in the Royal Pavilion in April 1885 to launch the appeal, a Mr. C.T. Lucas of Warnham Court stood up and, as the magazine recorded, proposed that 25 gentlemen of Sussex 'should guarantee £1,000 each and endeavour to raise it amongst their friends, promising himself to be one of the twenty-five'. Who he was remains a mystery, except to say that in 1895, the year of his death, he was elected a Vice Patron of the College. The accounts for 1886-7 record two governors as giving £500 each (Richard Bevan and Henry Griffith). They also show £60 as donated by the 'old boys' and another £50 by the founder's widow, Mrs. Soames. Thus, in total, the Completion Fund raised £11,821.

The debenture issue raised £9,000, but the share scheme was a complete flop. Between 1884 and 1886, just two were sold. Had a substantial number been taken under the 1884 proposals, the 1885 idea for presentations could never have been launched. The days of proprietary schools were over. Shares no longer seemed right in the context of education. The College's proposal was out of sympathy with the feelings of the 1880s—which does not speak well of the Council's acumen. As for the presentations, there is equally a complete silence. Was that too a great fiasco?

Against £11,821 given between 1884 and 1887, the Council laid out:

Viscount Hampden

£	s	d	
9,120	17	4	on the Playground
8,911	0	10	on House A
14,331	8	3	on House B and the Gateway
774	3	1	on the Sanatorium
33,136	9	6	

between 1883 and 1887, an excess of £21,315 over receipts (which shortfall was covered by mortgages). First came the additional £14,000 in 1884 already noted. A further £17,000 was borrowed in 1886. Thus in three years, College indebtedness more than tripled to £44,800—requiring a surplus of £1,224 18s. 8d. a year on the revenue account simply to pay the interest. How could they afford such a debt burden? As ever, everything depended on the number of pupils in the school. Expansion was needed to draw in more boys and more boys were needed to pay for the expansion.

Numbers in College

	maximum number	total entrants	dayboy entrants	boarder entrants	leavers
1880	144	58	18	40	58
1881	150	38	14	24	82
1882	138	72	25	47	42
1883	145	57	35	22	46
1884	149	48	19	29	44
1885	167	60	18	42	40
1886	204	82	20	62	53
1887	213	63	21	42	53
1888	219	54	21	33	62
1889	201	56	23	33	71
1890	201	64	30	34	56

The slump of the later 1870s continued to trouble Belcher's first years. The net loss of 44 boys in 1881 was the very worst of any year before 1914. Then, suddenly, each year from 1882 to 1887 showed positive growth. The College roll during those six years showed a total net gain of 103 boys. In 1886, numbers made a spectacular, almost miraculous leap. For the second time in the College's history there were more than 200 boys in the school. The previous record of 207 boys (1863-4) was exceeded in 1887-8, the new peak being 219 boys in 1888. At first, the line was held by the dayboys, as it had been in Bigg's first half decade. Boarding admissions during 1881-5 fell by 13 per cent compared with the previous five years, while dayboys joining increased 10 per cent. The particular drop in new boarders in 1883-4 might have been influenced by another strong attack on Brighton's sewers in *The Lancet* during 1882.

This pattern was more than reversed between 1886 and 1890 as the new emphasis on boarding began to have the desired effect. While day admissions rose by 4.5 per cent, boarding entrants jumped by 39 per cent. How was this growth achieved? Most certainly it was the result of deliberate effort. At the Old Boys' dinner of 1881, a member of Council made the following appeal to the assembled company: 'The success of the College is very greatly in your hands and if you will only do your duty and send sons to Brighton College ...'. Perhaps it was no

[OCTOBER 31, 1885.]   PUNCH, OR THE LONDON CHARIVARI   215

THE BURMESE TOAD.

The Burma Field Force of 1885 was commanded by Sir Harry Prendergast VC (1849-50).

accident that a formal old boys organisation was founded the following year. The Council's declared target was a College of 300—not the 600 of 1845—and from the four new boarding houses planned we can deduce that they intended five-sixths of the school should be boarders. New boarding houses opened in 1883 and 1887, with more planned. All were built to the specifications of the latest theories on boarding requirements. These must have been a spur to many a prospective parent.

So too was an overdue restructuring of the Lower Department. If the Juniors could be expanded, not only would admissions rise but, the bugbear of the last forty years, pupils would stay longer in the College. Ever since Metcalfe had been sacked and the office of Headmaster of the Lower Department abolished in 1849, the youngest boys had formed merely the lowest classes of the College, enjoying an identity and routine no different from their elders. Now in 1882, an entirely separate Junior Department was reconstituted, and the age of admission cut by one year to eight. Henceforth, the juniors lived a separate existence. Their own boarding house was set up in St George's Lodge, diagonally opposite on the corner of College Place and Eastern Road. Three years later, the junior boarders moved again, to 1 and 2 Walpole Road. Belcher's policy paid a handsome dividend. Between 1884 and 1886, junior numbers rose from nineteen to sixty.

Was Brighton College becoming a national rather than a provincial school? That was certainly the Council's intention. Regular advertising in Leeds, Manchester and Liverpool newspapers was revived, but it did not work. Between 1887 and 1890, some eleven boys from the Midlands and the North entered the College (just 4.6 per cent of the total). Twenty years before, during a similar national push under Dr. Griffith, the number drawn in from the same areas had been little better at seventeen (8 per cent). If the comparison is extended, there were similarly no signs of progress:

Catchment areas (i)

	pupils admitted 1867-70		pupils admitted 1887-90	
South West	11	(5.4%)	5	(2.1%)
East Anglia	4	(1.9%)	2	(0.8%)
East Midlands	10	(4.9%)	3	(1.3%)
West Midlands	4	(1.9%)	4	(1.7%)
Yorkshire & N.E.	1		1	
Lancashire & N.W.	2		3	
Wales	0		1	
Scotland	0		0	
Ireland	0		2	
(Total admissions)	(205)		(236)	

So where did the increase of the latter 1880s come from? Small-scale growth occurred in the overseas market. Nine boys from the Empire were recruited, seven of them from India; the previous sample contained only one. Three boys came from the Continent (as against one in 1867-70), five from South America and two from

China. But primary growth was generated under the College's nose, in Brighton and Hove:

Catchment areas (ii)

	pupils admitted 1867-70		*pupils admitted 1887-90*	
the Empire	1		9	(3.8%)
Continental Europe	1		3	
the rest of the world	0		7	(2.9%)
Brighton & Hove	78	(38.0%)	100	(42.4%)
the rest of Sussex	11	(5.4%)	7	(3.0%)
the rest of the S.E.	78	(38.0%)	89	(37.7%)
(Total admissions)	(205)		(236)	

Some 2,800 prospectuses had been sent to selected Sussex homes. Advertisements had been placed on the railway stations of the Victoria to Brighton line. Local expansion generated the boom of the later 1880s. Brighton College remained a very provincial public school of the south east.

Never had expectations been so high. The right image at last secured success in the market place. The county nobility had agreed to grace the front of the prospectus as Vice Patrons. Finances as well as facilities seemed under transformation with fee income exceeding expenditure on salaries by 49 per cent. The Secretary, eminent librarian and numismatist Frederick Madden, even managed to sell the tons of surplus chalk generated by Playground levelling as in-fill for sea defences in Hove and harbour extensions at Newhaven (a narrow-gauge railway being laid across Sutherland Road for two months to ship it out via the Kemp Town station).

Led by Henry Griffith, the Council in 1884 opened negotiations with the borough to improve the surrounding area; 'It is of the greatest importance to the prosperity of the College that its approaches and neighbourhood should be as attractive and healthy as possible'. Sutherland Road was widened. A proposed tramline along Eastern Road was scrapped. Local sewer ventilation was improved. Not everything the College wanted was possible. Without purchasing and demolishing entire rows of houses, nothing could be done to improve Montague Place and

The College's first coat of arms, designed by Sir Thomas Jackson

Chichester House, 1886.

Crescent Place 'for a great widening of the approaches of the College from the sea front'. Had the site of Burlington Cottage already been sold? Neither could the Council evict Evershed's candle factory and the noxious smells it generated, just across Sutherland Road. But they still harried its manager and bombarded the town council with allegations about hazards to the health of the neighbourhood.

Long had Brighton College struggled to enjoy such success. During the slow watches of the night, most must have wondered if it ever would. But those days of weakness and caution seemed now to be the story of another school. Across the Empire, the Golden Jubilee of the Queen-Empress was marked in 1887. Beyond simple celebration, many looked back across the past half century and took enormous pride in the progress and expansion their own generation had brought about. In Brighton, such sentiments could mingle with similar feelings about the rise of their own public school, 40 years on from its opening. As House 'B' was completed and carriages drove through the half-finished entrance gate tower, who could doubt that Brighton College's place among the great schools was at last assured. Belcher reflected that mood perfectly in his report to the Council: 'I have every reason to be satisfied with the present condition of the School, and I look forward to the future with renewed confidence and hope'.

Jackson's design for the Eastern Road buildings, 1884

Five

1888-1895

Dark and cheerless is the morn

Shrewd observers of Victoria's jubilee noted that the gold of 1887 was autumnal. Britain's position in the world was waning. In Brighton College, July 1888 saw the retirement of 'Joey' Newton after 41 years of teaching mathematics, all but 10 of them as Vice Principal. He had been appointed by Macleane in the College's very first year. By his own description 'possessed somewhat of a re-served disposition', he was a figure held in the greatest affection. At OB dinners of the 1880s and 1890s he would be received with rapturous cheering. One former pupil, the eminent church historian John Neville Figgis (1881-85), spoke of his 'kindly glance, quick insight and genuine humour, reproving with satire half-playful, half-ten-der the indolence or the stupidity of his scholars ... No one was less didactic ... He was no prig ... His strength was inward. He kept order, but no one quite knew why.' Belcher called him 'the golden thread running throughout the life of Brighton College'.

John Neville Figgis
Aged 30

Newton left at the peak. Numbers hovered around the two hundred mark in 1889 and 1890, and then began to slip. In nine years, the roll proceeded to drop by 98, or 45 per cent. Slip turned to slide when the greatest expansion the College had known turned into the most serious collapse it had suffered. As in the later years of Dr. Griffith and Dr. Bigg, so now under Mr. Belcher, protracted bust followed brief boom.

Admissions in 1886-90 almost matched the record set in 1861-65, but those for 1881-85 were the worst for 30 years:

Numbers in College

	maximum number	total entrants	dayboy entrants	boarder entrants	leavers
1887	213	63	21	42	53
1888	219	54	21	33	62
1889	201	56	23	33	71
1890	201	64	30	34	56
1891	196	51	24	27	71
1892	176	66	25	41	84
1893	148	40	22	18	48
1894	147	45	23	22	50
1895	132	24	12	12	38

Decennial averages

	Admissions per annum	Pupils in College per annum
1860-69	60.8	180.6
1870-79	55.0	158.1
1880-89	58.6	165.1

Growth there was, but its significance was wholly misjudged. After just two or three years' improvement, the Council could not know that expansion was now perma-nently-rooted. Indeed, experience suggested that the roll was likely to behave capri-ciously. Hope danced for the briefest of seasons.

Retrenchment began as early as 1887 when the capital account was 'closed for the present'. Rather than the red brick and tile-hung 'Queen Anne' style sanatorium Jackson had designed, a corrugated iron structure was erected at the south-west corner of the Playground, next to the observatory (Brightonians of the 1930s-50s knew this as the Physics laboratory, next to the Engineering Shop). Jackson's entrance gate tower had a temporary roof laid above the first floor chamber–in which truncated form it stands to this day. The third and fourth boarding houses were abandoned, along with Big School and the new chapel. As an iron sanatorium symbolised reality so a lone chimney stack, standing for the next 42 years to the east of the entrance archway, spoke of vain faith.

The financial situation by January 1888 was already dire:

mortgage indebtedness	£44,800
debentures	£9,000
floating debt	£3,009
annual interest charges	£1,380
	£58,189

For income to exceed expenditure, the Secretary calculated that the College needed 250 boys on its books. But that was a figure greater than the school had ever known.

Initially, therefore, the objective had to be the covering of working expenses. Economies were made everywhere and, naturally, they fell hardest where outlay was the greatest: salaries. The secretariat was cut. Belcher took a voluntary pay cut. Redundancies among the teaching staff were planned, but the Vice Principal offered to retire and his post was abolished. (Naturally this, the real reason why the golden thread was severed, remained a well-kept secret.) Fees were also altered. The concession on tuition for clergy sons was abolished. Fee levels were altered so that, rather than rising at age thirteen and again at fifteen, the only threshold was above or below thirteen. While the package appeared to aid the parents, in fact it netted the College an additional £70 per annum. Finally and most dubiously, the Council began playing fast and loose with the scholarship funds. Nearly all the scholarship capital was stolen to pay debts and running expenses. Scholarship provision collapsed, which in turn must have contributed to further falls in the roll:

	number of awards	total value	free day places that represented
1881	8	£120 pa	4.0
1883	9	£360 pa	13.3
1885	6	£150 pa	5.5
1887	4	£80 pa	2.9
1889	3	£60 pa	1.8

Junior Department classroom, *c.*1890

'The strictest economy consistent with efficiency' became the Council's watchword. Economies alone would not, however, suffice this time for, as numbers continued to slip away, the College was crushed by the unyielding sum due yearly to service the debt. Back in 1883, the Council had judged interest of £638 8s. 8d. as 'an annual charge which greatly cripples the resources of the College'. Six years later, the sum due on borrowings stood at £1,760 13s. 4d. Fortunately for the school, some loans had come from friends: the Treasurer Richard Bevan, the solicitor Henry Griffith and the Headmaster himself. In April 1889, all three offered to forego the interest due over the next two years, saving the College £347 10s. 0d. per annum. For the future, they also cut their rate by 1 per cent, to 3 per cent. Such generosity gave precious flexibility to the Secretary. Yet the College would

Richard Bevan [Photo: Cuckfield Museum]

still have to find £1,413 3s. 4d. and regularly Mr. Belcher pleaded with the Council to make 'a strong effort by some means or other to reduce the debt and lessen the load'.

With the roll at 201 in 1889, the College's predicament remained partially masked. In June of that year, the Headmaster could still talk of the debt burden as 'a most serious drawback to further development'. From Christmas 1889, however, the facts could no longer be ignored. The Treasurer had to warn his colleagues that, with their overdraft currently standing at £3,613 3s. 5d., the bank was likely to refuse to honour College cheques. Again, friends came to the rescue. Four members of the Council and the Headmaster immediately provided a loan of £200 each to meet that term's salary bill–a most generous but extraordinary procedure, repeated annually until 1893. Short-term loans and hand-to-mouth measures must, however, be temporary and in 1890 the fateful decision was taken to restructure College debts. In place of the seven extant mortgages, one single loan of £40,000 at 5 per cent was taken from the Phoenix Fire Insurance Company.

Did the Council understand the risk they were taking? They were not being forced to redeem any of the old mortgages, yet they were placing themselves entirely in the hands of strangers who charged 1.5 per cent above standard rates. If the accounts showed an operating deficit of £939 in 1888 and £1,158 in 1889, could there be hope of a surplus in 1890? What would happen then? Interest due would not be waived or rates cut next time. The background to this calamitous decision is wholly obscure. In all probability, the key player was again Henry Griffith for he took the prime rôle in the school's financial affairs. Since he was also the Phoenix's local agent, that perhaps explains the choice of lender. Did he receive commission? Whoever proposed the consolidated loan, it rapidly proved a lethal error of judgement.

Miraculously, the Secretary delivered an operating profit of £20 in 1890. College supporters were also still to hand. At Christmas 1890, they offered a 'temporary advance not exceeding £1000'. The following Christmas, Griffith and the Headmaster produced £2,100. In April 1892, 'friends of the College' lent another £900. Such loyal generosity was remarkable, but the bank accounts of these good gentlemen were not inexhaustible, the roll was dropping faster and a deficit of £2,000 was forecast by July 1892. The Council did try to act. They ordered the Headmaster to cut the salary bill and one assistant master was sacked. Beyond that and a significant surrender in his own salary Belcher refused to go, arguing 'that the school could not be carried on if the staff were further reduced' (below fourteen). Simultaneously, the Council went cap in hand to an unknown number of old boys and local gentlemen. Those approaches netted, however, the promise only of £395. Again, one has to ask why Brighton College did not look to all its friends. Among the Vice Patrons were Lord Leconfield, reputedly the richest man in the land, and the Duke of Devonshire who, on inheriting the title in 1891, had come into a fortune of nearly £2 million. All his life, Woodard solicited large gifts from such men to fund his schools. The College Council would not and instead appealed to the Phoenix, which granted a further advance of £5,000 at 4 per cent, repayable in five years.

Salvation could come now only if the roll went up again. Despite every effort, however, numbers dropped 40 per cent between 1888 and 1895. The rise of 1885-88 had been linked to vigorous advertising as Belcher pushed boarding. The school even began to offer accommodation during the holidays for overseas pupils, with the vicar of South Cerney, Gloucestershire. The promotion of the Junior Department had brought in more younger boys who would stay longer. Belcher called this 'building up the school from the right point, viz. the foundations'. One wonders what the seven- year-old Francisco Brenes made of Brighton College when he joined in 1888, straight off the mailboat from Costa Rica. So what was going wrong from 1887-88? Problems with bullying in 1884 cannot have been the start since numbers went on rising for another three years. At various points between 1889 and 1895, the Council explained the leakage as being the consequence of recent influenza epidemics in the town, a new down-turn in Brighton's fashionable ranking, the level of College fees and the economic depression of the time. Towards the end, they also blamed public knowledge of the school's financial situation.

The question of fee levels is problematic for, perversely, they are a topic rarely mentioned in published school histories. As a contribution to a neglected field, Brighton in 1889 charged annually:

	day	boarding
aged over 13	£33 0s. 0d.	£105 0s. 0d.
aged under 13	£26 5s. 0d.	£89 5s. 0d.

Day places were indeed expensive. Kings College Wimbledon and St Paul's both then charged 24 guineas per annum. Even if in part that explains the 8 per cent fall in day admissions between 1886-90 and 1891-95, we are little the wiser because day numbers were not the ones to crash.

The number of new boarders admitted in 1886-90 and 1891-95 showed a decrease of 41 per cent. Renewed advertising could not stem this haemorrhage. Neither could the revival of a reduction on tuition fees for the sons of Anglican clergy (now set at one-third off), or extending that offer to the sons of army and navy officers, or even granting the Headmaster discretion to reduce the tuition fees of new boys by five guineas per year. By looking at the addresses of new boarders, we can identify where the losses were occurring:

Home address of new boarding entrants

	1887-90		1893-96	
Brighton & Hove	100	(42.4%)	74	(47.7%)
rest of Sussex	7	(3.0%)	7	(4.5%)
rest of south-east	89	(37.7%)	44	(28.4%)
rest of England	18	(7.6%)	17	(10.9%)
rest of U.K.	3		2	
Continental Europe	3		3	
the Empire	9	(3.8%)	6	(3.9%)
rest of the world	7			
total	236		155	

Brighton College had never been able to draw significant numbers from across the kingdom, but had always been rooted first in its home town and then more generally across the south east. During the current crisis, recruitment from Brighton and Hove shrank less critically than from the Home Counties.

To say that Britain was suffering economic depression is misleading. What was being experienced was a period of price deflation, caused by rising industrial output and international competition. Profits were falling, but so were prices. It is estimated that, between 1860 and 1890, real wages rose by at least one-half. The sole area really to suffer was agriculture where land values, rents and income all fell by over 20 per cent. Brighton College drew very few, however, from the landed gentry. As a significant cause of the Brighton College crash, the general economic climate will not do. Yet the public schools found these hard times for, as general population growth faltered, the great rise of the middle classes ended. Having doubled in number between 1841 and 1881, the middle classes grew by only 50 per cent between 1881 and 1911. The proportion of the population aged under 15 decreased from 36.3 per cent in 1861 to 30.8 per cent in 1901. At Lancing, the roll collapsed from 200 to just 90 between 1886 and 1899. At Cheltenham, numbers dropped from 660 to 489 in the seven years from 1882 (losses of 55 per cent and 26 per cent respectively). These were tough decades for middle-class fee-paying education. Even a Cambridge College (Cavendish) went bankrupt and collapsed. Brighton College could not have picked a worse period to borrow heavily against projected demand.

Of course, there could be winners. Malvern College saw its roll expand by 72 per cent between 1887 and 1891 (188 to 323 boys). Most interesting of all was what happened at Eastbourne College, founded in 1865. At the very moment Brighton peaked and then slumped, numbers entering Eastbourne rose by 300 per cent to 207. Were these two patterns directly connected? Had a newer local rival stolen a march

Rev. Robert Halley Chambers

on its nearest competitor? If less in the dark than Belcher and the Council, we have to accept that we do not understand what was going on. Perhaps we need to remember that the choice of a school is as individual as the way we decide to vote. Certainly we must allow for the possibility that there was no specific cause. Evanescent patterns there were, but answer there was not.

As the future prime minister Asquith might have said, the Council was in a state of funk. Inability to pinpoint the problem must have been infuriating. All that effort; all that growth; all those hopes; and now mystifying failure. Dogged by disappointments and mounting difficulties, Belcher was so very tired, aged prematurely by the worry. Shortly before his forty-fifth birthday he sent in his resignation. His wife was ill. He was weary. 'The arm of flesh will fail you', he is reported as telling the Treasurer shortly beforehand. Great achievement is assured, however, of subsequent recognition. More than any of his predecessors, he put the College on the map. For the first time, Old Boys found that people had heard of their school. Before 1881, Brighton College had been a somewhat idiosyncratic institution. After 1885, it was a typical small public school. In rural Hampshire the Belchers both made a good recovery and, until his death in 1919, Rev. Thomas Hayes served as vicar of Bramley.

Hopes turned to his successor. The early years of each of the previous three Heads had seen an upturn in College fortunes. A new man would bring fresh vitality and ideas, so he must be offered a good salary: £400 per annum plus capitation at £3 per head over 200. Together with his own boarders, after rent and taxes, that meant a net salary of around £1,000 per annum. Few clerics could match such a sum outside schoolmastering, and the average GP received £500 to £600. Junior barristers regarded an income range of £500 to £1,200 as normal. With a basic salary more than it could rightly afford, Brighton College expected to entice a good man. From a mere 15 applications and a shortlist of six, the Council rejected Matthew Bayfield, then an assistant at Malvern who in 1895 became Headmaster of rival Eastbourne College. They also turned down Haighton Chappel from Marlborough who in 1896 became Headmaster of Worcester Cathedral School. Instead, for the first time they picked a candidate who was already a serving headmaster, Robert Halley Chambers. After teaching at Repton and King's Canterbury, he had for the past 11 years been Principal of Victoria College Jersey.

In Chambers the Council was playing safe, going for a proven track record. With his first in mods and second in literae humaniores, he could not match the double firsts possessed by several of his rivals. Naturally, he came highly recommended. The influential Frederick Walker, then High Master of St Paul's (who in 1853 had taught at Brighton College), classed Chambers as 'a Candidate in the maturity of his bodily and mental strength. He is an exceptionally powerful man.' The former Headmaster of King's Canterbury declared 'in his management of boys, he showed force of character, decision and common sense', while the Dean of Jersey spoke reassuringly for Brighton of his churchmanship as 'strictly moderate, firmly loyal to the Church of England and her doctrines and discipline'. His trump card was, however, the growth of the roll during his reign at Victoria College from 100 to 180 boys.

Chambers knew what he was taking on. During his interview, he said he had 'heard that the financial position of the College was a matter of some anxiety' (which probably goes far in explaining the small field). At that stage, of course, the Council was willing to reveal little. Indeed, the job details sent to enquirers declared disingenuously that there was 'no reason why the number of Boys should not in a short time be brought up to 300'. When Chambers was offered the post, he told the Council bluntly that he hesitated 'on financial grounds'. Quite reasonably, he needed to know the truth. He was told it, was shown the accounts and went over them with the Treasurer. Only then did he accept.

Chambers was a brave man. Burstow paints him in Olympian terms as one who chose to work 'tirelessly for the good repute of the school' even though 'he could expect little glory'. This self-denial is too pious. He did indeed work tirelessly, but he went into the job with his eyes open. He must have relished the challenge and quite probably aimed to make his reputation as the man who saved Brighton College—much as, at that very moment, Dawson was about to do in the two other headships he held before coming to Brighton. It was a gamble, with his own reputation as much at stake as that of the school, but here was the hope of glory. Within his first year, Chambers saw numbers drop from 174 to 148, and that was after he had brought seven boys from Victoria College. Thereafter, the rate of loss began to slow and the slump bottomed out at 119 in October 1897. Given time, Chambers might have turned the College round. But time he never had. College debt repayment could not be sustained with further net losses of pupils every year from 1891 to 1895.

As if financial crisis was not enough to burden the new Headmaster, two months into office Chambers had to deal with what Burstow in 1957 coyly termed 'serious moral trouble'. Our only source is the Council Minutes and while, not surprisingly, they record little of substance, there can be no doubt that what had come to light was schoolboy homosexuality, centred in Hampden (then a boarding house) and extending into School House. Chambers can have taken little comfort from senior boys in his own House assuring him that 'the hovering demon was now less prevalent than the year before'. Boyish wickedness haunted schoolmasters in this era more than in any other part of the Victorian age, for this was a time bearing the unmistakable whiff of decadence. In *The Sign of Four* (1890), Conan Doyle made Sherlock Holmes a cocaine addict. Hardy's *Tess of the d'Urbevilles* (1891) had a seduced woman as its unrepentant heroine. 1894 saw the first *Yellow Book*. From the Cleveland Street Scandal of 1889, when a male brothel was discovered in London, to the trial of Oscar Wilde in 1895, homosexuality was the 'vice' of greatest concern to those working to protect the bulwarks. This was a time of moral panic.

Chambers expelled seven boys, including two prefects, and another four were removed at the Headmaster's request. In addition, as the Headmaster told the Council, 'I found it necessary to flog several boys in the presence of their houses'. The rôle of Hampden's Housemaster, Walter Bazett, is unclear for his conduct was never commented on by the Headmaster to the Council. Did he really suffer a nervous breakdown when the story broke? Another member of the staff, William Lattimer (1900-06) made passing reference to these events in the notes he sent to Burstow, saying that Bazett 'fled the country' during the investigations. Certainly he went to Paris and is said to have attempted suicide. Perhaps he simply could not cope with the shock of what he was told had been happening in his House. We shall never know. Hampden House was broken up, the boys being split between School and Chichester, while its name and building were transferred to the hitherto nameless dayboys; until 1893, they had been squeezed into the tiny room to the left of the passage to the back quad. How 69 boys must have rattled round in all that new space! Had the reason for these changes become public knowledge, we may presume that the spring or summer of 1894 would have brought nemesis. As it was, not a hint of the trouble leaked out and the College was able to stagger a little further.

December 1892 saw the last application of first aid when Messrs. Bevan and Griffith returned interest received over the past four years, totalling £849 17s. 5d. But the patient was now beyond help. By March 1893 the roll had dropped to 146, and that July the Secretary was unable to make the £1,000 repayment due to the Phoenix. Brighton College was not the first public school to be bankrupt. Bradfield College crashed in 1881 owing £160,000. But that was no comfort. Like any sensible lender, the Phoenix tried to be accommodating and a temporary reduction was agreed. But when in April 1894 the College again defaulted, this time on a half-year interest payment of £1,092, they pulled the plug by demanding repayment of the principal in three months. On that the Phoenix would not budge, refusing to meet a deputation from the Council. In desperation, the College pointed out that 'as soon as it is known that the Phoenix ... propose to take legal proceedings to enforce their security, that must put an end to the institution and must depreciate very materially the value of the property which they quit' and added a clear warning, 'Neither the teaching staff nor the boys would continue at the College with the knowledge of such circumstances and the members of the Council do not see how they could take any other course than to inform the Masters and the Parents of the boys'. The Council threatened to go public at the Company A.G.M. on 30 July.

Behind the scenes; Henry Griffith worked frantically, visiting individual Phoenix directors to persuade them that, with a little time, regular repayments would be re-sumed. But the Phoenix seemed obdurate. Why should they consent 'on the chance of the College proving a success, to submit to an immediate further indebtedness'. As the deadline approached, they suggested the College make a public appeal among its friends for monies sufficient to pay both the overdue interest and 'to reduce the capital sum due to such an amount as would adduce them [the Phoenix] reasonable time to prove whether the anticipations of the Council were well founded or not'. Here was the first glimmer of hope. Perhaps the Phoenix would bargain, rather than foreclose and bring in the demolition men to clear the ground for housing.

With nothing now to lose, the Council maintained an unyielding stance, writing back that the proposal would give insufficient time for parents to arrange alternative schooling if the College closed at the end of term. Further, to launch such an appeal would undermine at a stroke all credibility the College possessed 'and so prove fatal'.

This was brinkmanship. If the company would not be reasonable (as the Council saw things), they would bring down the College and ruin the Phoenix's chances of recouping its investment–the loans exceeded the value of College land by £18,000–by turning the site into terraced houses. The Phoenix must agree to preserve the school so that, in time, it could be sold as a going concern.

It worked. The Phoenix did not foreclose in July 1894. Instead, letters were exchanged at a furious rate for six months, drawing and redrawing the future of the College. Meanwhile, a new threat was raised as the Charity Commissioners, carrying out a routine investigation of charities connected with Brighton, became aware of the school's predicament. Thus began a six-year contest between Commissioners and College over control of the scholarship funds. They summoned details of the trustees and their meetings, past accounts, scholarship examination papers and the school's articles of association, concerned to establish the independence and thus the safety of all funds should the College go bankrupt or be taken over. The Commissioners were outraged to discover that there were no trustees and often no trust deeds. Whether they ever discovered that most funds existed only on paper is uncertain but, for a while, it looked as if they would seize what remained. Eventually, they insisted merely that the funds be invested with the Official Trustee of Charitable Funds, in India 2.5 per cent stock. Further, the College was forced, none too soon, to comply with charitable trust law by separating scholarship funds and their management from the Council's control. As for that other battle for control, the Council in November 1894 offered £300 towards interest due, and the Phoenix agreed 'not to put in force any of their powers until the end of the first school term in April 1895.' The Council exploited this and, rejecting a term-by-term 'spasmodic prolongation of the life of the College', requested a reduction in the rate of interest payable. When that was refused, they raised the stakes by threatening to close the school at the end of the current term. Indeed, the governors issued formal notice of dismissal to the Headmaster and staff on 22 March. That was too much. The Phoenix were not going to be pushed any further by a creditor owing them £54,063 1s. 9d. Written notice was delivered to the Council on 21 May stating that legal possession of the College would be taken the following day.

Urgent clarification revealed that the Phoenix would not shut the gates and demolish the buildings. Rather, it would seek the continuance of the College 'as one of the leading educational establishments of the County'. Such are the rich rewards of incompetence. Under terms dictated by the Phoenix, the proprietary company of 1845 went into voluntary liquidation on 22 May 1895. While the College and its Council would carry on, the new owner would appoint a Bursar to act as its official representative. He would have a seat at the Council table and exercise what the Phoenix described as 'the ordinary powers of a managing director'. That was polite understatement for he possessed 'absolute power of veto on all questions'. Outwardly, everything was done to mask what was really happening. Bankruptcy would carry such stigma that both sides needed to play this charade.

We should not be tempted to see this saga in Dunkirk terms, when all was lost but then gloriously retrieved. Neither was this the mischance of the hour. This was a disaster whose seeds had been sown across the previous 12 years and whose fruits were not hope triumphant but a ruinous inheritance. The College Council lost control of their own school through their own irresponsibility. The name of Henry Griffith

The Junior and Chichester Houses, when brand-new

would be linked to calamity and forgotten, not remembered as a second founder. The bragging times were over. There were precious few heroes now. What a way to mark the golden jubilee of Brighton College.

Daily school life continued as if nothing untoward was happening. The boys themselves knew little and understood even less. Vergil and football were their concerns. Yet constant financial worries, the Hampden scandal and the perpetual need to guard the College roll from further harm meant, Chambers ran a solemn, dour régime. One of his assistant masters, 'Old Bird' Lattimer, suggested that 'he never recovered confidence' after the Hampden business. In the words of Francis Bond (1892-1901), 'he quickly became anything but popular'. The boys knew nothing of the great burden which kept him from that active involvement with the Playground for which he had been noted in Jersey. His apparent lack of interest in their activities weighed against him. So too did his de-gowning of two prefects, the immortals of the school (one was Arthur Belcher, son of his predecessor and himself Headmaster from 1933), at a ceremony before the entire College for smoking in their study. To the boys, it was a gross over-reaction and proved him alien to their values. After the 'genial, approachable and understanding' Old Tom, Chambers seemed stern and remote. 'He certainly did not inspire affection' (William Tindal-Atkinson, 1887-94). They could not relate to him. Neither could many of his staff. Fortunately, he decided that life under the Phoenix was not for him and he sent in his resignation on 21 May 1895, the day before they took over.

What a Council meeting that must have been: a letter arriving from the Phoenix announcing their takeover and another from the Headmaster resigning forthwith. Chambers reminded the governors 'that for a long time past I have desired to lay down my charge as soon as this could be done consistently with honour and with the interest of the College', which means he was looking for a way out within a year of taking the job. For him, the Phoenix takeover thus represented the very opposite it meant for the College. As the school was incarcerated, its Headmaster was liberated. Their parting was cordial and, before long, Chambers secured the headmastership of Christs College Brecon, succeeding one of his rivals for the Brighton job. There he stayed until 1921 when he was appointed vicar of Llandevally in Brecknock, subsequently becoming a canon of Swansea. He died in 1934. How could Belcher's *History* have described the brief reign of our most forgotten Headmaster as 'uneventful'?

Part of the chapel's great East window (glass by Clayton and Bell). Was Scott's design (1858) inspired by Lincoln Cathedral?

Six

1895-1906

Lead, kindly light

T he hour was now come. Chambers' letter of resignation and the printed circular announcing the appointment of his successor bore the same date: 21 May 1895. Both were in the planning for some time and, wisely, the Council had decided not to advertise. In the middle of liquidation and repossession, continuity was absolutely vital. The Phoenix must be given no occasion to rethink intentions. Thus the new Headmaster was discovered through private soundings. How extensively the Council searched is not recorded, but among the assistant masters of Radley College they made a precious discovery, the 29-year-old Rev. Arthur Fluitt Titherington. A keen evangelical and compelling preacher, he had emerged from Oxford with a double second in literae humaniores and modern history as well as a rowing blue (stroke, 1887); his own son Geoffrey (1902-3) rowed in the Oxford boat of 1914.

Titherington is the first Head we can really know, for in the 1950s Burstow col-

lected reminiscences from survivors of those, even then, distant days. George Hobson (1898-1900) wrote that 'he always struck me as unsympathetic and dictatorial', but his is a lone voice. Every other contributor offered a very different portrait, each remembering with obvious pleasure their Headmaster's brisk walk, his habit of running up staircases, his patience in the classroom, his mischievous sense of humour. Titherington was no ineffectual softie, but a muscular man, standing six feet three inches tall. John Thornton (1899-1904) remembered how 'his eyes would flash when he was displeased'. Parker Harrison (1899-1902) testified to a glance 'that put the fear of death into small boys'. Contemporaries noted with respect that this schoolmaster did not *need* to use his cane: to the boys, he was quite simply 'the Chief'.

Harold Ogden (1900-02) wrote that, 'to me he had the great and glorious gift

Arthur Fluitt Titherington

of knowing how to treat boys properly: one doesn't forget this kind of thing even after half a century'. No teacher could ask for a better epitaph. Ogden went on to describe his Head as 'a giant, but of a genial nature'. That seems to catch the man. He was famous for 'an expansive beam at the slightest provocation'. Harold Playne (1897-1904; Bursar 1939-40 and 1944-46), told how when translating Aristophanes–they were reading the scene in *The Frogs* where Bacchus rows across the Styx–Titherington took over and suddenly inserted into his declamation, 'Oh those frogs, confound and rot 'em, I've a blister on my bottom'. Playne's narrative continues, 'He had a merry twinkle in his eye as he quoted and we thought it pretty good for a clerical Head-master'. Another delectable reminiscence was offered by Victor Roy (1899-1904):

At that time there was a very popular Musical comedy melody called 'The Honeysuckle and the Bee'. One afternoon, I looked into the Chapel: there was nobody about so seating myself at the Organ I began to play by ear 'The Honeysuckle'. Something caused me to look over my shoulder: close by was the Head, listening. Nothing was said and after a few moments he moved away, a ghost of a twinkle in his eye.

After so dour a predecessor, Titherington was as a breath of sweet air. His wife, known affectionately to the school as 'Mother', was as popular as he, beloved by

The Chief and Mother
Mr and Mrs Titherington

small, tearful boarders as much as by those who had left Eton collars far behind. They entertained extensively. Ever-hungry boys were always being invited round to tea, to be plied by 'Mother' with plates stacked high with muffins and cake. Among the staff, invitations to frequent 'At Home' evenings were much antici-pated for their ladened table, jolly com-pany and song-singing round the piano. Famous also were bicycling expeditions into the lanes of Sussex, the Chief and Mother leading the way on their tandem.

Titherington accepted the post in full knowledge that the College had only 128 boys (121 when he arrived in Septem-ber), was bankrupt and owned by an insurance company. His salary would be lower than any of his predecessors, as long as the College remained small: £600 basic plus £5 capitation for every boy over 150, together with the profits of School House. Perhaps that was the idea. Given the College's situation, it was a package the Phoenix had to guarantee if someone even half good was to be found. The difficulties Titherington faced were gar-gantuan. He knew the statement issued by the Council that

> the financial difficulties which have hitherto hampered the development of the College have been
> entirely removed ... and there is every reason to hope that under the new arrangements the College
> will now enter upon a period of uninterrupted growth and prosperity, and will be enabled to take
> its place among the Great Public Schools of the Country

was grossly misleading. What had been removed was not the financial difficulties, but the school's independence. The new arrangements regulated the operations of a bankrupt owing £44,580 principal and £10,480 interest.

In two respects, however, the situation had changed. Perpetual financial worry had been lifted. Bankruptcy brought with it a certain stability. Second, the way had been opened for the Headmaster to take a more active rôle in College decision-making. The Council had lost the powers it once guarded so jealously against earlier Principals. The axis of power now lay between the Phoenix Bursar and the Head-master.

To some degree, the crisis of Brighton College mirrored that of its mother town. The heady days of rapid expansion were over. Brighton was stagnant, lacking direction. Parts of the seafront were semi-derelict, especially Kemp Town which had become a tatty east end. But revival was at hand. The entrepreneur Harry Preston, who took over the *Royal York Hotel* in 1901, spared no pains in restoring the reputation of his adopted home. Regular visits by Edward VII in 1908-10, the first by a sovereign since 1845, brought desperately needed respectability. Brighton College played its own part in this recovery. On taking possession, the Phoenix had insisted there be 'no restriction of admission'. From May 1895, the school for gentlemen ceased to exist. No longer did it matter if a parent was a shopkeeper or a theatre manager. Ability to pay the fees would, henceforth, be the sole qualifying criterion for parents.

Soames and his supporters would have been outraged. Like the College President in 1872, they knew that 'the different classes of society, the different occupations of life, require different teaching'. The Victorians were snobs, but only up to a point. Social harmony between the old and the new ruling groups was strong. Matthew Arnold, son of the good Doctor, summed it up perfectly in *Friendship's Garland* (1871):

> it is only [in] England that this beneficial salutary inter-mixture of classes takes place. Look at the
> bottle-merchant's son, and the Plantagenet being brought up side by side. None of your absurd
> separations and seventy-two quarterings here. Very likely, young Bottles will end by being a Lord
> himself.

The ethos of Eton could not, however, sit with the bourgeois pretensions of Brighton College's foundation. Even with the barest trace of blue blood, Brighton had been the most socially exclusive school in the kingdom, and almost paid with its life for the privilege. Then came the Phoenix who removed the single most inhibiting factor restraining growth and prosperity. Every cloud has a silver lining.

The declaration in Belcher's *History* that Titherington's era 'was obviously a time for consolidation rather than for experimentation ... not marked by any external progress' is mean. The first experiment and progressive step has just been described, necessity once again being the mother of invention at Brighton College. Bursar and Headmaster then developed the school in two strategic areas: the juniors and the dayboys. In December 1895, Titherington moved the juniors into the old Hampden House where, until 1918, they would live and be taught in much superior

Junior House, *c.*1890

accommodation. Prep schools as we know them were then the new growth area in private fee-paying education, a development not unconnected with the introduction of a minimum school leaving age: set at 11 in 1893 and raised to 12 in 1899. Most public schools took the opportunity to shed their juniors. Belcher and Titherington marked out a different course, and were fighting for market share.

According to William Tindal-Atkinson (Juniors 1887-8), the Juniors possessed 'a happy, homely atmosphere' under their Headmaster, Dobree Charles Wickham ...

> a kindly man, even if, under severe provocation, apt to go off the deep end. In Summer he used to take us for a day out at 'The Black Rabbit', Arundel–an unforgettable day's outing. I have a grateful memory of his many kindnesses ... I said farewell with real regret.

Mrs. Wickham was, as in every prep school, an equally crucial figure. Francis Bond (Juniors 1892-4) testified that she 'combined a quiet natural dignity with charm and beauty and was an effective foil to her somewhat volatile husband. All the small boys loved her'.

After 14 years in office, Wickham left to open a coaching establishment near Crowborough. Then followed an uncomfortable series of short reigns: F.G. Lushington (1897-98), William Southcombe (1898-1902), T.H. Bayley (1902-06). Was anything the matter? Information is too scant to tell. Wickham and Southcombe are recorded as being hot-tempered. The magazine credited Bayley with 'a measure of success not attained for many years'. Otherwise, we know only of daily life from a pupil perspective. Frederick Firmstone (1889-1900) recounted an evocative story:

Junior House Dining Hall,
*c.*1890

After a heavy fall of snow in the Winter Terms, it was customary for The Senior School to raid The Junior. The latter put up surprisingly good fights. Indeed, so fearless were they that matters were brought to a climax one day when a boy of 12 committing the heinous offence of hitting The Captain of the Senior School behind the ear with a snowball was captured, taken prisoner and, as a reprisal, dragged by his heels round the snowbound Playground, finally being deposited at the School Entrance in Walpole Road, bloody but unbowed. Following that episode, the Junior School was out of bounds.

He spoke of the boys' love of fighting 'Wrestling was '*The* CRAZE'. I found it beneficial to become expert in that one was put to the test at all times of the day by boys of all ages and sizes.' But he also revealed a darker side of

organised fights in the Playroom after school hours (To which–I believe–the Housemaster turned a Blind Eye)' and 'Hunting with Packs (Boys not Dogs) after Evening Prep–all matured in the brain of 'The Cock of the Dorm' who had in attendance minions all too ready to gratify the whims of their Idol.

An early Hampden antic was recounted by Leonard Spong (1894-95):

I came from Hove by train leaving about 8am, changing at Brighton for the Kemptown train which had open carriages so you could climb over the backs of the seats from end to end. This train usually brought in the Grammar School boys, who were our great enemies, and if by chance they left their school books in the train it was our great pleasure to hurl them over the Lewes Viaduct.

Steady boys, steady! While numbers never jumped, the Junior Department proved a lifebelt as much during the Phoenix years as it had under Belcher:

	Junior Dept. admissions	as a % of total College admissions
1897	13	37
1899	23	57.5
1901	17	38
1903	25	54
1905	16	39

By contrast the drive to promote Brighton College as a school for dayboys marked a radical reversal of policy. Did the idea come from the Phoenix or the Headmaster? Was the decision purely pragmatic, or was Titherington the first Head since Cotterill to see dayboys as contributing something beyond fees? Both are key questions, but we know the answer to neither. When the College was located in a large town, was short of pupils and it was the boarding side which had collapsed, the initiative at least made sound economic sense:

	dayboys	*boarders*
1887	75	138
1896	67	61
1905	74	61

No substantive dayboy expansion could be hoped for until the College showed that it took dayboys seriously. From the foundation, they had survived in one tiny room off the passage to the octagon. At Christmas 1895, therefore, Titherington moved them to the only large extant space: the Council Chamber, with a garret above as a changing room. What symbolism! The once almighty Council, victor over Macleane and Bigg, broken by the Phoenix and now giving way to Cinderella. Thereafter, Titherington pressed for a new building and in 1905 the Phoenix eventually agreed, butting a small block clumsily in the angle of the Back Quad between the

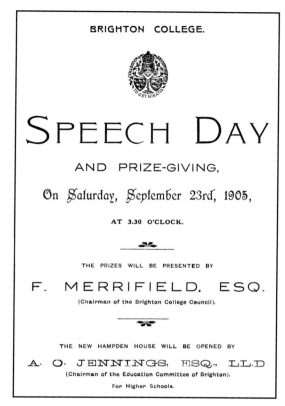

BRIGHTON COLLEGE.

SPEECH DAY

AND PRIZE-GIVING,

On Saturday, September 23rd, 1905,

AT 3.30 O'CLOCK.

THE PRIZES WILL BE PRESENTED BY

F. MERRIFIELD, ESQ.

(Chairman of the Brighton College Council).

THE NEW HAMPDEN HOUSE WILL BE OPENED BY

A. O. JENNINGS, ESQ., LL.D

(Chairman of the Education Committee of Brighton).

For Higher Schools.

Main Building and the Chapel. Downstairs was a changing room, upstairs a prep and reading room. Today, it serves as home for just a few of the dayboys, but the hotch-potch of rooms and corridors added in 1959-60 to create Aldrich House (as the 1905 block is now called) stands testimony to the bastard status so long the lot of their predecessors.

Burstow states the architect to have been Thomas Jackson, designer of the great 1880s schemes. He was not. The new building was designed and built by the company owned by the Phoenix Bursar, Arthur Thwaites. How much it cost we have no idea–the Council and College were not involved–but its erection shouts out the confidence of the Phoenix. Another positive sign was a request in 1903 from the newly-established Brighton Borough Education Committee for the College to admit 'municipal scholars'. The first really good news the Phoenix had heard from Brighton, it goes far in explaining why they sanctioned capital expenditure on the dayboys the following year. It also provides a unique glimpse into the working relationship between Company and College. The decision to accept or reject the Borough proposal was taken in London by the Phoenix directors. They then allowed the Council to determine precise arrangements. In other words, this was the same separation of powers in use before 1895, only now the College Council stood in the place formerly consigned to the Principal. Wisely, they used it to inject academic quality. Under the terms of the agreement, all municipal scholars were to be 'of sufficient promise in ability and attainment to fit them for a course of study aiming at distinction in the Universities or in examinations leading to the Civil Service or Army'. Had the Phoenix captivity lasted longer, the Borough might well have bought the College in 1912, merging it with the Grammar School to establish the united institution in Eastern Road (instead of moving the overcrowded Grammar School from the town centre and building entirely new premises on the Old Shoreham Road). In which case, Brighton College would now be the VIth Form College.

Another name must be linked to the renaissance of the dayboys: their first proper Housemaster, William Lattimer (1900-06), subsequently Headmaster of Queen Elizabeth Grammar School, Barnet. The project only gathered to a head because of his ability to forge the dayboys into a real House, which then proceeded to beat the boarders in the various games competitions and to dominate the College's scholastic successes. One of his boys, Sir Sydney Roberts (1902-06), explained what happened:

Old Brightonians' Dinner, June 1903

The day-boys were still pretty good mud, and the idea of a Day-boy House was still a little strange. Thanks to Lattimer's drive, the situation was transformed, and in 1903 we won about four cups. Familiarly known as 'The Old Bird', Lattimer, a tough North-countryman, created a remarkable spirit in the House ... Looking back I am struck by the number of boys in Hampden at that time who attained some distinction in later years. And it must be remembered that the School was very small.

Sir Bernard Blatch (1900-05) agreed, stating that 'the Old Bird was the provider of all the driving force and the creator of a real 'House' spirit'.

Dayboy strength underpinned Titherington's years. In 1896 and then consistently from 1899, they made up just over half the College. In 1901, they constituted almost two-thirds of the school:

Numbers in College

	maximum number	total entrants	dayboy entrants	boarder entrants	leavers
1894	147	45	23	22	50
1895	132	24	12	12	38
1896	128	46	27	19	35
1897	131	35	21	14	42
1898	138	57	34	23	49
1899	135	40	26	14	56
1900	124	39	26	13	29
1901	137	45	32	13	31
1902	145	62	24	38	51
1903	153	46	35	11	53
1904	140	44	27	17	50
1905	135	41	20	21	42

Sir Bernard Blatch

If we are not careful, the roll will be misread as indicating only an era of great weakness. Admissions between 1896 and 1905 averaged 45.5 per annum, the smallest for any ten-year period in the school's existence. Boarding remained very fragile. Only 83 boarders joined between 1896 and 1900, the lowest ever five-year total. Look again. The fall in boarding admissions was halted and then reversed, 1901-05, showing an increase of 21 per cent on 1896-1900. As for the dayboys, some 134 entered in 1896-1900, and another 137 between 1901 and 1905. By any standards, those totals were exceptional, better than anything experienced during the previous thirty years (23 per cent higher than 1886-95, 29 per cent higher than 1876-85, 15 per cent higher than 1866-75). Here was something wondrous. The roll had remained unbelievably calm across a ten-year period for the very first time in the College's existence. Sustained by dayboy and junior expansion, it was further bolstered by a third achievement: boys were remaining longer in the school:

Length of stay in College

	pupils entering 1879-81		pupils entering 1899-1901	
1 year or less	54	(39%)	34	(27%)
1 to 2 years	24	(17.5%)	22	(18%)
2 to 4 years	41	(30%)	41	(33%)
4 to 6 years	13	(9.5%)	21	(17%)
6 to 8 years	4		3	
8 to 10 years	1		3	
	137		124	

The change was not spectacular. The proportion attending three years or less fell by 8.5 per cent (to 64.5 per cent), those staying for one or two terms by 12 per cent.

But high leaving rates had so weakened Brighton College that any improvement had to be significant.

Healthier numbers brought greater revenue, stabilising the College and bringing a regular surplus to the current account. So improved were prospects after five years of occupation that the Phoenix guaranteed not to close the College 'without three years notice'. Much of the credit belongs to Arthur Thwaites but he, alas, remains trapped in the shadows of our ignorance and it is Titherington's share in the transformation which we see. Burstow is right to assert that 'no Headmaster at Brighton College seems to have been more successful as a schoolmaster or to have won a deeper love and respect of those he taught'. He cut a splendid figure of a man. Kind courteousness sat well on him. 'Old Bird' Lattimer, who worked for eight headmasters during his career, wrote

I never met one whom I respected and admired more than Titherington. No one could have been more considerate to his Staff than he ...

Sir Henry Cotton (1859-61). Chief Commissioner of Assam, Sir Henry was a fine Victorian Radical. He espoused the cause of Indian home rule and was President of the Indian National Congress in 1904. In 1906-10 he was Liberal M.P. for Nottingham East.

The Chapel, *c.*1900

I know that there were some would have wished for more austerity in his rule, but his choice of complete friendship with his boys was part of a deliberate policy.

Major-General James Campbell (1899-1906) suggested that 'he worked too hard teaching too much himself, and probably had not sufficient push'. This may come close to the knuckle, for he was unprepossessing and is reported as suffering anxious torments in Thwaites' presence. But it was inspirational leadership and VIth Form teaching that the Phoenix required of him, not business acumen. Most, looking backwards, have compared him with his successor, unfavourably. No other should be compared with Dawson, and we do Titherington an injustice merely to see him as the one who prepared the way.

College tradition affirms that, in 1897, Radley approached their former assistant master and offered him their Wardenship. Instead, he stuck by Brighton and exhausted himself in the war of attrition. By. the autumn of 1905, his health was in a parlous state. When, therefore, his old Oxford College offered him their Hampshire living of Bramshott, he had the good sense to accept. He had ruled wisely. He had ruled benevolently. He had ruled well. In the magazine, Arthur Belcher (1886-95), then in his third year as an assistant master, penned a charming Latin valedictory:

> What parting word shall be said to you who for eleven years have ruled our school with kindly wisdom? Never sparing yourself, you with a father's care have steered our ship through stormy seas—always with affection, in anger never. To you, who cared for us in work and play, we offer now our sad farewell. May the years bring you ever deeper happiness.

BRIGHTON COLLEGE SEMI-CENTENARY ANNIVERSARY.

➤●◄

THE COUNCIL AND MASTERS OF BRIGHTON COLLEGE

Request the pleasure of the Company of

---

to Luncheon, on Tuesday, the 27th July, 1897, at One p.m.

CHAPEL AT 12.

PRIZE-GIVING AND RECITATIONS IN THE GYMNASIUM AT 12.20.

THE PRIZES WILL BE DISTRIBUTED BY

G. W. E. LODER, ESQ., M.P.

The Old Brightonian Cricket Match will be played in the Afternoon.

THE BAND OF THE FIRST VOLUNTEER BATTALION ROYAL SUSSEX REGIMENT

(By kind permission of Colonel Hugh J. Verrall and the Officers) will attend.

THE FAVOUR OF AN EARLY ANSWER IS REQUESTED.

Please reply to THE SECRETARY, BRIGHTON COLLEGE.

Part III

Solid joys and lasting treasure

Details from the memorial window to Rev. Arthur Titherington (Headmaster 1895-1906)
[glass by Morris & Co., 1923]

SEVEN

1847-1905

Life in Brighton College

Part (i): In the Classroom

When Soames called his school Brighton *College,* he was not blindly following contemporary fashion. Neither Marlborough (in its earliest days) nor Rossall used that term. A collegiate foundation, a society of people living and working together for the promotion of a common purpose, was precisely his vision. The presence of dayboys and off-campus boarding houses did not subvert the ideal, even if both made it more difficult to attain. Indeed, some have seen provision for dayboys as the founder's curse. But this was the design and, a collegiate structure, the whole would be greater than the sum of its parts.

Hours and holidays

Any modern pupil would find the Victorian rhythm of work, rest and holiday remarkably familiar. The day always began at 9am with shortened mattins. Morning lessons commenced at 9.10 or 9.15 and the day ended between 5 and 6pm, afternoon hours sometimes being shorter in the winter. One element only caused constant discussion: the length of the lunch break. Until 1877, it lasted two hours, but then began endless tinkering which steadily extended its duration. By 1889, the gap between morning and afternoon school was three hours; during the winter terms of 1894-95 a further ten minutes were added. Lunchtime was presumably of great importance to the masters. It certainly was to the boys. Here was their chance to relax, to let off steam, to talk, to read, to go onto the Downs and gather specimens for egg or butterfly collections, to play football or cricket or fives. As has already been noted, and as will be explored in the next chapter, school life outside the chapel and the classroom was informal. To the Victorian mind, that was an important principle, the proof of which is seen in the amount of time the College allocated to voluntary activity.

The first permanent change to routine was made in 1867 when the ancient system of dividing a school year into two 'halves' was replaced by a three-term year. The second was the introduction of morning break, normally of ten minutes' duration, in 1882. On the other hand, boys and masters never enjoyed a half-term; that novelty appeared as recently as 1947. School always lasted for six days, but the number of half holidays varied. Usually there were two (one of which was always Saturday), but from 1869 to 1876 a third existed, as it did again every summer term from 1894. These and other small changes can be summed up in one simple statement: the number of classroom hours fell and the length of holidays increased:

	classroom hours per week	holiday weeks per year
1847	30	12.5
1857	30	12.5
1867	29	12-15
1877	29	15
1887	27.5	15
1897	26	15

As far as can be ascertained, nobody complained.

Curriculum

The first prospectus, issued to attract shareholders in December 1845, staked out clearly the academic ground the new College would occupy:

> The Institution to be established for the purpose of providing an efficient course of Education ... comprising religious and moral instruction ... the Greek, Latin and Hebrew, the French and German Languages and Literature; History, Geography, Mathematics, and such other branches of knowledge as it may be found practicable and advantageous to introduce. The Institution to include a naval and military Department.

Upper West corridor, *c.*1895

That statement told prospective parents two crucial things. First, Brighton College would offer the traditional 'liberal education' of the ancient public schools—Latin and Greek (in that order)—without which entry to the universities and most professions was impossible. In 1847-48 at least, that also meant the teaching of Hebrew to senior boys, in line with the best Renaissance precept. The other novelty in 'liberal education' was the College's method of teaching Classics. Macleane, Cotterill and Long would have spent their own schooldays engaged in an endless rote learning of grammar. In the best of the new schools, however, mastering grammar was balanced by translating and reading critically classical literature. Hard as it is for us to appreciate the difference, the testimony of Thomas Jackson quoted in chapter 1 shows its revolutionary consequences.

Second, the prospectus announced that a progressive spirit determined the rest of the curriculum, shaping it to meet the needs of a career in the army, in banking or in business. 'Utility' was to be valued in this school, but separate streams were *not* on offer. As the prospectus of 1859 explained, the 'sound liberal and religious Education' was 'so modified as to meet the demands for practical knowledge of the present age'. The 1866 prospectus made that even clearer

[The College] recognises the general principle that the basis for a good education must be the same, whether to prepare for the Universities, for the Learned or Military Professions, or for the higher class of Mercantile or Manufacturing Employments.

Even when a formal distinction was drawn in 1864 and boys joined either the Classical Department or the Civil and Military Department, a unity was retained. Every boy took Latin. Every boy studied English Literature, French and Science. What varied was the amount of time devoted to each. And while 'Modern' boys could drop Greek, 'Classical' boys had to study Mathematics.

Priorities are here laid bare. Latin and Greek were important. They had to be. But at Brighton there was never a Classical hegemony. Its founders had drunk deep of criticism condemning the narrowness of the old schoolroom, summarised neatly in 1809 by Rev. Sydney Smith whereby

a young Englishman goes to school at six or seven and remains in a course of education until twenty four at the university. In all that time, his sole and exclusive occupation is learning Latin and Greek, and results in his holding scarcely a notion that there is any other kind of excellence.

The way had been pioneered in 18th-century Dissenting Academies and some private schools, like that run by Blimber in *Dombey and Son*. When, therefore, the Clarendon Commission called on the ancient public schools in 1864 to make French and German, Mathematics and Science integral to their work, Eton and Harrow were being summoned to a ground which had been occupied for twenty years by upstart institutions like Brighton College.

Principal Bigg asserted in 1873 that 'Classical study exercises and disciplines the mental powers in a way matched by no other'. In saying that he repeated a commonplace of his age. None of his predecessors or successors under review would have questioned the potency or the value of 'liberal education'. Yet only his immediate successor would (probably) have endorsed that sentiment without qualification. Macleane, Cotterill and Griffith were all Cambridge men with double firsts in Mathematics and Classics. The last two were also keen amateur scientists and, like Chambers and Titherington later, did much to promote the Modern Department.

The Library, *c.*1895. Until 1887, this was also where the Council met

Chambers made it his practice to teach Modern I in addition to his time-hallowed place as master of the VIth Form. A highly unorthodox practice, it was continued by Titherington who held a double second in Classics and History.

Modern Studies

Reference back to the quotation from the 1845 prospectus shows that Modern Languages, History, Geography and Maths (in that order) were on offer. The first thing to observe is that the subject order is wholly misleading. The second is the absence of Science. Until the 1870s, the prime 'modern' subject at Brighton College was Mathematics, which meant mostly geometry and algebra, taught to an exceptionally high standard by the first three Principals (all wranglers), by the redoubtable 'Joey' Newton (1847-88) as Mathematical Lecturer and by a series of other assistants, almost all wranglers. Dr. Griffith worked out a new proof for the Binomial Theorem. Of Newton, John Neville Figgis (1881-85) wrote 'His life was in his teaching. Everything was to him the source of mathematical problems ... He taught lessons of high endeavour, of intellectual enthusiasm'. Every Brighton College boy could have sung with Gilbert's modern major-general (1880), that 'I'm very well acquainted with matters mathematical, I understand equations both the simple and quadratical. About Binomial Theorem,

I'm teeming with a lot o' news, with many cheerful facts about the square of the hypotenuse'. By contrast, Maths was still a voluntary extra at Eton in the 1850s.

Next came Modern Languages. As the *Illustrated London News* noted in October 1849,

> the education [at the College] is not materially different from that of the public grammar schools; a more systematic attention to Mathematics and Modern Languages in subordination to classical training being perhaps the chief distinction in the institution.

French was always compulsory for all, as was German within the Modern Department. Between 1847 and 1870, Italian was also on offer. In the earliest days often termed 'professor', the language teacher was invariably French, German or Italian himself. Degrees in Modern Languages came extraordinarily late to English universities and natives were automatically presumed capable of teaching their mother tongue, its literature and their nation's history.

For us, the notion that English Language and Literature might not be taught is unthinkable. In 1845, however, the suggestion that they should be was far from universally accepted. Championed by Matthew Arnold and John Stuart Mill, lessons of English were roundly condemned by William Morris as 'vulgar' and Oxford introduced a final honours school only in 1894. At Brighton College, instruction in English would seem, until the mid-1860s, to have been limited to a 'Writing Master' and, for a short while, a visiting elocution teacher. If custom was followed, the Writing Master's classes would have involved grammar, handwriting and reading aloud. That situation changed around 1864 with the appointment of a further two visiting specialists, a 'Lecturer on Literature' and a 'Teacher of English Language'. 'The importance of our language was at length being recognised', the Chairman of the Council declared proudly at Prize Day 1875. 'Before, it had been eclipsed by Latin and Greek.'

For the years 1865-70 we are fortunate to possess printed class lists which spell out briefly what each form was to study. In English Language, reading aloud from the New Testament was important, but most time was devoted to spelling and grammar. As for literature, the course seems bizarre: a book of poetry, Walter Scott's novel *Marmion* (1808), Byron's epic poem *The Destruction of Sennacherib* and a steady working through the first three books of *Paradise Lost*–and that is all, unless one counts the annual prize competition to render a specified scene from Shakespeare in Greek iambics. Milton's dominance should not surprise for then he was regarded as *the* supreme christian poet; the College bought his complete works in 1847. Shakespeare's absence from the classroom reminds us that his rediscovery came well into the 19th century. Scott was safe. Byron's presence is the other shock for, by mid-century, the Romantic poets had been associated firmly with false attitudes, with anti-social and Bohemian behaviour. Twenty years later, the class lists again provide syllabus detail. Chaucer remained in limbo and boys were still taken through Milton. The old-fashioned Scott and the bad Byron had been banished, to be replaced by Shakespeare. Finally, in an echo of the old days of the Writing Master, shorthand was made available as an optional extra in 1889.

History appeared in Scripture, Classics and in Modern Language classes as well as on its own. The ancient history of the Mediterranean world was thus covered more than thoroughly. History's presence in the College curriculum from the foundation was inevitable. For the Evangelicals at the helm, history was the record of God's dealings with men, so the study of human progress was of great moral value. None before the 1890s would have questioned the notion of history as progress. For the Victorians, history also appealed to their sense of the romantic, their love of ruins (preferably ivy clad). Honours schools in History were instituted at Oxford and at Cambridge early in the 1870s.

Even if we put to one side the study of Old Testament kings, of Hannibal and Alexander the Great, the College's historical coverage in the later 1860s was remarkably broad. A boy working his way up the classes would have studied Louis XIII and XIV, Napoleon I and Peter the Great as well as William the Conqueror, Richard I, the Wars of the Roses, Elizabeth I, Charles I, the Civil War and the Commonwealth, and finally William IV. Highlights of English history focused sharply around biography, as was the Victorian way, seem exactly what might be expected. Perhaps the same is true of the Sun King and Bonaparte for they were an *entrée* to Marlborough and Wellington. But all of this was novel. Modern History at Harrow in 1805 ended with Alfred the Great. A tsar and near-contemporary domestic history were even more adventurous. That valuable breadth had gone by 1887 when post-Biblical and Classical history involved nothing but English affairs prior to 1815. The subject was fossilising.

Science

Mechanics and magnetism may have been taught from 1847 within the compass of Mathematics, but that is only a guess. The first evidence we possess for Science is Principal Cotterill's raising of a subscription to purchase and set up an 8-inch (15-foot focal length) refracting telescope, thereby beginning a strong tradition of astronomy which lasted into the 1890s. His initiative was followed after three months by securing the 'Head Assistant in the Royal Chemistry Society' to give a series of quarterly 'lectures with experiments' on 'Chemistry and subsequently Mineralogy, Geology and other subjects'. Later the same year, a classroom was converted into a laboratory for Astronomy, Chemistry and Physics. Scientific study had arrived at Brighton College and Cotterill, a wrangler with a laboratory of his own at home, was its midwife.

Many an 18th-century gentleman had a laboratory and the inclusion of Science within the secondary curriculum was a constant demand of much reformist agitation from the 1770s. By Science, most thought of the experimental chemistry of Joseph Priestley and the work on magnetism and induction by Humphrey Davy and Michael Faraday. None of these men was a specialist. Science had not yet been compartmentalised into separate disciplines. That proved a problem when it came to teaching Science in schools for the sheer breadth of the subject (in an already packed timetable) was as much an obstacle as its novelty. So too was cost. Early Victorian governors and headmasters were not used to subjects which required more than books, paper and pens. The ancient public schools lagged far behind. The Clarendon Commission (1861-64) found that only Rugby took Science seriously. But a new spirit was abroad. Cambridge introduced an honours degree in Natural Science as early as 1848; Oxford and London followed in 1853 and 1859 respectively. The Great Exhibition (1851) amply demonstrated the need for scientific and technical education. Science was coming of age.

Brighton College was the first English school to erect a purpose-built laboratory, in 1870-71. Yet Science never appeared among subjects to be taught in the many draft papers of 1845-46 and the College opened without it in 1847. When first we do encounter College Science, it is in a whirlwind of activity in 1851-52. Cotterill seems to have been in a hurry, wasting no time on succeeding to the Principalship to launch the subject. Is this the key to its previous absence? Macleane had drawn up the scheme of education in 1846, and omitted Science. Now, very suddenly, it came rushing in. The first Principal must have opposed its inclusion and the inaugural Council cannot have felt very strongly about its presence, since they let him do it. If true, this serves as a timely reminder that educational reform was no single movement but a delta of ideas and issues. Macleane and Cotterill might disagree over Science, but both could be genuine reformers. Cotterill's enthusiasm was, however, no one-man-band. So keen was Rev. William Grignon (1850-53) that, whenever he was not teaching Latin and Greek, he attended the lessons and demonstrations himself— knowledge later put to good use when Headmaster of Felsted.

Cotterill was Principal too short a time to leave Science in a strong position and one senses that in the early years of Dr. Griffith, himself an amateur astronomer and chemist who won a council medal at the Great Exhibition for inventing a scientific barometer, the subject marked time. Then came a second abrupt change to the fortunes of this subject when, from 1868, all pupils started to learn 'elementary Natural Philosophy, falling bodies, elementary hydrostatics and optics, astronomy and chemistry'. The first Science prize was instituted; by 1872 there were three. Doubtless it was to foster this renaissance that Griffith presented the College with the new laboratory on his resignation. Dr. Bigg maintained the momentum by appointing in 1873 the first full-time Science master. Under James Davies FCS (1873-79), Chemistry and Astronomy flourished, and these developments helped launch the Modern Department. Perhaps also they reflected that climate of concern in the 1860s that Britain was falling behind. Bismarck's victories over Denmark, Austria and France (1864-71) led the War Office to demand a basic scientific grounding in all officer recruits.

Pressure for modernisation soon sank beneath a suffocating complacency. When Davies accepted appointment as an HMI, Bigg replaced him with a series of part-time lecturers. Only in 1883 was another permanent post created, filled by Walter Woollcombe FRAS, FLS who like Davies was an Oxford graduate. He arrived to find only Chemistry taught and equipment scattered, neglected, rusted or broken. But at least the College had finally bought a copy of Darwin's *Descent of Man*, 10 years after its 1871 publication. Woollcombe himself linked the lab to the porters' lodge by 'Bell's Telephonic communication'. He secured funding for a full-scale lab refit in 1882, but pleas for a larger laboratory were put at the back of the queue in the Council's great redevelopment bonanza. He decided gloomily that, without another lab, Physics should not be reintroduced and he left the following year. The fact that he was replaced by a part-time lecturer reinforces his prognosis. The College could not make up its mind about the status and significance of Science.

Thenceforth the subject was restricted to Chemistry, Astronomy and Theoretical Physics. From some point in the 1880s, it was also limited to Modern Department boys, although that is not as serious as it sounds for, as will be observed shortly, the Modern Department by now comprised the bulk of the school. Within those horizons, the subject enjoyed its second renaissance under a series of four eager young Cambridge graduates. Titherington wanted to build another lab and to introduce engineering, but the tight rein by which Thwaites and the Phoenix held him made such developments impossible. All Titherington could do was extend the lab by finding a new home for carpentry. At least he was trying and the 1905 prospectus even went so far as to advertise 'the excellent School of Engineering attached to the Municipal School of Technology in Brighton'. Titherington's stand was as a beacon in glowering skies. Across the public schools, the curriculum was stagnating. Science had failed to become a mainstream subject worthy of automatic study by the brightest. Schools like Uppingham, Oundle, Dulwich and Brighton were the exceptions. There is nothing new about English prejudice against 'practical', non-bookish subjects.

The Masters

Reference has already been made to the laying down of a first-rate classical tradition. We have already noted the reputation won for the young school by Newton and Long, whom Matthew Arnold praised for treating Roman History 'not as a dead and

G. SAMPSON.   D. C. WICKHAM.   THE REV. A. F. TITHERINGTON.   A. T. HAY.   H. TAYLOR.

Photo by]   A GROUP OF MASTERS.   [Donovan

dry matter of learning, but as a side of modern applicability and living interest'. Virtually all the full-time masters were graduates, from Oxbridge. Until the late 1870s, over half were also clergymen, whereas from 1889 to 1905 none were ordained. These men were, with inevitable exceptions, a most impressive group, especially in the 1850s-60s and again from around 1890. Of those appointed by the first three Principals, around two-thirds had a first-class degree. Under Chambers and Titherington that proportion was over half. Master to pupil ratios were (usually) most favourable:

	pupils per master
1847	18.6
1857	13.7
1867	18.4
1877	15.7
1887	17.7
1897	11.9
1905	12.3

Indeed, the demand for such and therefore also for the use of small, separate teaching rooms were important factors behind the founding of the new schools; Eton in 1834 had a ratio of 63:1. With young, intelligent and talented masters teaching small classes, it is no wonder that Victorian and Edwardian Brighton College, for all its inherent financial and thus institutional instability, carved out a considerable academic reputation.

One test of staff quality has traditionally been to look at their subsequent careers. If applied to Brighton College, every decade during these years produced some headships, like that of A.E. Pollard (1878) to Oxford High School, D.E. Norton (1887-90) to Kings Bruton and the always dapper C.J. Mayne (1891-98) to Government School Karachi and then Rajkumar College where, to this day, his statue stands and his name is revered. Applied to those appointed to Brighton between 1850 and 1861, the number who became headmasters is exceptional for so small a school:

Rev. W. Grignon (1850-53) : Sheffield Collegiate; Felsted
S. Kingsford (1851-55) : Chard and Ludlow Grammar Schools
Rev. E. Hawkins (1851-61) : St John's Leatherhead
F. Walker (1853) : Manchester Grammar; St Paul's
Rev. E. Dowland (1858-61) : Salisbury Cathedral School
Rev. H. Day (1859-61) : Sedbergh
E. Marshall (1861) : Brighton Grammar School
Rev. F. Heppenstall (1861-64) : The Perse; Sedbergh

A couple returned to university where they carved out distinguished careers, notably H.L. Drake (1897-98) who for many years was a sought-after Classics tutor at Pembroke Oxford. In a different vein, E.S. Thomas (1903-04) went off to be Secretary of the Egypt Exploration Fund and chief assistant to Howard Carter's excavations. Others became eminent by dedicating many years to the College, as with 'Joey' Newton (1847-88) already encountered or the Australian 'Old Jack Straw' A.T. Hay (1884-1906, Second Master from 1897). Different again were two *literati*: Grant Allen (1870-71) and Frank Harris (1876-77). Allen was a minor novelist who acquired

Grant Allen   Frank Harris

temporary fame with *The Woman Who Did* (1896). On his departure, the magazine paid tribute to his 'indefatigable coaching for the last Recital ... [and] the great loss the Reading Club sustains in his departure'. As for Frank Harris, what does one say about this notorious author, traveller, intriguer and fantasist, debunker of everything sacred to the Victorian era. That he found being a schoolmaster restrictive and tedious is no less surprising than his notion that he would enjoy the life and should apply for the post in the first place.

Academic standards

The staff engendered extraordinary levels of scholarship. For a school whose size ranged normally between 120 and 160, many of whom were juniors and whose Sixth Form usually comprised between 10 and 26 boys only, the achievement was all the more remarkable. Most years there was at least one university scholarship and/or high placing in the competitive exams for Woolwich and the Indian Civil Service, marked invariably by the grant of a 'free half'. Without universal public exams, there was no external hurdle, no absolute standard against which schools and their pupils could be calibrated and, by the wisdom of current monomania, pigeon-holed in a league table. Very few College boys ever took a public exam. London matriculation seems only to have been sat by certain individuals a year or two after leaving the College. As a yardstick, therefore, all we have to go on is the Oxford and Cambridge Higher Certificate, sometimes called the Leaving Certificate, which dispensed with the need to take 'smalls' or 'little-go', the entrance exams to the two universities. These Brighton College introduced in 1874 to the Classical Side; three years later to the Modern:

	average number of candidates passing per annum	minimum/maximum candidates per annum	
1875-79	5.2	4	6
1880-84	5.2	3	8
1885-89	8.4	7	10
1890-94	7.0	5	9
1895-99	5.6	3	10
1900-04	6.4	2	10

To our eyes, those numbers look horrifyingly low. That is our error. Only the *very* top boys took this exam and Brighton, for its size, stood shoulders high with its competitors, as a chart compiled by Belcher shows. His list is all the more interesting because it includes Oxbridge open scholarships and confines itself to other recent foundations:

	O & C Highers	Open scholarships	School population
	1889	1886-89	1889
Lancing	4	4	200
Radley	6	6	155
Eastbourne	7	1	187
Marlborough	8	25	570
BRIGHTON	8	4	201
Bradfield	9	4	164
Malvern	10	7	233
Cheltenham	14	4	450
Rossall	14	20	300
Clifton	16	34	480

As early as 1851, the Council dared to state publicly:

the success which has hitherto attended students from the College to the Universities and elsewhere is sufficient to assure its friends that, in course of time, it will not be inferior in that respect to any Institution in the kingdom.

It was a bold claim, but one justified by events. Wherever we apply a yardstick – entrance to all forms of further education, success in competitive examinations for the Royal Artillery and Royal Engineers, for Sandhurst or the Indian Civil Service—the result comes out much to the credit of the young College. Standards were high and boys were stretched. Continual anxieties about numbers in the school and the size of the overdraft made no difference. As an institution, Victorian Brighton College was permanently weak, at times wholly unstable. As a place of education, Victorian Brighton College was perpetually robust, at times vigorous and sprightly.

Classical v Modern?

Career intentions determined the choice between the two sides and Brighton College always mixed these twin components of Victorian secondary education. Doubtless they cohabited with some discomfort, sometimes with disdain for or resentment of the other. Of such Common Room tensions we know, however, nothing. In due time, the Modern came to swamp the Classical. Our earliest surviving class list (1864) shows that the Civil and Military Department contained 21.7 per cent of the boys. As our survey draws to a close in 1905, it was the Classical Side (as it was then termed) which made up 23.5 per cent of the school:

	Classical		Modern	Total boys
July 1864	162	(78%)	45	207
July 1874	103	(68%)	49	152
July 1884	60	(40%)	89	149
July 1894	43	(41%)	61	104*
July 1904	28	(32%)	60	85*

*The figures for 1894 and 1904 are the Senior Dept. only, the Juniors no longer being divided.

Parental and occupational demand, reflecting opinion at large, voted with its feet and, for a long time, the College was happy to oblige. The establishing of the Civil and Military Department (1864), of an entire Modern Department (1868) and of a special Army Class (1880) fitted well the ethos of the young College. Malvern had no Modern Department when it opened in 1865 and Lancing established none until 1885. The College took the Modern seriously, stressing in prospectuses of 1871-77 that 'its system is not exclusively Classical', and from 1878 to 1881 declaring that 'special regard is paid to pupils who are not intended for the Universities'.

Yet the last few pages have also demonstrated a certain waning of the reformist, progressive spirit. Had a new conservatism come to replace it? At first sight the answer seems to be 'yes'. College scholarships were not available to Modern boys for a long time. The failure to upgrade scientific facilities and to provide even elementary technical and engineering facilities, financial stringency notwithstanding, must challenge the

College's commitment to the new after 1880. That successive Principals, Headmasters and Housemasters were to some degree biased against the Modern Side is suggested in their selection of praepositors. Plenty of Modern boys stayed on beyond their sixteenth birthday. Even allowing for the unpredictable spread of talent in specific years, that pattern is too strong to dismiss:

	Classical	*Modern*
1865	5 *	0
1870	8 *	0
1875	12 *	0
1880	6 *	3
1885	8 *	2
1890	8	3 *
1895	5	6 *
1899	8 *	2
1905	2 *	6 *

*represents the Captain of the School

Push the argument any further, however, and it starts to crumble. Clear distinction between the Classical and the Modern had become blurred. In 1885, John Neville Figgis won a Mathematics Scholarship to St Catherine's Cambridge from the Classical Side. When in 1907 Alan Carr (1902-07) won a Mathematics Exhibition to the same college, he came from the Modern Side. Even more perplexing, Arthur Shallow (1902-06) and Geoffrey Manooch (1904-08) both won high placings in the Indian Police examinations, the first from the Modern (as one would expect), but the second from the Classical. Histories of education assert firmly that the new public schools lost from the 1870s-80s their modernist edge as they scrambled desperately to ape the ancient public schools. Most certainly that scramble took place, at Brighton as elsewhere. But was the curriculum damaged? The evidence from Brighton seems distinctly unclear. Another test could look at the degree subjects studied by former pupils, even though university was the ambition of only a minority of boys before the 1960s. We know of 636 boys who entered the College 1848-1905 and then proceeded to university. Alas, their degree subject is recorded in a mere 192 cases (30.2 per cent), so we are left only with impressions. *Very* limited evidence, this does, however, suggest that Modern subjects continued to be popular and successful. Alongside Classics and Theology, the 'new' subjects seem fairly well represented:

Known degree subjects

year of graduation	classics	theology	maths	history	moral science
1850-59	6	2	5	3	-
1860-69	11	4	9	1	2
1870-79	8	4	5	1	1
1880-89	6	4	3	7	-
1890-99	3	5	-	3	1
1900-05	6	2	3	2	2

The Modern had rapidly become a new orthodoxy, but had the modern really won through? The real test (as ever) comes with Science, and that takes us close to the heart of a great historical issue: the reasons for the economic decline of England from around 1870, and the rôle in that of the public schools:

year of graduation	natural science	engineering	veterinary science	dentistry
1850-59	1	-	-	-
1860-69	3	-	-	-
1870-79	2	-	1	-
1880-89	2	2	-	1
1890-99	1	1	1	-
1900-05	-	6	-	-

By definition, the universities then catered for only a part of this rapidly expanding area. Other institutions are equally relevant:

year of qualification	Royal Indian Engineering College	Crystal Palace Engineering School	Cambourne School of Mines	Central Technical College
1870-79	2	-	-	-
1880-89	2	2	-	-
1890-99	1	2	-	2
1900-05	-	1	2	-

The same need to go beyond the universities is even more true of medicine, which caught on very slowly as a degree subject, especially in England:

year of graduation or qualification	university	hospital
1850-59	1	5
1860-69	1	9
1870-79	6	12
1880-89	15	14
1890-99	6	6
1900-05	2	2

The conspicuous failure of Victorian Oxford and Cambridge to take seriously subjects like Medicine and Engineering only emphasises the different attitude of Brighton College. To study Classics or History, its VIth Formers flocked almost exclusively to Oxbridge. For Medicine and Engineering, however, they had to go in large numbers to London and to the Scottish universities, especially Edinburgh. Here is evidence more than sufficient to assert confidently that Brighton College promoted the modern with skill and conviction.

The view from the Headmaster's croquet lawn, c.1895

But that is only part of the answer. Most boys went into the law, banking, accountancy and stockbroking, as well as the church and the army. As a good public school, Brighton College fed the professions with plain, honest English gentlemen, instilled with an ethos of public service. Much has been written about the economic and industrial decay of Britain during the years 1870-1914, and of a marked rejection by the middle classes of manufacturing business as a worthy occupation. Royal Commissions in 1870 and 1885 pointed out that the nation was falling further and further behind Germany and America. Both identified the root problem as the gross deficiency in the provision of scientific and technical training in secondary and higher education. Brighton College was most certainly deficient in this area by 1880, but does not seem to have been infected by the reaction against Science prevalent from around 1890 in the public school world. As we have seen, Chambers and Titherington worked with some success to circumvent the school's financial inability to build further laboratories and workshops. In a world of national decay where each public school looked and sounded increasingly like every other public school, Brighton College had found again something of its progressive spirit. Brighton College had kept faith with its foundation, even as the school bell tolled to mark the death of Queen Victoria.

EIGHT

1847-1905

Life in Brighton College

Part (ii) Refreshment and Amusement

There are repeated complaints about the disuse of the library... The present day mind cannot for ever soak itself in the monumental novels of fifty years ago. The root of the evil is that there exists no subscription which would allow of the purchase of new books. As it is, we are dependent upon the charity of those who are generous enough to present us with that *rara avis*–a recent work.

From the anonymous sub librarian, who penned this battle cry in 1902, we may deduce that the College Library had limited appeal as a centre of recreation. Things had been better. The magazine of December 1881 printed a list of 102 books missing, mostly fiction. Gone were three novels by Dickens, four by Walter Scott and eight by Captain Marryat (including *Mr. Midshipman Easy*, and *The Children of the New Forest*), *Mansfield Park, Vanity Fair, Westward Ho!*, poetry by Elizabeth Barrett Browning, Burns and Tennyson. Somebody had been reading avidly. Juniors perhaps saw things differently in 1902. *Treasure Island* (1883), *King Solomon's Mines* (1885), *The White Company* (1891), *The Jungle Books* (1894-5) and *Kim* (1901), endless adventure novels by Henty and Jules Verne, appeared on the shelves at or soon after publication, courtesy of benevolent masters.

The Magazine

Some boys found recreation in writing for and editing the school magazine. Indeed, Brighton College is credited with producing the first ever such publication. This appeared in November 1852, written by 'senior boarders at the house of the Principal'. William Foster-Melliar (1850-54) was the founder-Editor, but it lasted only two issues. The urge to see one's efforts in print was, of course, too strong and a second attempt, launched in 1853, ran for eight numbers. Both were essentially journals of literary and academic pretensions, filled with learned essays, weak poems, and corny jokes. Readers were presented with a broad range of articles: 'Formation of Cliffs between Brighton and Rottendean [sic]', 'The Steam Engine', 'Etching', 'Geoffrey Chaucer'.

Alternatively, they could be inspired during the Crimean War by odes to national heroism like 'To England', or be touched by sentimental pieces such as 'The Hospital at Scutari' which sang of 'A mortal only, yet divine possest, by man beloved, by angels blest'. Two budding schoolboy poets even wrote and published (by subscription among masters and parents) a volume of their own verse entitled *Lays of 1855;*

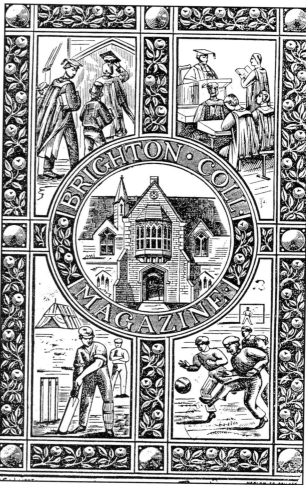

The original cover of the Brighton College magazine, 1869, designed by Sir Thomas Jackson. Without the pictures it remained in use until 1933.

the authors are thought to have been Foster-Melliar and Lewis Frazer (1855-58). Literary endeavour continued until the 1870s when, fairly abruptly, it disappeared almost completely from the magazine, not to return until the 1930s.

Societies

With the advent of regular magazines we hear of the doings of the societies within which the boys pursued and developed their enthusiasms: the Art Club, the Chess Club, the Debating Society, the Glee Club, the Entomological Society, the Literary Society, the Meteorological Society, the Musical Society, the Natural History Society, the Photographic Club, the Reading Club, the Scientific Society. Of course, such clubs came and went, sometimes two or three times, for they were wholly dependent on pupils' tastes. According to the magazine of October 1878, societies flourished because they 'so greatly help to while away the long evenings of the winter months'. But that is mean, for it ignores the commitment put into these recreational and, in many cases, intellectual activities. The Art Club put on exhibitions of its members' work. The Glee Club gave concerts to their fellow pupils. Members of the Reading Club, in evening dress, took part in the Christmas Recital and on Prize Days.

Some societies made up for the deficiencies in the curriculum. Others supplemented school work. The marginal position occupied by Music will be examined shortly. Art existed even more tenuously. Between 1847 and 1889 there was always a part-time 'Drawing Master'; the first, Charles Runciman, exhibited at the Royal Academy from 1836 to 1855. From 1889, one of the full-time masters took Drawing. All the time, however, it was a voluntary extra, charged at four guineas per annum (cut to three guineas in 1899). Drawing was important to the Victorians. They saw it as a valuable way of observing the world, but they perceived it as a social accomplishment, not a formal skill. An exceptionally high proportion of Victorians seem to have sketched and painted watercolours, but boys were taught by their mothers at home. Art as a school subject was regarded as fit only for girls.

Chess was rated highly in those days, being seen as intellectual rather than frivolous, and therefore an honest recreation for those of ability and energy. The very first inter-school match played by Brighton College was a postal chess game against Shrewsbury in December 1848; we lost. The next we hear of College chess is not until 1876 when a letter in the magazine, reporting that the game was 'a favourite amusement' in one of the Houses, called for a College Chess Club to be set up. Others must have thought so too, for such a club came into being in Lent Term 1877.

The dominant presence of scientific clubs takes us a vital stage on from the discussion in chapter seven to demonstrate that many boys themselves held a genuine interest. The Scientific Society, founded in 1875, met 'every ten days or so' in the two winter terms for members to read papers. There were five sections: Botanical, Entomological, Meteorological, Ornithological and Antiquarian. Meetings always ended with displays of objects. A rain gauge and barometer were employed to post daily weather reports. A College museum was soon under way. Summer outings took members to Devils Dyke, to Cissbury and Chanctonbury Rings to collect specimens –a jolly enjoyed as much as the annual choir picnic to Arundel or Bramber.

Prince among these schoolboy associations was the Debating Society, of which we have record from 1860. Each term the Vth and VIth forms organised between five and eight debates which frequently took on the questions of the day: the abolition of capital punishment, the conduct of Garibaldi or Abraham Lincoln or Bismarck, the introduction of compulsory education, the abolition of field sports, the legalisation of cremation, votes for women. On political questions, these young men tended to be Conservative, condemning Palmerston's and Gladstone's policies as regularly as endorsing those of Lord Derby and Disraeli. College boys are recorded as helping the local Tory candidates in the 1884 Brighton by-election and at all three General Elections between 1885 and 1892.

On questions that pushed the frontiers of Victorian society they were also conservative. The retention of transportation for convicts was approved in 1863 and 1868. The secret ballot was rejected in the year before parliament introduced it. A motion to let women vote and become MPs was overwhelmingly defeated in 1892. Proposals to abolish capital punishment failed every time they were suggested. A Channel Tunnel was twice voted down during the schemes discussed nationally in the 1880s. But some debates produced results that would surprise us. A motion to make elementary education compulsory was carried in 1869, the year before the Liberals enacted it. A debate in 1872 favoured the admission of women to higher education. Another in 1876 called for the abolition of field sports on account of their cruelty. Perhaps there is an explanation for this. Debate summaries across these years give the firm impression that Brighton College schoolboys were less open-minded in 1895 than they had been in 1875. Yet even then there could be exceptions, as the motion won in March 1890: 'That the attitude of the dockers during the late agitation deserved the sympathy and support of the nation'. Did any group of College boys hold such advanced views again until the later 1960s?

Lectures

Speakers came fairly regularly to inform and entertain. Their subjects ranged from butterflies to 'Rustic Songs', from the Solomon Islands to the work of The British and Foreign Bible Society. New standards in entertainment arrived in March 1889 with the lecture by Professor E.D. Archibald, who illustrated his talk on Edison's phonograph not only with magic lantern slides (explaining the physics of sound waves), but with the machine itself, recording on the spot 'a speech' and a rendition of 'John Brown's Body'. 'All his words were reproduced with wonderful clearness. After the lecture, many of the audience went up to the platform to hear the low records through the ear tubes'. Were we able to go back and sit among the audiences at these lectures, we might well pick that last performance for its historical significance. The dictating phonograph, which the professor appears to have brought, had been developed by Edison only the year before Brighton College boys heard it. Another not-to-be missed lecture would have been that in 1893 by Edward Whymper, the legendary mountaineer, who spoke with lantern slides of his conquest of the Matterhorn. What could have challenged, for excitement, for significance or for topicality the twin lectures in 1892 and 1897 by Fridtjof Nansen before and after his voyages into the Eastern Arctic. On the latter occasion, so many from the town wanted to hear the famed explorer that the venue was moved to the Dome.

Guy Fawkes Night

One highlight of the boarders' year until the 1860s was the magnificent celebration of 5 November. The boys spent much time collecting firewood to build, ever higher and higher, a great bonfire in the Principal's garden. George Barber (1858-65) tells us:

> Our bonfire wood filled the whole place ... I never saw such a big one in all my life. There were five big waggons filled up double the height of themselves with wood and furze.

The Housemasters paid for fireworks, for food and hot punch, but the boys provided an essential ingredient of their own, described for us again by Barber:

> We had lots of flaming balls. They are composed of large balls of tow wound round with wire very tight and then soaked in turpentine. You light them and kick them about. It is a most awful lark.

Each year, one of the masters delivered a stirring anti-popery oration while, in turn, each assembled boy circled round the mountainous pile, lighting his torch from the flaming brand of his neighbour. With the circle of flame complete, the boys then struck up the national anthem and at the point in verse two where they sang

> O Lord our God, arise,
> Scatter our enemies,
> And make them fall ...

the orator thrust his torch into the pyre.

Unfortunately for the boys, the celebration was too successful, attracting ever more attention from the neighbourhood. In 1869, the Principal had to hire three constables and an inspector to keep order. Defeat had to be admitted and, with very considerable vitriol against 'the hordes of Edward Street', the ceremony was suppressed in 1870 or 1871. Thereafter, praepositors took the juniors to see a public display in the town. It was not the same. Perhaps, however, it helped to kill off anti-catholic feeling in Brighton, both town and College. When in 1856 Dr. Woodard had held a public meeting locally to raise funds for Lancing, College boys took a prominent part in the crowd which jeered and yelled, booed and hissed this 'nursery of popery'. At the bonfire ceremony of 1858 described by Barber, 'our Guy Faux [sic] was an imitation of Cardinal Wiseman. He had a roman candle in his mouth and one in each hand'. Here was the populist end of the Council's firm evangelicalism.

In later years, pyrotechnics were again enjoyed. Parker Harrison (1899-1902) tells us that, at their hut on Small Field [the site of the present Great Hall], the Juniors 'fired off a small brass cannon, the explosive being the heads of matches laboriously scraped and powdered, and exploded by a hot pin'. What the authorities thought we are not told, but at least he does not mention any casualties (though who can say about the long-term effects of the phosphorus).

Public celebrations

In what manner the College made formal celebration of Victoria's Golden and Diamond Jubilees the magazine does not record, beyond reference to the holiday granted (in 1887, a four-day exeat). Similar silence will be found on that other event which produced a spontaneous outpouring of national joy, the Relief of Mafeking (1900). We know, however, that the Corps took part in a parade in the town. Spencer Batchelor (1898-1902) tells us he was taking an exam the morning the news came through ...

and, in the exuberance of the moment, wrote at the top of my paper: 'Hark the Herald Angels sing Tis the Relief of Mafeking', and was threatened with being kept in for the afternoon, though this was changed for a modicum of lines.

Detail does survive concerning two events. For the wedding of the future George V in 1893,

the Headmaster kindly allowed the School to repair to the Playground during the last hour of the morning. During the evening, a few favoured members were allowed to accompany the House Masters on to the Front, to view the fireworks displayed on the Chain Pier, while the others were permitted to watch from the top storey of Hampden House.

Photo by]   THE "TUCK SHOP." ICES!   [*Donovan.*

As for the funeral of the Duke of Wellington (1852), the whole school was given a half holiday, while those who wished to witness the event itself were allowed two days leave of absence. This generosity was the result of royal command. Prince Albert, very much the brains behind the state funeral, was determined that 'every Englishman shall have time and opportunity to take his humble part'. In the wave of mourning that swept the kingdom, the College authorities duly complied (unlike their successors a century later who granted no such leave for Churchill's state funeral in 1965). It was one of those brilliant winter days and around two-thirds of the College were among the million and a half who packed the streets of the capital to witness the cortège of the man described by Queen Victoria as 'the last great Englishman'.

College slang

Victorian public schoolboys displayed a marked tendency to invent their own languages. In some schools, enough terms have come down to fill a phrase book, but from Brighton only three survive:

    a *wolley* – the rough jostling of the crowd around the tuckshop
                [there was also a verb 'to *wolley*' and the expression '*wolley up!*']
    a *tight* – cricket fielding practice
    a *mill* – a schoolboy fight

Plays

Drama played a small part in the life of the Victorian College. Sir Thomas Jackson (1850-53) refers to painting scenery for a play, but there then seems to have been a hiatus until 1880 when The House put on the farce *Ici on parle Français* and the choir performed in costume Gilbert and Sullivan's *Trial by Jury*. Puritanism probably explains this state of affairs. An aversion to acting was by no means a Brighton peculiarity. In their early days, no plays were put on at Cheltenham or Malvern either. Once more, we need to recall the College's church-evangelical foundation. We know that Dr. Griffith vetoed proposals for a play and that Rev. Henry Venn Elliott considered that theatre and opera 'risk the everlasting salvation of those who exhibit them'.

    Does this explain why Lancing began drama *much* earlier than Brighton? The closest College boys were allowed was the reading of excerpts from a Classical, a French and an English play each Prize Day. From 1868, there was also a Reading Club which, beyond poems and extracts from novels, often tackled scenes from plays, usually Shakespeare, Sheridan and Goldsmith. But *Lear* was not selected until 1880, *Hamlet* not until 1891. Neither on Prize Day nor at the Club were costumes or scenery employed. This was not drama. This was recitation.

    Eventually, the smell of greasepaint worked its magic and, from 1883, extracts from several plays, often Sheridan, were performed at the end of each Lent Term. Christmas 1885 should have seen the production of the first three acts of *Julius Caesar*, but the show had to be abandoned when both Anthony and Cassius were taken ill. Yet even this was not full drama. Beyond the one-act comedies, no complete work was staged until December 1901 when, with hired scenery, costumes and footlights, *The Yeoman of the Guard* was performed. The audience, we are told, 'were most

The Cyclops: frontispiece to the magazine, April 1904

enthusiastic in their applause, and insisted on a great many encores'. No full play came until 1904: *The Cyclops* by Euripedes, performed in Greek. This was an extraordinarily ambitious project for a school of only 140 boys and shows, as Burstow noted, that 'the Classical Side was by no means dead'. One-act comedies continued and a Dramatic Society stammered briefly in 1910-13. No full play would be staged again, however, until *The Merchant of Venice* in 1919. Only then can College drama really be said to have begun.

Music

College music was a recreational activity, not a curriculum subject. Before 1888, the 'Organist and Choral Master' was a part-time man whose name appeared at the bottom of the prospectus staff list, alongside the Drawing and Fencing Masters. Thomas Ingram, formerly Sub-Organist of Ely, held the first such appointment from 1847 to his death in 1869. His job specification was to give singing lessons, coach the chapel choir and play for services. Within a year, he had started a Choral Society, which gave its first

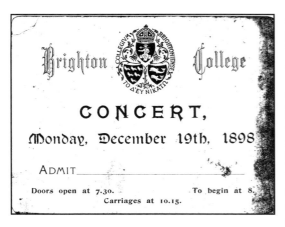

concert in June 1848. What they sang is not recorded, but we are informed that it 'passed off brilliantly'. By 1859, singing was compulsory for all boarders; from 1866 to 1881 for all in lower forms. We hear vaguely of a band in 1862, of an orchestra in 1879 and again in 1891. Piano lessons were first advertised in 1875 when the College bought three upright pianos. Violin tuition was added 14 years later. Otherwise, the only available instrument would seem to have been the chapel organ and, at £1 10s. 0d. per term for tuition, the accounts show six boys (out of 145) were being taught in 1883.

Within the magazines we can follow the repertoire of the Annual Concert. Until 1877, its programme was divided between 'part i - sacred' and 'part ii - secular'. In the former, programmes relied almost exclusively on Handel, supported by Mendelssohn, and occasionally works by Haydn and Spohr. Part ii saw far greater variety, but an exceedingly high proportion of the works were by composers now wholly forgotten. Traditional English songs appeared frequently in the earlier years, for example *The Vicar of Bray* and *Men of Harlech*, but never any of the new parlour songs which would have been very out of place; perhaps *Come into the Garden Maud* and the like were sung in the rooms of 'Burney' Belcher (staff 1886-93, brother of Rev T.H.) where Philip Le Febvre (1892-94) remembered, 'we were kept warm for an hour or so on wintry evenings once a fortnight with chorus songs'. At the Concert, more 'highbrow' pieces were attempted from 1874 when a trio from *Così fan Tutte* made its debut. With the scrapping of the oratorio section in 1877, a vigour seemed to overtake the Concert. Instrumental items appeared for the first time: Beethoven's First Violin Sonata in 1878, Haydn's Toy Symphony in 1879. The chief innovation was, however, a contemporary English element. This usually took the form of a song or two by Parry, Stanford or Sullivan (almost never from the Savoy Operas). More ambitious was a performance of Sterndale Bennett's cantata *The May Queen* in 1878. From 1897, there were pieces by Edward German.

All of that was very accesssible. Conspicuous by its almost complete absence was Continental music of the second half of the century. There was a little Grieg, a little less Brahms and a single work by Dvorak. Wagner was played twice, once in 1890, but for the first time in 1879 (the Bridal Chorus from *Lohengrin*). If that was progressive, it was a solitary exception. So too was an *Ave Maria* by Mascagni, the only work from a Continental composer born after 1850. Were opportunities for music-making and the quality of musical education better or worse elsewhere?

The College Home Mission

Brighton College set up its mission late, Uppingham leading the field in 1869. On the initiative of the Headmaster, Brighton followed in June 1885 by linking itself to the slum parish of St Augustine Stepney, where both vicar and curate were old boys:

The Brighton College Mission, Stepney (The church was gutted in the Blitz and later demolished, but the Club House still stands)

Harry Wilson (1862-72) and his brother Richard (1867-72, later known as 'The Hoppers' Parson'). The origins of public school and university missions lay in a combination of practical christianity and growing unease about levels of destitution. How could Britain, the leading imperial and industrial power, still possess extensive slums? Urban poverty was an affront to the nation, but missions were designed to alleviate more than 'bodily distress'. They aimed to christianise what the Bishop of London called 'the inner-city wilderness' and, if their rhetoric can be believed, to re-integrate the two nations.

The Mission supported a boys' Club which provided washing facilities, cheap food and relaxations such as football, swimming and cricket (the latter played in the moat of the Tower of London) for 'lads of the poorest class [who] had to work hard for their livelihood. Some of them worked as boiler cleaners, others at the Docks, but all were working at the hardest and lowest kind of labour'. The Club also offered spiritual instruction in a parish where, from a population of 8,000 souls, only around 100 attended church each Sunday. Indeed, Club membership was limited to those who would go to church. Old boys living in London were asked to come over 'and help to amuse and instruct the lads'. But the prime need was money. In 1885, the

College collected £74 11s. 9d. By 1890, fund-raising had pushed that up to £118 10s. 4d.–the equivalent of 1.18 boarding places at the College. The fund helped to pay for the Brighton College Mission Curate and the complete renovation of the Club. Each summer, Club boys came down to Brighton, swam in the sea and visited the College. By 1894, the vicar estimated, 'more than two hundred boys have passed through our hands ... This Easter, out of 306 communicants, about 130 were men and lads, and this large proportion was due chiefly to the influence of our Club'. Then, suddenly, the trail goes cold. We know that in 1896 the parish was supported by the Oxford Christ Church Mission and all reference in Brighton College sources ceases after 1899. Wilson continued as vicar until 1902 and need had not been diminished. Had enthusiasm waned? Only £67 5s. 0d. was collected in 1893. The apparently inglorious end to the mission needs further investigation.

The Rifle Volunteers

Another short-lived affair was the College's first attempt to put pupils into uniform. In 1859-60, Britain was gripped with Volunteer fever as a French invasion scare sent almost the entire nation rushing to become part-time soldiers. Among the many public schools which responded was Brighton College where a corps began in November 1860, attached to the 1st Sussex (Brighton) Rifles as the 4th Company. According to Mowbray Gray (1855-62), 'every schoolboy over the height of 4ft 2in thought it necessary to offer his services to his country'. That meant an initial muster of 66 from a College roll of 173, supplemented by 'sixteen little fellows who form the Fife and Drum Band to the Corps'. At the inaugural inspection the following month, they played *The British Grenadiers* 'in capital style' as Mrs. Hawkins, wife of one of the masters (and the mother of Anthony Hope Hawkins who wrote *The Prisoner of Zenda*), presented them with a red silk colour of her own handiwork. Burstow's *History* (1957) notes that this colour and a band uniform had 'recently been discovered'. Typically, however, both have again disappeared, almost certainly thrown out in the 1960s. Gray tells us something of the short life and ignoble demise of this unit:

We were armed with percussion carbines which had seen service in the Crimean War ... We used to take long marches over the Downs, led by our band ringing the changes on the only three marches they knew, *Gary Owen*, *The Girl I Left Behind Me* and *The British Grenadiers* ... Things went on well for a time with the B.C.V.R.C., and it seemed as if we could not get enough soldiering, but gradually and inch by inch our legs came further through our trousers and our arms through our sleeves ... We applied vainly to our parents for new uniforms, but were met with the old cry—they must be let out unless we could pass them on to our younger brothers. In these depressing circumstances, our ranks thinned considerably and we practically confined our manoeuvres to our parade ground but, when here, we were under the continual witticisms and criticisms of the Brighton Hooligans, for whom in those days we had another name. Physical courage we might have had, but our moral courage failed lamentably.

The Volunteer movement remained a prominent feature of Victorian middle-class life, but not at Brighton College. The 4th Company had gone before 1869.

The pros and cons of a new corps were debated in the magazine from time to time each decade thereafter. Then in 1896, the War Office wrote to the Headmasters' Conference calling all public schools to the colours if they did not already have a corps. Revived enthusiasm for the Volunteers was under way, generated by alarm at the size of the German army and by mounting evidence that the population was not physically fit. The new movement really took off when military failure in the Second Boer War (1899-1902) shattered confidence in British military capabilities. On Speech Day 1900, the Headmaster announced that

all arrangements for the establishment, or rather revival, of a Cadet Corps were now completed, and the Corps was going to be established next term. A great deal was heard of the loss of time for volunteering. The way to avoid such loss of time was to train boys to the use of the rifle at school

adding at the OB dinner in July 1901 a clear sign of the new realism: 'It was a part of a boy's training to which he attached great importance with a view to the future and the requirements of the Empire'. Enough equipment had arrived to enable the boys, this time attached to the 1st Volunteer Battalion, Royal Sussex Regiment, to take part in the local ceremony proclaiming the accession of Edward VII in January 1901. Three obvious differences between 1860 and 1900 explain why this second corps survived:

A pupil's sketch of the original Band uniform, drawn on its rediscovery in the 1950s

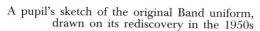

Photograph by Messrs. Fry. Brighton.

INSPECTION BY MAJOR-GENERAL TURNER, INSPECTOR-GENERAL OF AUXILIARY FORCES.

The Corps drawn up for its first Inspection, 1901

parents did not have to buy uniform; College masters commanded the unit; the company was set up by the enthusiasm of the Headmaster, not the boys. Before long, that also meant something else. Despite the corps' official title, it had by 1905 become compulsory. Supplied with Lee-Metford rifles and resplendent in scarlet tunics with blue trousers, they practised on a range at Mile Oak, went off to camp and in 1902 entered for the Ashburton at Bisley. For their first field day, the cadets joined forces with regulars from the Royal Sussex Regiment and the Rifle Brigade 'to hold Clayton Tunnel against the attack of the French, whose object was to blow up the tunnel and occupy the London Road'. To exercise with professional troops must have been exhilarating, but one has to wonder at the competence of a War Office which still planned war against France.

The Boer War made everyone take stock. Old boys had fought in numerous colonial wars before and their deeds of daring had duly been recorded in the magazine. From the issue of December 1899, however, the war in South Africa was given the kind of attention hitherto reserved for the XI. Updated lists of OBs at the front were printed, along with their letters, details of their actions, their medals, their wounds and their deaths. In July 1900, the magazine appeared with a frontispiece displaying the portraits of the first five killed. Inside was news that Bertram Simpson (1891-94, better known by his pen name Putnam Weale) was trapped in the Peking Legation by the Boxer Rebellion, that Harry Moorhouse (1882-87, later Lt. Governor of Nigeria) was on active service in the Third Ashanti War and that Col. Charles Maitland (1869-73) had been killed during the Somali Expedition. 'It's a thin red line of heroes when the drum begins to roll.' The burden of Empire suddenly seemed very great. Some began to question a reliance on sentiment and tradition. That same July 1900 issue carried a poem by William Eggar (1882-84, staff 1888-90), then a master at Eton, entitled *Advice Gratis* and asking 'Is the Anglo-Saxon race down the hill of time declining?' Verses four and five are particularly interesting:

> How can we, the public schools
> Mend our scheme of education?
> If the officers are fools,
> What about the nation?
> If the army gets the best,
> Brothers, what about the rest?
>
> Let us drop our silly pride,
> Drop our airs and change our graces,
> Learn to shoot, and learn to ride,
> Learn our proper place.
> Games may suffer: what's the odds?
> We must worship other gods.

In Memoriam.

CAPTAIN A. R. EUSTACE, 2nd *The Buffs*.
Killed at Driefontein, March 10th, 1900.

LIEUT. R. C. B. HENRY, 2nd *Dublin Fusiliers*.
Killed at Colenso, December 15th, 1899.

LIEUT. P. W. TINDAL ATKINSON, *H.M.S Partridge*.
Died at Durban, July 11th, 1900.

LIEUT. H. D. SELOUS, 2nd *Bedfordshire Regiment*.
Killed at Paardeberg, February 24th, 1900.

LIEUT. T. B. ELY, 2nd *Dublin Fusiliers*.
Died on voyage home, on board s.s. "Orcana."

Part (iii) 'Such liberty as may form manliness'

Alcohol

Of school fare we know next to nothing. Until 1933, food was a private matter, organised by individual Housemasters, so no trace of dietary questions is to be found among the Council minutes. Neither do any of the reminiscences Burstow collected refer to food. Does that mean it was reasonably good? Doubtless the boys were always hungry and the tuckshop certainly did a very brisk trade in buns and biscuits as well as sweets. The magazine mentions that its turnover in 1886 was £450 (equivalent to 16 dayboys' fees!). Tuck boxes would have arrived crammed with provisions at the start of term, but prospectuses in the 1880s imposed the niggardly restriction: 'hampers from home are allowed occasionally'. An intriguing rider was then added, 'They must not contain wine' and suddenly we are jolted into remembering the great gulf between their world and our own.

For the first 30 years, the boys were given a pint of beer with lunch and again at dinner. Could this be one reason for the two-hour lunch break? In 1876, that ration was halved and by 1885 beer was offered only at dinner to senior boys who wanted it. To our way of thinking, it is not the reduction in availability but the presence of beer in the first place which calls for comment. Actually, the reason for both is the same. Water was far too dangerous to drink until the days of good drainage, proper sewage disposal and the clean water provided by municipal water boards. As we have already seen, that was never the case in Brighton before 1870. Many remained unconvinced ten years later. Only then could the morality of teenage drinking become an issue and temperance pressures have it removed from the (previously universal) diet of the young. What happened at Brighton College seems to fit very closely the timetable of social change set by technology and religion.

College bounds

More liberty is and ought to be granted at public schools than is allowed at private; more trust reposed in the honour of the boys and more local scope allowed them in proportion to their number and their character relative to other schools.

So spoke the first Principal in 1850. He takes us to the heart of a fundamental of 19th-century College life: the boys enjoyed very considerable liberty, far greater than anything their successors have been permitted. The masters were well aware that, as Macleane put it, 'the difficulty of restraining the ill disposed and removing from their reach the facilities for Vice which such a Town affords is proportionately enhanced' and so, unlike rural Marlborough, the College always imposed some bounds, but they were drawn most generously, stretching as far as Falmer, Stanmer and Lewes. Once boarders began keeping bicycles, the expanse of the Downs could really be exploited. Only Brighton was excluded, 'No student is allowed to be out after dusk, or to go into the town at any time, except when visiting his friends, or by the special leave of the Principal'. That was relaxed in 1887 when 'leave to visit friends in Brighton is granted on Sundays and half-holidays, under certain restrictions'. But the town was not entirely

BRIGHTON COLLEGE.

SCHOOL RULES.

1.—No boy shall go out of bounds on any occasion without a special leave, signed by his House Master ; to be retained as a pass, and produced on demand to any Master or Præpositor.

2.—Any leave out of bounds into the Town must specify the shop or house to be visited, and no other may be entered.

3.—Entrance is forbidden, under any pretext, into any Tobacconist's or Wine Merchant's shop, or any Billiard Room ; or, without a special signed leave, into any Hotel, place of public amusement, or on to either of the Piers.

4.—No boy shall be absent from his House Meals, or out of his House after lock-up, without a special leave.

5.—College Præpositors have authority over the whole College, and are expected to prevent, and if need be, punish offences against College or House Rules. But all punishments inflicted by a Præpositor must be entered in a book kept for the purpose. House Præpositors have authority only over their own Houses.

6.—During Term-time the College Ribbon must be worn on all week-days, and no boy may appear without it. On Sundays, before dinner only caps and gowns for gown boys, and tall hats for juniors are allowed ; after dinner, tall hats must be worn by all boys.

7.—Riding and driving, and sea-bathing, except by special leave from the House Master, are strictly forbidden.

8.—Every boy on entering the College shall be held responsible for making himself acquainted with the Rules and Bounds of the College. A map, showing the bounds, is hung in the Entrance Hall of the College.

9.—College Præpositors are exempted from Rule 1, requiring leave out of bounds.

10.—Day-boys dining at the Principal's House are subject to all rules for boarders between morning and afternoon school.

BOUNDS, &c.

1.—Before dinner the bounds are the Parade and Beach to the East of the Chain Pier, College Road, and Burlington Street or Crescent Place ; Eastern Road, East of the College, as far as the Hospital Gates.

2.—After dinner, the Downs, Walpole Road and Eastern Road, as above, are in bounds ; the Parade and all parts of the Town are not.

3.—Bath leaves may be obtained from the House Master, and include Booth's, but no other shop or house. Boys must go to and return from the Baths by the Parade only.

4.—All visiting leaves must be countersigned by the Principal, and will only be given on Wednesdays and Saturdays except under very exceptional circumstances. They do not confer exemption from evening work.

5.—On Sunday no boy may go West of the College at all without special leave, or East except on the Parade, and Downs East of the Gas Works.

T. HAYES BELCHER,
PRINCIPAL.

out of bounds. Three shops were permitted to the boys: a cake shop in St George's Road, a sports shop in College Road and a gentlemen's outfitters in St James Street. Naturally, the praepositors were exempt from all such restrictions and, of course, the boys were more than willing to break out, as Sidney Clayton (1889-92) remembered:

In the summer we used occasionally to go to Brill's Baths before the House was up. [We] had to get out by the window near the door— only the thin ones could manage to squeeze through the bars. As far as I remember, we were never caught. Two or three of the older boys used to go down the town and would pawn things to raise money, and also do the same for any of the others.

Uniform

In public schools, uniform is a 20th-century innovation. Previously, uniforms were associated firmly with charity schools. All Brighton imposed was 'academical dress' (ie black gown and mortar board) in the Senior Department, which dayboys were also required to wear 'in going to and from the College'. When Bigg enhanced the rôle of praepositors, he transferred these garments to the exclusive use of the prefects so, for the ordinary boys, there were then no regulations at all—although it went without saying that the families patronising the College would automatically dress their sons in a suit.

In the end, however, institutional desire for regularity and homogeneity began to get the better of the public school world. At Brighton, the first steps towards corporate identity were taken by T.H. Belcher. From 1882, the rules declared that, 'coats, waistcoats and neckties should be dark. For younger boys, the Eton Jacket and Collar are preferred. Tall hats must be worn on Sundays'. Three years later, recommendation was turned into requirement, but not all parents would appear to have co-operated. Frederick Firmstone (1889-1900) tells us that he was sent daily into the Junior Department wearing 'sailor suit, kilt or corduroy suit'. Another sign of the original deregulated ways was the wearing of beards by senior boys. This is noticeable in photographs until the 1870s. Did beards then go out of fashion or were they the first victim of that extraordinary late 19th-century attempt to prolong childhood? On the subject of attire, one final curiosity must be mentioned. The earliest surviving clothing list for boarders dates from December 1882. Among a host of unexceptional items like 4 nightshirts, 12 collars, 3 pairs of boots appears '4 Pairs of Drawers (if worn)'. 'If worn' was removed from 1883, but does that mean mid-Victorian convention, for all its efforts to cover and conceal the body, had still not turned the wearing of underwear into a universal custom?

'Boy Government'

As with bounds and uniform, so in the rest of school life College boys enjoyed very considerable liberty. The structure of a public school around 1850 was not that of an absolutist monarchy but that of a federal republic. Rights and responsibilities were clearly defined and separated. The realm of the masters was in chapel and classroom, while the boys governed the Playground. By 1900, the balance of power had shifted so significantly in the masters' favour that the boys had been left with almost no dominion. Between 1866 and 1871, the College prospectus announced that 'the principle adopted in discipline is to give such liberty as may form manliness of character and habits of self-control, without exposing boys prematurely or unnecessarily to evil'. No such statement could have been written 30 years later. Creeping centralisation had so curtailed liberty that the old federal constitution lay shattered.

So distinct is that world to us that it is sobering to pause and grasp the extent of what scholars term 'boy government'. As traditional school history has exaggerated the significance of the headmaster, so it has grossly undervalued the rôle of the pupils. At Brighton College, the Captain of the School was elected by universal suffrage among the boys. The senior boys ran the societies and collected subscriptions from among their fellows to fund any expenditure. The lectures mentioned earlier in this chapter were organised entirely by the prefects. On the Playground, captains of each first team were elected by the team members, and were invested with authority to appoint not just their own Secretary but also the captains of lesser teams. Honours caps (colours) were awarded by ballot among team members. The magazine was written and compiled by pupils under a pupil Editor, elected by the praepositors.

Everything was held together by the Finance Committee whose members in the 1870s were the Captains of Cricket, Football and Fives, the President of the Debating Society, the President of the Reading Club and the magazine Editor, under the chairmanship of the School Captain. The committee controlled *all* funds for all activities, selected opponents for school matches (transport and catering then being organised by the relevant Secretary). The College even paid over to the Committee monies to hire any professional coaches required, to purchase equipment and to have the pitches maintained.

Individual details might change from time to time—for example, secretaries of each sport were elected alongside the captains in the 1850s—but this system remained intact for the first thirty years. The great breach in 'boy government' was made in 1878 when Dr. Bigg introduced portentous changes. Henceforth, first team captains would be nominated by the Committee to the Principal, who would exercise a veto. Second, the Principal would select the Captain of the School from among the praepositors. Third, the choice of Editor was similarly subjected to the Principal's approval. Pupil sovereignty had been breached. Before long, the magazine Editor was supervised by a master, aptly entitled 'Censor'. Masters also began to take over the organisation of games. The pupils' power base contracted rapidly, but it was not in the interest of the masters to choke it off completely. Instead of a populist democracy, Bigg and then Belcher created an oligarchy of senior boys: the school prefects. Henceforth, they would be endowed with great status and an authority to match. Into the 1960s, Brighton College school prefects were (if *they* chose to be) as proconsuls. Outside the classroom, a Head of House would be far more important than an ordinary master. This was a revolution of the first magnitude.

Part (iv) 'Follow up! Follow up! Follow up!'

This final section surveys Victorian College sport. Remember throughout that only in 1883 did the Playground (as they called it, to us the Home Ground) reach the size and shape everyone has known in this century. Remember also that the school was very much smaller than at any time this century, excepting only 1940-44. In the earliest days when the College rented only a fraction of the current Home Ground, additional space was provided in the then private Queens Park by its owner Thomas Attree, a shareholder and good friend of William Soames. Further, some cricket matches were played on the Royal Brunswick Ground, Hove (on the site of Third and Fourth Avenues). In other words, there was never enough space.

When the College was founded, games were recreational, played purely for fun, of no official standing and totally voluntary. So it is no accident or quirk that the area behind the school was termed the Playground. Not until the final three years of this

Brighton College, 1851. (Note the game in progress on The Playground, centre left.)

BRIGHTON COLLEGE IN 1851- BY GEORGE RUFF

survey did games become compulsory (1902). Among the public schools, Brighton College may have been the very last to take that step.

Cricket

Other inferior games as Hockey, Football, etc. as winter comes on take its place, but Cricket will always retain its place as the head of all games in this country.

So spoke the magazine in 1852, anticipating the voice of Arthur in *Tom Brown's Schooldays* (1858) that 'cricket is an institution, the birthright of British boys'. Cricket was the premier game at most Victorian public schools, Brighton included. After all, it was well established by 1800 as an aristocratic pastime and alone among games had codified laws. Cricket was a sport for gentlemen. Early references show the Brighton College season extended beyond the Summer Term to include September. Most matches were played against local clubs, but two school fixtures crowned the season: the match against Tonbridge (instituted 1855) and the match against Lancing (begun 1859). At various times, one or the other was often referred to as 'the Eton-Harrow match of the South'.

The XI of 1855 must have been remarkable for it contained three future Cambridge blues: George Cotterill (1848-57), Edward Fawcett (1851-58) and Augustus Bateman (1852-58). They were not the first old boys to win a cricket blue; that distinction is held by Herbert White (1847-49). Together with Denzil Onslow (1855-58), however, they were members together of the 1860 Cambridge XI. For so tiny a school, that was a mighty crop. No wonder Burstow held that 'cricket in this period was at a high level'.

The rough state of the Playground caused problems. Tonbridge complained in 1858 about the wicket and, after a first levelling in 1868, about the outfield. At least by then the College had bought out a sheep drover's right of way across the pitch and the premises of a certain John Phelp who, just to the north west of the field, 'carried on the business of horse slaughterer in the lime pits'. But that still left scope for complaint about College Cricket itself. In 1858, Tonbridge accused Brighton of violating Law X which required the umpire to call 'no ball' if the bowler's hand was above the shoulder when letting go of the ball (over arm bowling had not then been legalised). One game from these years must be singled out: the Lancing match of 1865. In this, the College made 273 runs while dismissing their opponents for 21 runs in the first innings and 7 runs in the second. What is more, Lancing's top scorer, Frederick Lacon, was actually a Brighton boy (1861-65), the visitors having arrived one man short. Two members of that College XI went on to win their blue, Henry Cotterill (1862-65) and Avison Scott (1863-67). The other great cricketer of that era was Joseph Montague Cotterill (1865-69), half-brother to the second Principal, who went on to captain the Edinburgh University XI and whom *The Sportsman* of 1877 described as 'one of the very finest batsmen of the day, amateur or professional'.

The donkey pulled the mowing machine

The XI off to play Lancing, 1871 (Lancing won by 2 runs)

The Playground before enlargement, 1876

Cricket enjoyed another triumphant period in the 1880s on the newly enlarged Playground. More schools were added to the XI's fixture list (Dulwich and Highgate were regulars, St Paul's occasionally, Bradfield once), but two-thirds of the matches were still against clubs. The XI of 1885 was the first unbeaten side since 1859, and the feat was not to be repeated for another 67 summers. In the words of the magazine, 'for this glorious result we are mainly indebted to the fine batting of the Captain and S. Woods, and to the good bowling of the latter and G.L. Wilson'.

All three were remarkable all-round sportsmen. The Captain, George Huth Cotterill (1878-86), a nephew of the second Principal, later played cricket for Sussex and captained both Cambridge and England at Association Football. George Wilson (1883-87) played Cricket and Football for Oxford—Wilson's House, opened in 1920, was named in his honour when, that year, he bequeathed £1,000 to the College. As for 'Sammy' Woods (1884-86), what didn't he play? He captained Cambridge and Somerset at Cricket, played Association Football for Australia and Rugby for both Cambridge and England. In his first-class career, he scored 15,499 runs and took 1,079 wickets. There was a fourth star in that 1885 XI, Norman Cooper (1882-89), who subsequently played Cricket for Surrey and Association Football for Cambridge and England.

'Sammy Woods'

Slightly later came Leslie Gay (1887-89) who represented Cambridge and England at Cricket and Football, and Hampshire at Cricket. Who can say what alchemy produced so fine a brood? Such triumphs are, however, seasonal. If Lancing only once beat Brighton between 1889 and 1912, the rest of the fixture card usually recorded a very different picture. A single win was all the XI of 1894 could manage. But all was not lost. The College beat the MCC in 1904 for the first time in 19 years.

Football

One of the best indicators of the original influences on the College foundation was that its boys played not Rugby (the game of the movement emulating Dr. Arnold) but Football, the game of Winchester. For centuries a rowdy, dangerous test of strength played out by peasants, Football was adopted by schools in the later 18th century and

---

The Football Song.

The primitive man, he built his boat,
He cooked his dinner and made his coat,
He thrashed his corn and he ground his wheat,
And he kept the ball at his own dear feet.
Chorus: Then here's to the fame of the passing game
         That is played with the oval here;
         Its wealth may stand in the northern land,
         And its home and health are here.

But civilisation is now his fate,
And division of labour has raised his state;
And farmer and miller and smith unite
To pass it out on the left and right.
                    Chorus.

Which things are a parable, friends, and yield
A type of the Brighton football field;
Where each is ready and each is keen,
And each is part of the great machine.
                    Chorus.

And every man on the side must feel
A reverent love for the common weal—
Glad ciphers all in the total sum
Of back, three-quarters and halves and scrum.
                    Chorus.

So give good heed to the virtues hid
In the game of the prolate spher-o-id,
In joyful hope to attain, *not* here,
To the perfect game of the perfect sphere.
                    Chorus.

---

turned into an honest game for gentlemen. So various were the games and rules played, however, that inter-school contests were nigh on impossible until codification was undertaken at the behest of public school old boys (the Football Association being formed in 1863, the Rugby Football Union in 1871).

The earliest reference to College Football comes from 1852. The game played for the next 21 years is, however, difficult to reconstruct for no rule book survives. A team was 12 strong. Points were awarded for 'rouges', 'rouge goals' and kick goals'— terms reminiscent of Eton but, unlike Eton, the rouge seems to have been a kind of scrum. By winning the ball there, a team gained a rouge which in turn entitled them to a place kick, and hence a rouge goal. The original value of these remains unknown, but rule alterations made in 1869 fixed them at one, three and five points respectively. Each game had two umpires, one for each side. The field incorporated the bank along the eastern edge of the Playground, which feature visiting teams found most disturbing. Unique also to Brighton football was 'scragging', until forbidden in 1869. Precisely what that was remains a mystery, but the magazine's report on the rule-change gives a slight clue:

No 'Scragging' is allowed but the player running with the ball must drop it directly he is fairly caught. Though this change may not meet with universal approbation, it must be remembered that the practice of 'scragging' is of comparatively recent date and was unknown before 1860.

A match report (v Lancing, 1870) yields further information on how the game was played:

Although the direct success of a game depends on the number of goals, rouges, etc., obtained yet, indirectly, its ultimate success is in a great measure dependent on those who 'play back'. Without a good 'back' player an otherwise excellent team is often defeated by one inferior to it, and we do not hesitate to say that to the general success of the Twelve this year although his name does not appear often as having made goals or rouges, no one has contributed more than Newton by his adroit and judicious back play.

Custom was changing. Lancing abandoned its own two (different) games for Association rules in 1871. Malvern changed in 1873. So too did Brighton College. Not that everything was altered immediately. For one more season, Brighton fielded a XII with six forwards and encountered opponents playing by different rules. Such contests must have been messy, as the report of one match from this transitional period makes clear:

The Football XII, 1878

The Wasps play the Rugby Union rules, the College twelve have lately adopted the Association rules. On this occasion the Wasps having choice of rules played their own, which being very different to those played by the College, placed the College twelve at a disadvantage especially as the Rugby ball is oval and to kick it straight requires much practice.

But the new game caught on fast. Football remained very popular. The XI was unbeaten in 1875 and again in 1878–feats never again repeated. The old boys started a club in 1881 while Chichester House had, from its foundation, a game of three-a-side indoor football played in the junior common room.

The first 10 Association seasons (1874-83) proved to be the best. Of those in College during the 1880s, 18 are known to have played for the county, several while still schoolboys. Four won their blues and played for England, as already noted in the Cricket section. Cotterill and Cooper captained Cambridge, Wilson Oxford. These three were also Corinthians. The XI reached the final of the Sussex Cup every year between 1885 and 1889. Lancing was beaten each season from 1889 to 1895. The lengthening of the season which after 1884 ran from October to April must have helped. So too did a succession of keen masters, most notably A.T. Hay (1885-1906), B.O. Corbett (1897-1902) who played for England and his brother A.L. Corbett (1902-36, 1942-47). But the best days had passed before any of these had arrived:

G. M. Robinson. A.L. King.   F. Savory.   L.A. Gay. A.J. Say Esq. R. Young.   F. G. Parsons.
          G. W. Picton.   K.C. Cooper.   [Sussex Cup]   A.C. Holland.   F.E. Whitley. A.G. Cavendish

The XI, 1888-89 (winners of the Sussex Cup)

	won	lost	drawn
1874-1883	62	31	13
1884-1893	68	46	25
1894-1903	58	67	15

Fives

The Lent Term was different from the others in that, until 1885, it had no major sport. All sorts of games were played but, from its inception in 1851, Fives was always regarded as more significant than any other. That in itself says something about the way games were then viewed, for this was a sport where inter-school matches were impossible and which could only occupy ten boys at any one time. At Brighton, Fives resembled the Eton rather than the Harrow variety, but it was a unique game; only with rule changes in 1954 did matches become possible. There was no step but, at back left, each of the courts had a box, known to the College boys as a 'pepper pot'; Box Court, however, had its 'pot' on the right. One player stood behind the other and only the server could score points. Fives went into rapid decline once Football took over the Lent Term in 1885. Within ten years, every court was reported to be semi-derelict. The invasion of Football was symbolic, however, of something else. As school games became more and more serious, Fives came to be seen as the wrong sort of sport. Again, *Tom Brown's Schooldays* explains the point succinctly:

Arthur	... Cricket and football are such unselfish games. They merge the individual in the eleven.
Tom	That's very true, and that's why football and cricket, now one comes to think of it, are such better games than fives or any other where the object is to come in first or to win for oneself.

In the Fives Court, *c.*1880

Brighton College Athletic Sports & Foot Races.

EIGHTH MEETING, FRIDAY, MAY 17, 1861.

STEWARDS: H. ALLEN,   A. E. BATEMAN,   R. S. BLAINE,   J. M. IMAGE,
J. M. McCORMICK,   C. C. THORNTON,   G. H. WRIGHT.

JUDGE: Rev. E. C. HAWKINS.   **STARTER**: H. C. MALDEN, Esq.
A. C. ROSS, *Hon. Sec.*   G. WARD, *Hon. Treas.*

At 2 0 p.m. Putting the Stone, 14lbs.—Prize, an Opera Glass
1. R. S. Blaine   3. T. G. Moilliet   5. J. C. Ross   7. G. H. Wright
2. M. G. Fox   4. J. H. Pollard   6. C. C. Thornton
Distance,   1st,   2nd,   3rd,

**At 2 10   Flat Race, 100 yards, for those under 14 years of age.—
Prize, Batting Gloves**
1. H. Acworth   6. B. P. Ellis   11. C. H. Griffith 16. C. C. Ross
2. G. C. Barnes   7. H. Gardner   12. A. C. Hall   17. S. G. Scott
3. F. Barratt   8. B. P. Garbett   13. E. Madden   18. T. B. Scott
4. T. W. Darling 9. A. C. Garbett   14. C. E. Maudslay 19. W. F. Williams
5. A. R. Dunnage 10. R. Gill   15. H. Ord
Time,   1st,   2nd,   3rd,

**At 2 20   Flat Race, 120 yards, given by the Vice-Principal;
2nd Prize, a Gold Pin**
1. H. Allen   7. G. C. Hilbers   13. H. Master   19. R. Ramsden
2. R. S. Blaine   8. J. M. Image   14. W. E. Master   20. J. C. Richardson
3. E. Bourdillon 9. W. J. Gill   15. J. M. McCormick 21. A. C. Ross
4. R. Crockett   10. J. R. Griffith 16. C. R. Oriebar   22. J. C. Ross
5. J. B. Curry   11. W. Griffith   17. J. H. Pollard   23. C. C. Thornton
6. M. G. Fox   12. J. R. Margary   18. A. S. Preston   24. G. Ward
Time,   1st,   2nd,   3rd,

At 2 30   High Jump, for those under 15 years of age.—Prize, a Telescope
1. B. P. Ellis   3. C. Higgens   5. A. R. Margary   7. E. H. Walters
2. A. C. Hall   4. C. P. Lack   6. F. Rouquette
Height,   1st,   2nd,   3rd,

At 2 40   High Jump.—Prize, a Gold Carbuncle Pin
1. M. G. Fox   3. J. M. McCormick 5. C. C. Thornton   7. H. E. Wilmot
2. W. J. Gill   4. J. C. Ross   6. G. R. Thornton
Height,   1st,   2nd,   3rd,

Athletics and Paper Chases

Brighton College once claimed to have invented the athletics sports meeting. This is not true. The distinction belongs to Cheltenham, which staged the first-ever sports day in 1852. Oxford and Cambridge copied in 1855, Brighton College the following year. As for cross-country running, it took the form of 'paper chases' or 'hare and hounds'. Usually, they seem to have been a run back to College from Falmer, Lewes or Bramber railway stations (the latter a staggering 13-mile course). That may explain why, around 1900, 'several boys developed hearts' and paper chases were abolished.

Gymnastics

Gymnastics was introduced to the curriculum at Sandhurst and Woolwich in 1822, but another 40 years passed before schools and town societies began building gymnasia. Brighton College was ahead of them all, beating Uppingham by a few months to the honour of setting up the first gymnasium in an English school (now the Hordern Room). Given that the room was small, the choice of 'German' rather than 'Swedish' gymnastics was curious—the latter emphasised free-standing exercises without apparatus, while it was the former which employed poles and ropes and bars. Did the team (the VIII) or the classes adopt even elements of the Swedish system around the turn of the century? The question is more than academic because the Swedish variety was introduced officially to both the British Army and all public elementary schools by an Old Boy, Sir George Fox (1858-63), Inspector of Army Gymnasia.

Other Sports

Gymnastics included boxing and fencing as well. Fencing was an obvious activity, being firmly classed as a gentlemanly accomplishment and so obviously suited to potential military officers. In fact, Fencing long enjoyed a status unique among College sports for, until 1871, the prospectus made no reference to any other sports, and the Fencing Master was listed among the masters. Where the *salle* was we do not know, but Fencing took place twice a week and for many years was taught by Messrs. Angelo, the most distinguished professors in the land.

Sporadically from 1877, there was a Lawn Tennis Club, existing always on the margins. At first, boys could play on the Principal's personal court (opposite his house). In 1884, however, an asphalt court was laid behind the Main Building. Various other games came and went in the Lent Term, before Football took it over from 1885. The magazine regularly published letters suggesting the latest bright idea. Lacrosse and Cycling would seem never to have been tried out, but there were sporadic flirtations with Hockey and Rugby. When we recall that these were pupil-organised Playground games, it is not out of place to mention reference in 1852 to 'Prisoners Base' or to Bagatelle, a form of Billiards then very popular. Indeed, a Bagatelle contest that year between the boarders of Mr. Cotterill and the boarders of Mrs. Vipond is the first recorded College House match.

For a seaside school located in a spa town where salt water was regarded as beneficial, swimming was an obvious activity with twin purpose. From 1847, therefore, College boys swam in the sea and at Brill's Baths. Both were used for swimming contests, the Baths for diving competitions. For much of this period, boys could join a pre-breakfast swim off

Sgt. Reynolds, Gymnastic Instructor, 1896 (the gymnasium is now the Hordern Room)

the beach held daily in the Summer Term. Some evenings throughout the year, there was another at Brill's. Reference to the sea leads to the great mystery in College sport of this period: Rowing. An activity apparently unnoticed by earlier College historians, a solitary reference indicates that in 1858 there was a Brighton College Boat Club, while a letter in the magazine in 1873 called for its 'reinstitution'.

Philathleticism?

Much would be claimed for sport. At the Old Boys' dinner of 1885, Dr. Griffith declared 'cricket is intimately connected with success in almost everything. A good cricketer, having an eye and an arm constantly practised, has the very education which is the supplement of book education'. He might have believed that in 1856 on becoming third Principal, but that is unlikely. Nonetheless, the cult of games grew fast from the 1860s and, well before 1914, wholly preposterous notions had become general currency. At the 1888 dinner, Henry Smith Wright (1856-58), then Conservative MP for South Nottingham, linked sport and Empire: 'Our national sports seem to be the one feature which distinguish us from all other nations on earth. Germany and France can not colonise much because they have no cricket or football'. The origins of this nonsense lie not with Dr. Arnold but with Charles Kingsley, author of *The Water Babies*. His disciples promoted one of the most crucial ethical codes to influence later Victorian and Edwardian Britain. Known popularly as 'muscular christianity' (a

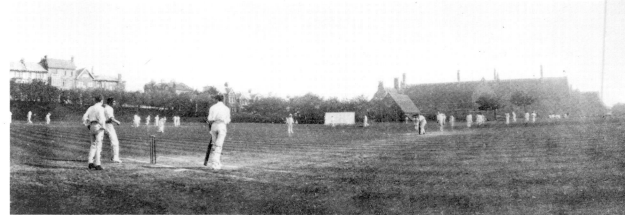

The Playground, *c.*1893

term coined in 1858), scholars call it 'philathleticism'. We are talking at first only of a new attitude to the sports field. Competitive and organised sports began to be played from the 1820s in the belief that they offered healthy exercise. To that, Kingsley grafted the notion that team games served a morally uplifting purpose. Henceforth, cricket and football would be taken as character-building activities, promoting self-discipline and encouraging reliance one upon another, teaching boys to command, to obey, to co-operate. In time, this ethic, ideally suited to an age of empire, would oust even the christianising ambition of the original school reformers.

To ethics must be added morality, for philathleticism also had roots in a new distrust. Schoolboys had always had too much energy. They had always got up to pranks. But the High Victorians, in revolt against Regency frivolity and debauchery, came to fear adolescent energy, especially emerging sexual consciousness. Boys must therefore be occupied in wholesome pursuits, not left to themselves. If organised every waking moment and exhausted in the process, they could be, as Kingsley put it in a private letter, 'saved from the evil of self-abuse'.

When did such ideas infiltrate Brighton College? The answer would seem to be remarkably late. Marlborough and Uppingham pioneered muscular christianity in the 1850s and there are some tell-tale early signs at Brighton. Inter-school matches, instruments in the new cult of forging school loyalty, began in the mid-1850s. From around the same date, some masters began to be active in Playground games (although never actually playing *in* College teams, as at Marlborough until 1872). The first masters with blues were appointed in 1865 and 1866, both old boys: Rev. G.E. Cotterill (1848-57) and Augustus Bateman (1852-58). But there are serious obstacles to fixing so early a date. One is the marked absence of official interest in College sport. Masters who joined in games were the exceptions until the 1890s. Athletic enthusiasm came from the boys, not the staff. A second is the rarity of inter-school contests throughout the period under review. A third is the absence of House cups to be won or colours awarded. But the real clue is the attitude towards that apparently dangerous commodity, spare time.

At Brighton College, games playing remained wholly voluntary until 1902, when cricket leagues were introduced. From 1883, all below the VIth form were compelled to do either gymnastics or drill for half an hour per week, but neither counted in the philathletic creed. The 1880s certainly made a difference. Games received more attention in the magazine. An increasingly complex hierarchy of colours developed. The Playground was enlarged and improved at great expense. Yet as long as the voluntary tradition remained intact, the philathletic movement would be stunted. Games were compulsory at Lancing from 1864, at Harrow by 1866 and at Eton from 1888. Was Brighton College the last public school to adopt the cult?

The write-up of a debate in February 1889 provides fascinating evidence. The motion was, 'That the amount of Athletics practised at Public Schools in the present day is excessive and to be condemned'. Most speeches were played out on predictable lines, rehearsing arguments that could have been heard in any public school over the next 75 years. Predictably, many speakers ignored the motion, arguing for the inherent or relative superiority of the classroom or the Playground. Much was made of 'the qualities developed at games—bravery, coolness, endurance—qualities essential to almost every walk of life'; the nascent England footballer N.C. Cooper added here 'the great quality of unselfishness'. His friend and future England goalkeeper, L.H. Gay, went so far as to claim 'the idea that games were practised to excess was impossible'. Charles Castellain (1886-90, master 1894), author of the College football song, touchingly added, 'surely the Masters would put down games if they were injurious?'

At the end, the Headmaster, himself a cricket blue, rose to speak. Belcher declared himself 'rather in favour of the motion, for he considered that there was an objectionable spirit in many fellows, which was inclined to sneer at honest hard work, and to cry out for games as the only thing worth living for'. Headmasters like Thring of Uppingham and Bell of Marlborough voiced the same misgivings, but in their schools it was already too late. At Brighton, however, pupil enthusiasm remained well ahead of official policy; the Debating Society supported compulsory games as early as 1876. But 'boy government' lay shattered and voluntaryism continued unchecked. The wisdom of 'Old Tom' Belcher meant that Brighton College around 1890 was perhaps a unique relic of an age already past: the last truly Victorian public school.

1. Brighton College.—2. The Cricket Pavilion.—3. General Sir J. Lintorn Simmons Unveiling the Gill Memorial.—4. The Memorial Tablet.

THE MEMORIAL TO THE LATE CAPTAIN GILL AT BRIGHTON COLLEGE

Part IV

Headmasters

William Dawson	May 1906
Arthur Belcher	March 1933
Christopher Scott	January 1937
Walter Hett	January 1939

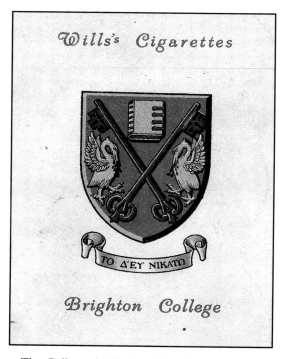

The College shield, issued by the College of
Arms, June 1920

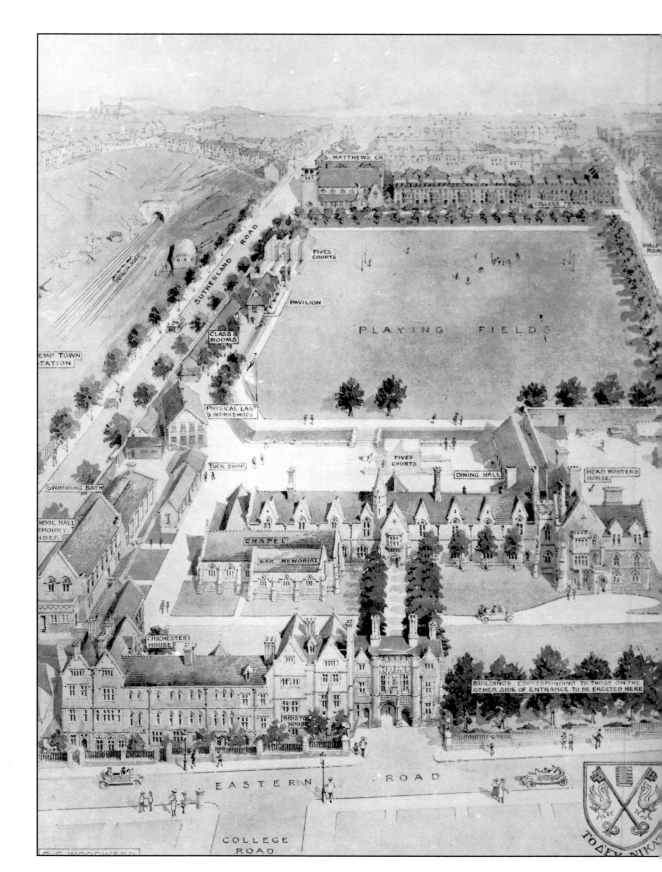

S. MATTHEWS CH.

COLLEGE TERRACE

WALL ROAD

FIVES COURTS

SUTHERLAND ROAD

PAVILION

PLAYING FIELDS

CLASS & ROOMS

EMP TOWN STATION

PHYSICAL LAB & WORKSHOPS

TUCK SHOP

FIVES COURTS

DINING HALL

HEAD MASTERS HOUSE

SWIMMING BATH

SCHOOL HALL ARMOURY UNDER

CHAPEL

WAR MEMORIAL

CHICHESTER HOUSE

BUILDINGS CORRESPONDING TO THOSE ON THE OTHER SIDE OF ENTRANCE TO BE ERECTED HERE

BRISTOL HOUSE

EASTERN ROAD

COLLEGE ROAD

C. C. WOODWARD

ΤΟ ΔΕΥ ΝΙΚΑ

NINE

1906-1933

Hark! a thrilling voice is sounding

By all that is wonderful! Who could have dared to dream such as this? Now sits expectation in the air!

The words of Lloyd George in greeting the Liberal landslide victory in the general election of January 1906 might equally have been heard at Brighton College on the election of Rev. William Rodgers Dawson as eighth Headmaster that same month. Beyond recording that 'many applications and enquiries were received', the Council minutes are silent on the selection process. Only one rival applicant is known, the Headmaster of Keswick School, who made his theme 'the transformation of the College into a great national public school for the co-education of boys and girls'. Bedales had admitted girls in 1898 and mixed secondary schools began to appear under the 1902 Education Act. But Brighton College was not ready for such ideas—it had not been that progressive even in 1845.

Dawson came with a not inconsiderable reputation, having by 35 already revived the fortunes of both schools where he had been Headmaster (Corby Grammar School and King's School Grantham). As in 1892, the Council was looking for a man with proven experience to lift numbers. So too, of course, was the Phoenix which wrote into his contract, 'There shall be no restriction as to the admission of boys' and gave Dawson the job for a two-year trial period at a salary calculated to make him work: £2 per boy per term, with a minimum basic of £600 per annum. But for the bankruptcy, Dawson could never have been appointed. Not being an Oxbridge graduate, he was unqualified under the old Company's amended rules.

Indeed, eyebrows were raised at this Manxman with his respondent's degree from Trinity College Dublin (i.e., he had done well in the pass degree). Since 1909, College Headmasters have only been required to be graduates of a UK university

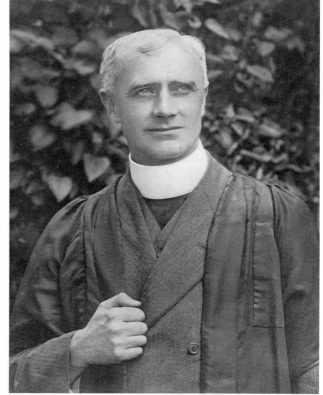

Rev. William Rodgers Dawson

Professor George Harrison

L.A.G. Strong

but, to this day, Dawson remains the only non-Oxbridge man appointed. Thus did chance bring Dawson within the selectors' grasp.

Did the Phoenix and the Council understand in 1906 that their new Headmaster had an ambition as dazzling as his track record? Dawson did not intend simply to add Brighton College like some trophy to the schools he had rescued. He saw potential and believed himself the one able to exploit it. The name of Brighton College would be spread through the provinces until the whole nation knew it. With William Rodgers Dawson at the helm, Brighton College would become the greatest school in England. This was no rhetoric. He believed it. He knew it must happen. What is more, most around him came to believe it too.

Professor G.B. Harrison (1907-13) has pointed out that 'Dawson was no scholar, nor did he have much interest in scholarship ... He had few theories of education'. The key to Dawson was, as Burstow observed, 'an enormous self-confidence and a complete mastery of the technique of leadership'. His vitality was boundless, his physical presence exceptional. Kenneth Robertson (1911-14) spoke of his 'very fine appearance, a magnificent head and in my time he used to wear grey flannel suits which matched exactly his eyes and hair and made him appear all the more remarkable'. He dominated every room he entered. L.A.G. Strong (1910-15, governor 1946-58) was categorical that 'I have never seen more natural, more determined, more autocratic leadership'.

Prospective parents were drawn to this Headmaster. When Mrs. Violet Fuchs was looking for a school for her son Vivian (1922-26), she found 'Mr. Dawson an expansive and fascinating person, Irish [sic], full of go and force'. Strong describes how his father and uncle arrived to look over the College, prepared to be hostile, but were charmed to ungrudging approval. In place of a conventional schoolmaster-parson they found a tall, powerfully built, young-looking man with brilliant eyes, a violent laugh, and gestures that spoke of enormous energy. He frankly answered their questions and, liking them as they liked him, confided in them the terms of his employment–adding with a grin that he proposed to increase the numbers drastically.

Sir Sydney Roberts

On his summer holidays in Torquay, Bournemouth or Scarborough, he would intercept families with youngish boys, enquire of their parents the school their son was down for, and proceed to convince them that Cheltenham, Malvern or wherever was quite the wrong place to have selected.

The College itself was stamped with his energy and personality from the day he took over. Sir Sydney Roberts (1902-06, governor 1933-66) was Senior Prefect the term Dawson 'descended on us like a whirlwind'. Over the boys, several elements combined to constitute his method of government. First, he instituted regular assemblies in which he addressed the whole school and left everyone in no doubt as to what was expected. Rarely did he have to harangue. 'A mere flashing glance or imperious word was enough to give him all the control he wanted', is how Alan Murdoch-Cozens (1902-12, staff 1919-33, Bursar 1933-38) described the style of Dawson's authority. Burstow picked out as another crucial trait 'a sarcasm which was no less dreaded than the big stick. He was a master of the art of making certain types of offenders seem ridiculous before the whole school'. As Peter Blake-White (1927-33) remembers, 'he appeared authoritarian at first acquaintance'. Dawson's disciplinary procedures could be unorthodox. He would put boys in the wastepaper basket, or make them sit on the floor with a duster over their face, or make them stand on their head. His insistence upon sober dress, good manners and correct speech was never relaxed. Neither was his obsessive campaign against long or greasy hair. Professor Harrison provides us with the psychological key, 'He had a great power over a boy's emotional responses and, however bitter one might feel with him, he would after an interview, leave one with the sense that one was an utter worm'.

Dawson tried to get to know every pupil in his school. He was always stopping the boys and talking to them. In a revolutionary break with tradition, he himself never taught the VIth Form. That was wise and left him free to take every class once or twice a week. In theory, they studied Divinity or English. In reality, almost everything under the sun except the official subject was covered. That did not matter. Dawson's aim was to be known. For the real magic to work, however, a boy needed to be in School House (the Headmaster was always its Housemaster until 1933) or to be a school prefect. Every School House boy was invited to breakfast once a term,

THE GREAT FIRE AT GIBBEY'S BREWERY, BRIGHTON. JUNE 9th 1907

and was left to consume a large cooked meal while the host dashed off to take chapel.

In the reminiscences of those in the College under Dawson, two things are very noticeable in what they say of him. Like those who came in the later 1920s when the College was over 500-strong and scattered in a diaspora of out-boarding houses, those who stayed only a few terms were rarely bewitched. Dawson's extraordinary personality worked its enchantments most effectively in a small circle over a period of time. As Peter Blake-White recalls, 'he grew on you'. That is why those old boys who speak most of the transforming power Dawson exerted were almost all school prefects. To Dawson, his prefects were colleagues and friends. Philip Burstow (Head of Hampden 1928-29) tells us that 'he cleverly talked to prefects as one man to another and temporarily gave the impression that he did not want to make any changes save with their permission' and that 'he was wont to treat the Head of School more nearly as an equal than anyone on the staff, save the Second Master'. Sir Alun Pugh (Head of School 1912-13) recorded in his diary how Dawson told him of his arguments with the Council. L.A.G. Strong (Head of School 1914-15) remembered how the Head-master 'proceeded to give me a confidential and highly indiscreet account of various crises which had arisen between him and various members of staff', an occasional habit confirmed by Pugh. Dawson went too far, but that is the point. Dawson relied very heavily on his prefects.

What is most extraordinary is that his staff were equally spellbound. Two he persuaded to be ordained. A third was weaned off the bottle. Dawson's hold over the masters is so remarkable because he offended virtually every one of them. He ignored them or he bullied them or he undermined them. He would throw them out of his study, literally. Excluded from the triangular axis of power between Headmaster, Second Master and Head of School, they were made to feel irrelevant. To disagree with Dawson was as useless as, in Haldane's description of Churchill, 'trying to argue with a brass band'. Professor Harrison tells us that those masters inherited from Titherington 'disapproved of him as a person of no academic standing; and some such as Duckworth [Housemaster of Chichester 1893-1908] did not conceal their feelings'. Once he was able to fill the Common Room with his own appointees, that was no longer a problem because (with precious few exceptions) they too were men of no academic standing. Their pay was bad and arbitrarily determined–there was no salary scale until 1934. Yet, as Burstow states, 'to a man they accorded him the right to be as rude as he liked'. They could be highly critical of him. 'Teddy' Lester (master 1927-70) called him 'a rogue, ever devious and lacking all morals. He would appoint

Sir Alun Pugh

The Masters 1923

a young master at one salary, then pay him at a lower one and accuse the man of disloyalty when he questioned it'. At the end he became almost irrelevant to them, as his last Head of School, Peter Blake-White, observed, 'the Chief seemed to have distanced himself from, or had been distanced by the staff. There was every appearance of most of the staff referring to HB rather than the Chief. He really appeared to become a loner'.

As with the boys, those masters who came to Brighton late in Dawson's career were far less susceptible to his allure. He was seriously ill and a shadow of his former self. He had lost his grip. Both Lester and Dorothy Fenwick (successively Matron of Stenning, School and Bristol Houses, 1929-47) accused him of cant and swore that he had a secret second family. As for the old timers, they stood by Dawson, however much they might grumble or complain or criticise. Many stayed with him for years —a remarkable testimonial. To masters as well as boys, he was their 'Chief'.

What was the source of Dawson's exceptional certitude? First, he held to an unswerving conviction that, as he told Strong, 'God had put him there'. Assured that he was a chosen instrument, he never looked back. It was his duty to remain in control and strive for the fulfilment of his mission. To use an old-fashioned phrase, Dawson believed in the guiding hand of providence. From that foundation, he then relied upon his own more than considerable strength to accomplish the Lord's work. 'Of his merely physical powers', as Burstow observed, 'accounts are of course legion.' For a headmaster to rest his authority upon his ability to bring to the ground any pupil of member of staff is certainly a singular way to proceed. But then Dawson was a unique individual—what other headmaster handed out signed photographs of himself?

Within two months of Dawson taking up the reins, negotiations had been opened with the Phoenix to buy the school back. For Burstow, the rescue of the College was perhaps Dawson's greatest achievement. Within a short interval, he achieved 'what no Council had hitherto been able to do'. To have ended the College's captivity was indeed exceptional, but Burstow is wrong in ascribing responsibility to the Headmaster. Sir Alun Pugh, elected to the Council the year after Dawson's resignation, spoke of 'the Council run by the Chief'. But things had been very different. Requests to the Headmaster to attend Council meetings were rarely issued before 1914. From then until 1933, he attended on a fairly frequent basis, but still at their specific invitation; A.H. Belcher (1933-36) was the first Headmaster to attend every Council automatically. It took time for Dawson to establish his ascendancy over the governing body. The minutes make plain that the buy-back scheme came from Col. Hugh Verrall (Council 1890-1908, College solicitor 1906-08, acting Secretary 1907-09). Dawson's contribution was the steady increase in the roll:

May 1906	128
May 1907	189
May 1908	203
May 1909	222

which opened the way for a revival in College finances. His boundless energy may even have reawakened in the Council the desire, dormant for eleven years, to rediscover its authority. But Dawson did not lead the Council, yet.

Negotiations lasted three years. Debtor and creditor argued over the price and terms of redemption. The College offered £25,000. The Phoenix pointed out that the school owed £55,000 and was valued at £70,000. The company's demand to nominate a majority of governors for 40 years was also problematic. The haggling was endless and, throughout, one has to admire the sheer cheek of the College Council. Beyond the basic bid price, they also proposed that the Phoenix should maintain responsibility for the College fabric and provide an additional £5,000 to build 'a swimming bath, science rooms and laboratory, and possibly an engineering classroom'. Why was the Phoenix prepared to negotiate at all? The reason is that, at last, the balance sheet looked so much brighter. The Phoenix might be able to cut its losses, sell at a good price and rid itself of this bad investment.

When talks first stalled in July 1907, Dawson intervened by threatening resignation, declaring:

it was essential that he should know not later than the end of next month whether the Phoenix would place the school in the position in which he alone was willing to continue as its Headmaster, or whether he would have to seek some other appointment as soon as possible after next Easter.

He was playing a lone hand, pushing the Council as much as the Phoenix. And he kept up the pressure, requesting a testimonial from the Council that November. But the Phoenix was not to be bullied and, in a state of deadlock, declared in March 1908 negotiations 'as having come to an end'. Further, they notified the Council that 'an offer they are prepared to accept has been made'. This was no mystery bidder. He was Col. Sir Charles Boxall (1861-68 and a Vice President of the Association of Old Brightonians). The Council had known of his interest for a year and had even discussed with him his intentions 'to bring the College into very close touch with the War Office under the Territorial Army scheme, without unduly interfering with its general system of education'. Boxall had secured the approval of the Inspector-General of Territorial Forces, the interest of the Secretary of State for War and the agreement of General Sir John French to

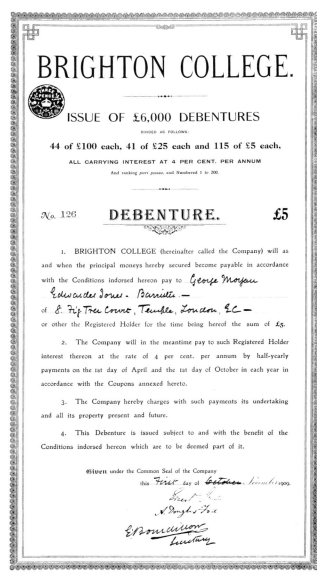

serve as a governor. All along, however, he had made it plain that he would never act if there was any chance of agreement between the College and the Phoenix. Once the Council informed Boxall that negotiations were not ended, he pulled out at once, determined to do nothing 'which would encourage the mortgagees in refusing the College's overtures'. The Colonel's loyalty to his old school and his determination 'in putting the College on its legs' were of the highest order. What is more, Boxall's withdrawal prompted both sides to bring a fresh realism to proceedings. If nothing else, it convinced the Phoenix that they must strike a deal with the Council.

Boxall played a straight hand. The same cannot be said for Dawson. His sabre-rattling in 1907 has already been described. At the very moment he was pressing the Council to settle with the Phoenix, he was also scheming with Boxall to do exactly the same thing. Indeed, with reference back to the events of 1907, Boxall told the Phoenix in 1908 that 'Mr. Dawson seemed so pleased with the idea and so glad to co-operate that I thought there were great elements of success'.

Amazingly, the Phoenix settled for a sale at £25,000 if the College made a capital downpayment of £5,000, followed by £500 per annum until 1949. They were washing their hands of Brighton College. Yet the annual accounts still showed an operating deficit. How were the Council to find £5,000 and accept this bargain-basement offer? Sir Charles Boxall had the answer. An appeal was made to the old boys to fund the deposit through a £5,000 debenture issue, paying 4 per cent; the Colonel himself contributed £500, members of the Council £600 and the academic staff £300. Within one month, redemptive generosity had produced £6,000, which stands proof to a powerful sentiment among the old boys, generated by the Association over its 27- year existence (contrast these events with the weakness of College appeals in 1885 and 1894). Debenture subscriptions also suggest that Lloyd George was right in claiming his budgets would not harm anyone with earned incomes under £3,000 per annum. The College company was reconstituted, but without proprietary admission, and with the debenture holders enjoying the right to nominate five members of the Council. Thus was a deal finally negotiated and Brighton College set free on 22 November 1909.

None of this would work unless the roll continued buoyant, which on the College's past record could not be taken for granted. This time, however, numbers went up and up. Dawson was a born recruiting sergeant and, never tied to a social status admission requirement, his talents were given free rein. He would take anyone. The son of a jockey and the son of a bishop were equally welcomed, as were sons of the prominent Brighton Labour councillors Milner Black and Herbert Carden. Neither did previous schooling matter. A significant number of new pupils never took common entrance (established 1903) because they came from the colonies or their parents worked over-seas in Chile or Argentina or China. Such boys, lacking a traditional Classics-based prep school background, were rejected by most public schools, but not Dawson's Brighton which eagerly gathered in the sons of the Empire. Foreign nationality was similarly no obstacle. Sir Vivian Fuchs, with a German father, was turned away by Tonbridge, but his mother recorded in her diary, 'Mr. Dawson writes kindly and does not mind about Ernst [her husband] being a German. Such balm to find anyone who prefers one to a pick-pocket'. When Head of School, L.A.G. Strong once asked Dawson why he admitted foreigners. 'He answered quite ingenuously

> I take them on my own terms: two years' fees in advance as surety for good behaviour. They're all highly sexed, and it's only a matter of months before they sleep with a house maid. Then out they go.

Strong's comment is that,

> I have no doubt of its truth. The foreigners had a way of suddenly being seen no more. I remembered asking a French boy what had happened to one of his friends. He smiled sweetly, shrugged his shoulders. 'Il aimait trop se coucher avec les belles filles.' I liked 'trop'.

Few 'foreigners' were actually admitted: 22 out of 293 between 1907 and 1910; 34 out of 628 from 1927 to 1930. Even so, Gordon House in its early days (*c.*1920-22) was nicknamed 'The League of Nations'. Not that many more came from the colonies—15 and 32 for the same periods, both representing 5 per cent of the school. Dawson recruited at home.

Numbers in College

1908	203
1912	245
1916	320
1920	483
1924	564
1928	571

The absolute peak was reached in September 1927 when 601 boys came to school. Growth seemed perpetual and effortless when, of course, it was neither. Since the first of three visits by Edward VII in 1908, Brighton had been enjoying something of a revival in popularity. The middle classes were expanding. The prosperity of London and the south east generated wealth sufficient to increase significantly the number of families looking to private education. Between 1924 and 1938, the proportion of salaried employees increased from 17 per cent of the workforce to 20 per cent. These were the voters who kept the Conservatives in power for all but three of the inter-war years. This was *the* era of public school fiction, of the stories of Frank Richards and Angela Brazil. The public schools enjoyed an Indian summer. But there was no intrinsic reason why parents should have so singled out Brighton College. Indeed, previous booms had passed Brighton College by. Between 1909 and 1929, Lancing's roll increased from 190 to 383, Rossall's from 279 to 448, Malvern's from 509 to 577. Dawson went out and drew pupils in. Recruitment continued unaffected by the First World War, in marked contrast to the College's experience during the Second. Every advance was a triumph. The fastest growth occurred between 1916 and 1921 when numbers rushed upwards from 320 to 516 (a 61 per cent increase)—and this at a time when under 20 per cent of children over 14 received any formal education at all. It also coincided with the earliest bout of 20th-century inflation which, for the first time ever, forced College fees up several times in rapid succession:

Increase in fees

	dayboy	boarder
	(£31 3s. 0d.)	(£93 3s. 0d.)
September 1917	£36 10s. 6d.	£105 13s. 6d.
January 1920	£42 10s. 6d.	£120 13s. 6d.
January 1921	£46 10s. 6d.	£130 13s. 6d.
September 1923	£58 17s. 0d.	£155 17s. 0d.

Given that the retail price index showed prices as doubling during the war, the first two increases must be judged remarkably modest. Overall, boarding fees rose by 56 per cent, day fees by 76 per cent, and perhaps their cumulative effect was to cut demand. The final jump, the steepest of them all, did coincide with a marked reduction in growth. Perhaps also that levelling off was due to increased competition from a series of new public schools, like Stowe and Canford. But the College had not priced itself out of the market. In 1921, Malvern, Lancing and Rossall charged a boarder £156, £150 and £145 per annum respectively.

The roll went onwards and upwards, beating every College record. Before 1906, there had only ever been 200 boys for two brief periods (1867-68 and 1886-89). Dawson came close to reaching three times that figure, and he did it when many boys still came for only a short time. Of the 482 boys who entered in 1915-18, some 37 per cent (179) stayed at most six terms; 20 per cent stayed for three terms or less. From September 1918, he also did it without the juniors. That February he had asked the Council their opinion 'upon the expediency of sooner or later abolishing the Junior School'. There were then only 25 boys under 11.5 years and he wanted the space they occupied for a new boarding house. Most Victorian public schools had already expelled their juniors as demand for places from older boys had grown, thereby creating one of the great modern gulfs between public and private education: differing ages of transfer to secondary education. When the upturn finally reached Brighton, pressure of numbers forced out the juniors there too.

Size was not the only fundamental alteration Dawson made. He achieved what Bigg and T.H. Belcher had failed to do. He made the College a boarding school. Almost all of the College's growth was in boarders. The impact was dramatic. From 1899, dayboys had formed a majority. Forty boarders brought with him from Grantham changed that immediately and, from the latter days of the war, the dayboys were overwhelmed:

Numbers in College

	boarders	dayboys
September 1905	59	72 (54.9%)
September 1910	136	104 (43.3%)
September 1915	172	116 (40.3%)
September 1920	387	96 (19.9%)
September 1925	466	123 (20.9%)
September 1927	488	113 (18.8%)

Across the Dawson years, the marked constancy of day numbers can only mean one thing: the Headmaster operated a quota.

Boarding was enhanced primarily by widening the College's recruiting beyond the Victorian reliance on greater Brighton and London:

Catchment areas (UK)

	pupils admitted 1887-90		pupils admitted 1907-10		pupils admitted 1927-30	
Brighton & Hove	100	(42.4%)	130	(44.4%)	148	(23.6%)
rest of Sussex	7	(2.9%)	23	(7.8%)	54	(8.6%)
rest of South East	89	(37.7%)	62	(21.2%)	235	(37.4%)
South West	5		3		14	
East Anglia	2		2		10	
East Midlands	3		27	(9.2%)	33	(5.2%)
West Midlands	4		2		16	
Yorkshire & N.E.	1		0		15	
Lancashire & N.W.	3		1		18	
Wales	1		4		9	
Scotland	0		2		7	
Ireland	2		0		1	
Total admitted	236		293		628	

Here too he achieved what Bigg and T.H. Belcher had aimed for. But it was not what Dawson had intended. He wanted Brighton College to be a national public school of the first rank. In terms of the school's name being known across the land, he achieved his goal. But he looked beyond that to something more permanent. For those three sample periods, the proportion of boys drawn from beyond the Home Counties rose from 8.9 per cent to 13.9 per cent to 19.6 per cent. He judged himself too hard. Such growth for a school which had always been local rather than even provincial in its recruitment was a very considerable triumph and testifies to the name he won for Brighton College.

Boarding numbers increased eightfold. How were they housed? Not by building any new Houses is the simple answer, in marked contrast to the strategy of the 1880s. Perhaps the two are not unrelated, given the bankruptcy which ensued. The College architect did in 1912 draw up plans for a new house beyond the entrance archway, costing £6,391, but it was instantly relegated to the bottom of the list of proposed capital projects. School House was split into two parts, called 'A' and 'B'. A series of new Houses was opened: Durnford in 1909, Walpole 1916, Bristol 1918, Gordon 1919, Wilsons 1920 and Stenning 1922. All but Bristol were located in one or more large houses in Kemp Town of which only School 'B' occupied premises bought by the College. The rest were purchased or leased by the Housemaster himself. Bristol alone was set up on campus, by thrusting out the Junior Department to three houses rented in College Terrace; the following year they were evicted again to Lewes Crescent,

Junior study, Stenning House, 1931

Chichester and Bristol Houses, 1922 [note the temporary north wall of Chichester (right), left in 1883 for Big School to join on and only faced with flint and terracotta in 1929]

to make way for Gordon House. Burstow described this last move as being the equivalent to 'achieving what amounted to Dominion status'. He was too polite. His beloved Juniors had been sold off to two College masters. Named Brighton College Preparatory School, it was in reality a fully independent institution, many of whose pupils did not go on to the College.

Beyond annual repayments to the Phoenix, the surplus which the College revenue account began to show yearly from 1910 was insufficient for large capital expenditure. At £4,686 (less £1,500 to the Phoenix) between 1912 and 1914, these profits did, however, give the College a flexibility hitherto never known. On that novel basis, the Phoenix advanced a further £3,500 at 4.5 per cent in 1913, secured personally on members of the Council. To that sum the College added a further £1,100 via a second 4 per cent debenture issue and another £1,415 subscribed by well-wishers. Together, these monies were employed in erecting two new pre-fabricated laboratories and a school hall–the 'Big School' planned by Gilbert Scott in 1848 and so longed for ever since. These years also witnessed a series of lesser capital projects: extensive drainage works in 1909-10; the reseating of the chapel, the provision of a new organ and the conversion of the building from gas to electric lighting in 1911; a new 'carpenters shop' (1911-12); the conversion of the rest of the main block of buildings to electricity in 1914–Chichester House was changed over in 1920, Bristol not until 1928. Meanwhile, Lord Francis Hervey (governor 1910-31 and nephew of Lord Alfred) obtained, from his brother the Marquis of Bristol, a 35-year lease on 8.5

Foundation stone of the Hall

Lord Francis Hervey [Photo: The National Trust]

acres at Manor Farm behind St Mark's church, at the generous annual rental of £5 per acre. Once levelled, the cost of which (£640) was defrayed by Lord Francis himself, the pitches created there were christened 'The New Ground'. With the school at 250 and rising, compulsory games had made their need desperate. Indeed, the New Ground itself soon proved insufficient and in 1916 a temporary lease was taken on additional land in Whitehawk. But for the First World War, a swimming pool would have been built in 1914-15.

*   *   *

When the Austrian Foreign Minister provoked war against Serbia in July 1914, the Officers Training Corps (as the cadet corps had become in 1908 under the Haldane reforms) was travelling to camp. On the British declaration of war (4 August), Kenneth Robertson (1911-14) tells us that 'half the tents were immediately struck and half the Regular cooks withdrawn'. He also adds the now fascinating perspective of a 16-year-old in that moment of European catastrophe: 'As schoolboys, the unsettled state of European politics did not worry us unduly ... The situation in Ireland seemed to many of us more likely to end in flare-up'. Not that these boys were unprepared. Sir Alun Pugh's diary for 24 November 1912 records: 'There is a report that Austria, Germany and Russia are mobilising. Chief gave us a long talk in Collect on the duty that lies before the present generation to defend their country'. That was a theme heard over and over again from the Boer War. Binyon's famous poem *For the Fallen* and Owen's *Anthem for Doomed Youth* were both written about those who were going to die; the former was penned almost at the outbreak of war. The generation of 1914 had been conditioned to join the team in khaki and been prepared for self-sacrifice.

In essence, the story of Brighton College and the First World War is one of 'business as usual'. The war barely disrupted school routine. It requires an effort on our part to remember that the Home Front experience of 1914-18 was so very different from that of 1939-45. There was virtually no bombing, no rationing until 1917, no conscription until 1916. The College was buoyant and, despite significantly increased taxation (the rate of income tax more than trebled to 6s. in the pound), continued to expand. With 402 boys in November 1918, the school had grown by 44 per cent since the war began:

Numbers in College

July 1914	280
July 1915	303
July 1916	320
July 1917	334
July 1918	409

Such growth was not automatic. At Malvern and Cheltenham the roll dropped in 1914-15. Yet the College had never been so full. Seventeen boys were refugees from France and Belgium, often taken in at reduced fees. One was a 13-year-old Belgian, Michel Gevers (Summer Term 1915), whose family had fled Liège. He drew a fascinating contrast with elements of his former world:

> The majesty of the premises made a great impression on me, as did the decorum of lunch [in School House]. The dishes were brought in on trolleys with silver covers. Custom decreed that to be served you had to offer the dish to your neighbour, who would reply 'Help yourself' very politely. The knife and fork were used quite differently from at home and your hand, when not employed in eating, was to remain under the table instead of on it as I was used to.

The OTC at camp, July 1914.

The Chapel *c.*1924, enlarged as the First World War Memorial (note the lectern donated by the
Sherwood Foresters)

The guns of the Somme were heard on the Playground during cricket in the last
week of June 1916. Insurance against aerial bombing was taken out the same year.
Social occasions were fewer in number, and Speech Day was abandoned after 1915
for the duration. Perhaps this war was first brought home to the College when various
training battalions, stationed nearby, began to use the school's facilities. One of these,
12th Battalion, The Sherwood Foresters, made the College their HQ during the Christmas holiday of 1914 and continued in residence until embarking for France the
following Easter. In gratitude, they presented the imposing brass lectern still in use in
the chapel.

The threat of requisitioning most certainly shook out any remaining equanimity.
The first scare came in 1915 with rumours that the College would, like the Grammar
School, be taken for a military hospital. Then 30 October 1916 saw the real thing. The
Headmaster was telephoned by the Chief Constable to be told 'that the College
buildings were commandeered by the War Office'. Wasting no time, Dawson went to
the central police station to remonstrate. In full flood, the Headmaster was not to be
trifled with and Mr. Gentle, the (perhaps aptly named) Chief Constable of Brighton,

BRIGHTON COLLEGE.

Brighton College has been requisitioned by the War Office. There are between three and four hundred boys there, and the decision, communicated suddenly in the middle of the term, has caused some perturbation to the school authorities.

BRIGHTON COLLEGE.

The Headmaster of Brighton College informs us that there is no foundation for the statement published yesterday that the College had been requisitioned by the War Office. He adds that official information is to the effect that such action has not even been contemplated by the authorities.

soon sent a message 'to the effect that other arrangements had been made and the matter was at an end'. Dawson had finished with Mr. Gentle, but he did not let the matter lie. First, he enlisted one of the governors, Charles Thomas-Stanford (1914-32), to recruit his fellow Brighton MP to write a joint protest to the Prime Minister. Meanwhile, the Headmaster travelled to London to see the College President, the Earl of Chichester, who was then working at the War Office. He agreed to 'put the whole matter before the Director-General of Quartering. Dawson's exploitation of contacts paid off. Letters were received from Lloyd George and the Director-General, declaring that

the College could rely upon not being disturbed except as a last resort under great pressure. In the event of its being taken over, the War Office would consider taking over any buildings in the neighbourhood such as a girls' school that would be suitable for the College.

Presumably neither St Mary's Hall nor Roedean knew the threat hanging over them in 1917 and 1918.

Naturally, the Officers Training Corps took on a heightened significance. Parades were increased from once to three times a week, with field operations on Wednesdays (lessons finished early to accommodate them), company drill on Fridays and recruits drilling on Mondays. Trench digging was practised regularly on the New Ground. Regulars also dug trenches, on Whitehawk Hill and around the racecourse. These the Brighton College OTC was to man if the Germans invaded. Increased activity was not easy for there was a serious shortage of officers and no sergeant-major. Four masters joined up in 1914, as did the Head Porter, while Lance Sergeant Weaver had been recalled to the 3rd Battalion, Coldstream Guards. Four more masters responded to Kitchener's call in 1915. All the OTC's ammunition was requisitioned, along with most of its rifles, to help supply the New Armies. None of this dampened spirits. The cadets were said to 'exhibit a keenness hitherto unknown'. They were eager to join in the big adventure. The Magazine of December 1914 printed a list of 349 old boys known to be serving in the King-Emperor's forces. These were days of optimism, of exhilaration, of belief in a brief cleansing war to test the nation's right to survive, to take youth and transmute it into something noble:

Honour has come back, as a king, to earth
And paid his subjects with a royal wage;
And nobleness walks in our ways again;
And we are come into our heritage'

Rupert Brooke

The top of the College was perpetually thin in 1914-15 as boys volunteered at 18 (or under), or went off at 17 to Sandhurst and Woolwich. Motivation altered irrevocably with conscription from January 1916 and any remaining innocence was extinguished by the Somme and Passchendaele. Those who went in 1917 and 1918 were different and theirs is the Western Front that continues to haunt us, not the August Bank Holiday lark of 1914-15.

The exodus of eight staff in 1914-15 caused obvious problems in the classroom and on the games field. As in 1939, older men were called out of retirement, not always with successful results. From September 1915, the Junior Department employed the College's first woman teacher, Miss C. Prichard. To some degree, however, the College was cushioned by the small number of young men on the staff in 1914. At Ardingly, 10 assistant masters and the headmaster had all volunteered before Christmas 1914.

As the U-boat blockade began to squeeze Britain from later 1916, food became difficult to obtain. Bread rationing was introduced in 1917. Retailers voluntarily established their own system of coupons. Official rationing did not come in until early 1918. This was not because food was in short supply—the wheat harvest of 1917 had been exceptionally good—but because the populace suddenly got it into its heads that food was scarce and began to stockpile. The illogical cause of shortages notwithstanding, Housemasters' wives had to go out of their way to find food sufficient to feed their boarders. In Chichester House, P.R.D. Spurgin (1915-19, master 1925-38) tells us that 'wartime catering was most difficult. The food was not of the best, but Mrs. Belcher's

smile down the room made everyone eat it! She used, according to rumour, to stand in queues in all weathers to get us something good'. There is no record of parts of the school grounds being turned over to food production as at Ardingly, but in 1917 the College rented 3.5 acres 'for the purpose of growing potatoes and other vegetables ... A certain amount of the work in connection with it has been done by the boys'. Within the year, 'the school allotment' had been increased by an acre. Direct assistance to the national effort was provided in the summers of 1917 and 1918 when two parties of fifty boys went to Mickleton in Gloucestershire for three weeks each to help gather in the harvest. Thirty boys also went for two weeks in July 1918 to help with harvesting near Rye. But there was no munitions work, as at Cheltenham, Oundle and Uppingham with the Armstrong Ordnance Volunteers.

Popular assumption presumes that public schoolboys, gentlemen already partially trained by the OTC, were

Gordon Belcher, pupil and master, killed 1915

automatically commissioned. This was not necessarily so, especially in colonial forces. Of the 146 old boys killed, we have details of 142. Twenty-three (16 per cent) were not officers. Seventeen were privates, three lance corporals. Perhaps the distinction needs to be drawn between the Victorian and the ancient public schools and the different social classes from which they drew. While the proportion of Lancing old boys killed serving in the ranks was similar to that of Brighton (20 per cent), only 1.5 per cent of Eton's war dead were not officers.

Most were indeed fresh-faced subalterns. Ninety-two (66 per cent) were aged 25 years or under. Sixty-one (43 per cent) had left the College less than five years earlier. But again, the popular image is not quite right. As there were 10 killed aged 18 or 19 so there were eight in their forties and one aged 51. In total, some 976 old boys are recorded as having served in British, imperial or allied forces:

British		Colonial units			Allied forces		
Army	747 (111)	African	6		American	4	
RN/RM	31 (6)	Australian	14	(3)	Arab Legion	1	(1)
RFC/RAF	75 (14)	Canadian	16	(6)	Belgian	1	
Red Cross	2	Indian	63	(3)	French	5	(2)
YMCA driver	1	New Zealand	5		Italian	1	
		S. African	3		Russian	1	

note: numbers in brackets are those killed

The last two items in the left column show us that there were possibly at least three conscientious objectors. There were also probably three or four serving in the German army.

'How will they regard this slaughter, they who'll live after us?' (Wilfred Owen). From the first wartime issue, the magazine was carrying a black-bordered roll of honour. Before long, portraits of the fallen were also a regular feature. Like the war that consumed them, it is so hard now to imagine them, the doomed sons of Edwardian England, in colour. Like the mud of Flanders, sepia was the dominant tone of this war. Details of war service were collated by Walter Hett (staff 1907-39, Headmaster 1939-44) and published in 1920 as *The Brighton College War Record*. For a permanent memorial, the old boys launched an appeal for £20,000 in December 1917, described as 'the lowest sum asked for by any public school'. At the same time, the College itself offered 50 per cent fees to the sons of any old boys killed on active service 'in cases where the need of assistance is seen to exist'. Sir Thomas Jackson (1850-53) was invited back to design a memorial extension to the chapel, but his plan to turn the existing building into the side aisle of a much larger church (with tower) had to be wholly recast when only £9,000 was forthcoming. The extension we now see was put up in 1922-23 and proved to be Jackson's last major work; he died the following year.

Across the Empire, many looked to powerful, demonstrative monuments testifying to the glorious dead. Unlike some public schools, Brighton College has no heroic bronze St George or Sir Galahad or youthful David. Limited by funds, Jackson wisely opted for total restraint. The gaunt litany of names carved into the wall is surrounded by no fuss or frill. Jackson's memorial works because of its very sternness. Attention

Lance-Corpl. H. E. NUNN,
R.N.D.,
Killed in action in Gallipoli.

Flight Sub-Lieut. J. F. W. AKERS,
R.N.A.S.,
Missing (presumed killed), July 20th, 1917.

Sub-Lieut. E. W. L. R. HULBERT,
R.N.D.,
Killed in action in France,
May 25th, 1918.

Lieut. H. D. WRIGHT,
R.G.A.,
Killed in action.

Private G. S. KING,
Canadian Infantry,
Died of wounds received in action, April 30th, 1918.

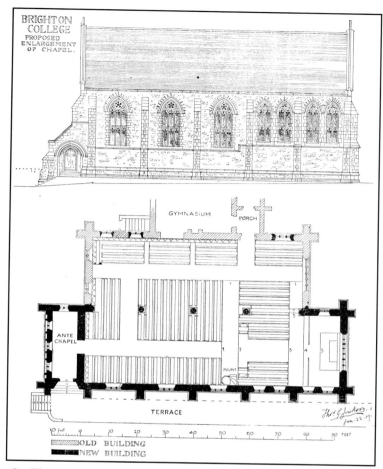

Sir Thomas Jackson's second design for the War Memorial Chapel
(abandoned for insufficient funds), 1919.

and emotion have no way of avoiding contemplation of the sheer scale of the killing:
146 old boys, the equivalent of one in every two boys who had come back to school
in 1914. When we realise that 119 (81.5 per cent) had left the College after 1900, we
glimpse the reality behind the truism that the Great War swept away an entire generation.

*   *   *

The years of Dawson's resolve to make Brighton College the greatest school in England matured in the 1920s. In pursuit of that quest, everything was done to create in
Brighton the image of a 'proper' public school (as determined by the opinion of the
day). The dayboys were downgraded and restricted. School prefects began to sport
their own distinctive blazer, tie and boater and also, for a short while, a silver-topped
black cane. An official coat of arms was acquired from the College of Arms. An old

boys' masonic lodge was founded. A new Home Mission was launched, to the nearby slum parish of St John Carlton Hill (whose vicar, Rev. H.H. Jones, had briefly been a member of staff in 1919). A biographical register of old boys was collated and published. The annual Lancing cricket match was transferred to the County Ground. Commemoration Day, a sort of founders' day, was begun as a grand focal point in the College year. At the same time, and certainly in reflection of this new triumphalist mood, the College's vitality made it possible to end Titherington's municipal scholars scheme. Brighton College would be beholden to none. In that same spirit, the Council used the introduction of a compulsory employers' 5 per cent contribution to masters' pensions (part of Geddes Axe in 1922) to withdraw from the Board of Education programme it had joined two years earlier and set up its own self-supporting scheme with the Equitable Life Assurance Society. The Council's motive is clearly set out in their minutes. This move would free the College

> from the supervision of the Board, which the Headmaster considered would be a great advantage. He feared it was quite possible the Board would sooner or later require a certain number of Elementary School pupils to be received without fees, which would be a great loss and detriment to the College.

Furthermore, withdrawal also ended the Board's right to nominate two governors.

The period 1916 to 1927 would appear cloudless. Triumphs followed in rapid succession. The school doubled in size and, for a moment, just topped 600 boys. From the effort concentrated upon sport, Dawson must have regarded it as the prime instrument for forging the school's reputation. Indeed, but even more was at stake, as Bishop Wand of London, a former pupil at Grantham, pointed out.

> Dawson's religion was of the Charles Kingsley type, a muscular and open air Christianity. His ideal was that of the Christian gentleman, with the emphasis rather upon the gentleman. Good sportsmanship was not merely next to godliness, but a direct manifestation of it.

The connection with religion is significant. As interest in religion declined sharply in the 1920s, and openly expressed religiosity among men came regularly labelled as effeminate, clerical schoolmasters worked to influence their boys through a crude, secularised morality, preached in terms of team spirit and loyalty, striving for the common aim and self sacrifice to achieve it. This was muscular christianity in almost pagan form. For Dawson, games thus served a twin purpose: the making of the Brighton College schoolboy as well as the making of Brighton College. Had Titherington not introduced compulsory sport in 1902, Dawson would have done it the moment he arrived. As it was, all he needed to do was to extend provision so that games were played every day except Friday (when the OTC paraded), supplemented by a 45-minute daily lesson of P.T. for every class. 'Keep clean, keep fit' was his own personal ethos. He himself did daily exercises and, as already noted, depended upon his own physical strength. This was not a man seen with books. Dawson was like the hero of a John Buchan novel. He was a man of the outdoors— hence his institution of the 'free half', an afternoon when everything was cancelled and boys had to go out, to hike across the Downs and breathe in the fresh air. This was, after all, the age of the rucksack and hiking, of the Youth Hostel movement, of 'strength through joy'.

Mr. and Mrs. Dawson

Burstow makes an important point when he says:

Brighton College was never as deliberately Spartan as some schools. But the powerful call of Sport, helped by the strong House spirit under the de-centralised system, made for an emphasis on hard bodies and cold baths. For the boys, the School with its intense overcrowding, was undoubtedly an uncomfortable place. The expenditure on fuel and carpets was not great, and central heating and hot showers were only slowly being introduced in the Twenties.

Team games flourished especially from around 1920 when the College was so vast. For a while, Association football even became the premier College sport, enjoying particular success just before the First World War. The XI of 1909-10 lost only one match and won the Public Schools Challenge Cup. The young bloods of the old boys' team proceeded to carry home the Sussex Cup every year from 1909 to 1914, and in 1913 triumphed over all other old boy sides in the Arthur Dunn Cup. In final tribute to a great tradition, Ronald Gandar-Dower (1903-10) won his Association blue and played for England in the 1920 Olympics.

Among the public schools, the Association game was a dying sport and Brighton changed to Rugby at the end of the 1917-18 season. Dawson himself had made that same switch at Grantham, but the moving spirit in 1918 at Brighton was his Second

OLD BRIGHTONIANS 1912-13: Winners of the "Arthur Dunn" and Sussex A.F.A. Cups. Names :— (left to right) Back row : W. McCowan (hon. sec.), G. M. Dawbarn, A. R. G. Roberson, G. Belcher, L. F. Dower, A. H. Belcher, (capt.) ; seated : A. J. Murdoch, P. Havelock Davies, M. H. Clarke, C. E. Hoffmeister (act. capt.), R. W. Dower, A. D. Cave ; in front : C. R. Shallow, W. S. Roos.

FIRST XI. 1917-18.

P. R. D. SPURGIN.   A. J. WALKER-LONGLEY.   D. F. A. APTHORP.   R. B. CAVE.   B. R. BENNETT.   E. GARLAND.

L. B. BARTON.   F. R. H. BEVEN.   C. C. RUTHERFORD.   M. H. TOLLIT.   R. NUTT.

This was the very last Association season

Master, Arthur Belcher (1885-95, master 1902-33, Headmaster 1933-36: always known as 'HB'). His reasoning takes us back to the cult of the English gentleman:

> Association football has been spoilt by professionalism. It is not the hard sturdy genre it was. The real honest charge with all a man's weight behind it is often penalised nowadays. There has been too much legislation—too much care for the financial aspect—too much of the idea that football is a spectacle for the people rather than a game played for the mere love of the game itself.

A few schools held out and still play by Association rules to this day (e.g. Bradfield, Lancing, Malvern and Repton). But not Brighton, which then was far too preoccupied with its own self image to stand against any tide or to notice that it was severing the last remaining link with its founding identity (as a school modelled on the image of

Bill Williams

Winchester, not according to the teachings of Dr. Arnold's disciples).

In their first four seasons, the XV won only six of their 48 matches but, coached by Rev. 'Bill' Williams (1919-45) and the England international Ernest Hammett (1921-46), the XV improved rapidly, especially once additional pitches became available in East Brighton Park from Christmas Term 1926. No XV ever managed the particular distinction of an all-victorious season, but the XV of 1925 came very close, winning 13 of its 14 matches with a style described in the magazine as 'fast and open'; they scored 502 points, and conceded only 43. One of their number, Peter Hordern (1921-26) went on to win his blue (Oxford 1928) and play for England. Over the next half dozen seasons, the XV remained exceptionally strong and produced two more blues (C.R.B. Birdwood, Cambridge 1931 & 32; J.M. Griffiths, Cambridge 1933). Out of all the fixtures, that against Christ's Hospital was regarded as the premier contest and, of the 21 played between 1919 and 1939, Brighton won fifteen.

Cricket similarly failed to see an unbeaten XI but, with Arthur Belcher as master in charge and two former Sussex players (the groundsman A.H. Mitchell and the Headmaster's Secretary Joe Vine) providing invaluable coaching, a fine series of batsmen emerged. Between 1920 and 1932, no less than 30 centuries were scored, in contrast to three between 1906 and 1914. Six stand out:

V.E. Bourdillon	615 runs	1916
W.R.N. Philps	521 runs	1921
G.W.F. Lyon	651 runs	1924
C. de B. Barnard	591 runs	1926
F.C. Jarchow	575 runs	1929
	628 runs	1930
C.R. Maxwell	565 runs	1930
	1,037 runs	1931

Of these, Gordon Lyon (1919-24, staff 1927-32) won a blue and played for Surrey, while Maxwell represented Middlesex, Nottinghamshire and Worcestershire, and toured with Sir Julian Cahn's XI. In addition to them, H.W.V. Levett (1922-26) kept wicket for the Gentlemen and toured India with the MCC. Curiously, no cricket blues were won after P.H. Davies (Oxford 1913-14) and E.C. Baker (Cambridge 1912 & 14), which for a good cricketing school the size of Brighton in the 1920s is bizarre—especially when we recall its record between 1850 and 1890.

FIRST XI. 1926.

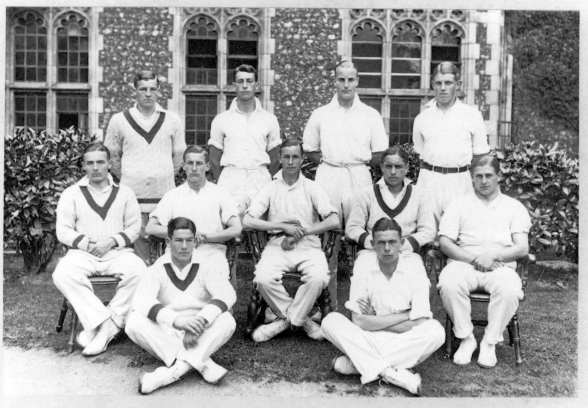

P. C. HORDERN.   U. H. HUNTINGTON.   E. L. TAYLOR.   J. A. P. BARTLETT.

C. A. R. LAWRENCE.   W. H. LEVETT.   J. H. GREEN.   C. DE B. BARNARD.   W. H. A. EVANS.

C. ODGERS.   J. M. WHITSED.

1st XI, 1926

Prior to Manor Farm's lease, the only way the whole school could be occupied on games afternoons had been the sending of large groups on a three-mile run around the racecourse–'HB' offered a pot of jam to the runner who was home first. From 1919, however, formal cross-country running was revived. Coached by two blues on the staff, it soon secured a prominent place among the 'minor sports'–until abolished for the second time on doctors orders, in 1934. Athletics similarly thrived as a purely internal activity, except for inter-school relays introduced in 1926. Another minor sport to come back out of the shadows was boxing which from 1920 surged forth anew as an Easter Term sport with Sgt. Major Beckett as instructor, the former Naval champion Rev. 'Bill' Williams as coach and the Brighton entrepreneur Sir Harry Preston as champion and supporter. The reappearance of fencing (foil and sabre) as an all-year-round sport in 1927 was a true resurrection after perhaps fifty years. Within three years, College fencers were entering the public schools championship and in

The Manor Farm playing fields

The Swimming Pool, *c*.1930

1931 a foil took part in the Dieppe International—the earliest known instance of a College team going overseas. G.V. Hett captained Cambridge in 1930 and took part in the 1936 Olympics. Most significant among the revived minor sports was swimming and (from 1926) its new adjunct, water polo, which developed apace with the opening of an on-campus, indoor heated pool in 1923. Why, therefore, was the competitive

Fives, *c.*1927 (in the background is the tower of St Matthew's Church)

season restricted to the Summer Term? Even without the Stock Exchange and Oxford University, the fixture list was impressive. In the public schools Bath Cup competition, the College usually came third or fourth (second in 1931). No less than six swimmers from Dawson's era went on to win half blues, as did four at water polo—by any standards, an exceptional achievement.

Some loved the emphasis on sport and revelled in the games they could play so frequently. Others of course loathed what they felt to be a hearty brashness. In previous College histories, their voice has always been overlooked. Professor Odell (1903-10) found 'the excessive adulation of team spirit smothered the appreciation of the intrinsic qualities of the individual'. Professor Harrison (1907-13) wrote that 'compulsory games for the less competent were for me the worst of all memories of school life; they existed only to keep us out of mischief'. Some were selective in their dislikes. Sir Michael Hordern (1925-30) who by his own description 'was no good at games at all' and captained the 3rd XV, points out in his autobiography at least one way the intelligent boy could circumvent the system. His pet hate was cricket and when his shooting test prevented escape via a different sport,

> spotted a way out, and that was to be a butt marker. This meant going down to the butts [at Mile Oak] three days a week and marking the targets as they were hit... This operation allowed you not only to avoid the cricket, but to smoke. So there we were, having a lovely time, puffing away in the butts on the Sussex Downs.

Something else should be noted. These three examples show that, even under Dawson, games never became the only thing that mattered. All three became school prefects. In schools like Rossall or Sedbergh, that would have been quite impossible. The front rank of College sport in the 1920s was held, arguably, not by cricket but by shooting, which had developed alongside the corps. Coached by 'Topliss'

The all-victorious VIII at Bisley, 1927

Practice in the Sheepcote Valley, with Sgt. Major Hawkins (1920-37)

(R.S.M. Hawkins), the VIII established a formidable standard and an immense reputation, winning at least one cup each year and heading the Bisley averages every year between 1926 and 1936, coming second in the Ashburton in 1929 and 1932. Their *annus mirabilis* was 1927 when they brought home all eight Bisley trophies, including the Ashburton–a still unequalled feat.

After the war, the OTC went back to one parade per week: 'sandpaper knicks on Friday, as we called it' (Sir Michael Hordern). The size of the College meant that the corps was one of the very largest in the country, with over 400 cadets in the second half of the 1920s. Sir Michael had another military memory: 'Oh those bloody puttees that had to be smoothly wound, and of course wouldn't wind smoothly and were always overlapping the wrong way'. There was neither a naval nor an air section and the only variety was Fusty Bennett's signals platoon or the fife and drum band. In the early twenties, the OTC was far from popular, suffering as in all schools from a post-war rejection of militarism. Indeed, the magazine write-ups contain an extraordinary number of complaints about low attendance at summer camp and the small numbers seeking Territorial Army commissions. Equally uncongenial were the House drill competition and the slog on so many Fridays to pass 'Cert A'. When Lt. Col. Homfray RMLI (1920-27) lectured cadets over and over 'that it was their duty to obtain a commission in the T.A.', their minds turned instead to the League of Nations Association and contemporary moves to international disarmament. The OTC was its own worst enemy.

OTC Inspection (date unknown)

Dawson put Brighton College on the map in the mid-1920s. As numbers went ever higher, word spread ever further that here was a dynamic school with a great Headmaster. His appointment to the Prebend of Bishophurst in 1924 was regarded within the College as a great accolade because it was proof that his stature was recognised beyond the College walls. The miracle at the 1927 Bisley meet drew considerable newspaper coverage. The annual meeting of the Headmasters' Conference at the College in December 1926 was itself a singular honour, and the direct result of the school having championed the cause of charitable tax status. Until the 1920s, only the nine 'Great Schools' (like Eton, Harrow and Winchester) were exempt from tax. All other schools, even if like Brighton College registered with the Board of Trade as 'associations not for profit', were deemed in law to be carrying on a trade. Any profits were therefore liable to tax. Led by George Morgan Edwardes-Jones KC (1869-77, governor 1913-36), Brighton College set out in December 1915 to claim for itself the privileged position in tax law of the élite nine. Naturally, progress was slow, but several significant skirmishes were won along the way. Action in the courts, reinforced by parliamentary lobbying, brought exemption from income tax schedules A and C through the 1918 Finance Act.

The primary contest was, however, over income tax schedule D: balance of profits. In the High Court in June 1924, Mr. Justice Rowlatt found in the College's favour [40 TLR 763-5] but judgement in *Brighton College v Marriott* went in favour of the Inland Revenue in the Court of Appeal and in the House of Lords [1926, AC 192-204]. Since all would benefit, the College had received financial support from HMC to take their case to the House of Lords. On defeat, they assisted Brighton College in orchestrating a parliamentary lobby to have the law changed. This they duly accomplished by section 24 of the 1927 Finance Act, which exempted all registered charities from tax on profits. To this day, the key precedent in determining the charitable tax status of any organisation is *Brighton College v Marriott*.

George Edwardes-Jones

*   *   *

Burstow drew a dividing line in Dawson's reign at the First World War, commenting that, while 'both the Chief and the College continued at the height of their powers for some time after 1918, the changed character of the post-war world was reflected profoundly in the whole life of the school'. The war had changed everything. For headmasters like Dawson, the faces of pupils lost at Ypres or Jutland could never be banished. For many who came back (and there was a significant influx of masters recruited straight from the forces), victory was hollow. It had come too late. Few were the combatants who, for all the zest they mustered, could keep at bay memories of their dead comrades. Yet jazz and inflation and flappers declared to everyone that in the 1920s here was a new world. At Brighton College, continual growth created a powerful mask of continuity. The division Burstow observed was forced by another factor, one that in 1957 he was too discreet to record: Dawson had been struck down. The significance is explained by L.A.G. Strong. 'In 1922 he had a minor paralytic stroke, which left him outwardly undamaged, but changed him drastically within. From that time on, he was a parody of himself, and in some respects worse than a parody.' Dawson was never a manager and, at 540 boys, the College in 1922 was already larger than it had ever been. 'Despite all that HB could do as Second Master, it was run on no discernible system. Unable in his later years to criticise the decisions he made, or understand the full import of what he was doing, the Chief clung to a few maxims and pushed them almost to disaster'.

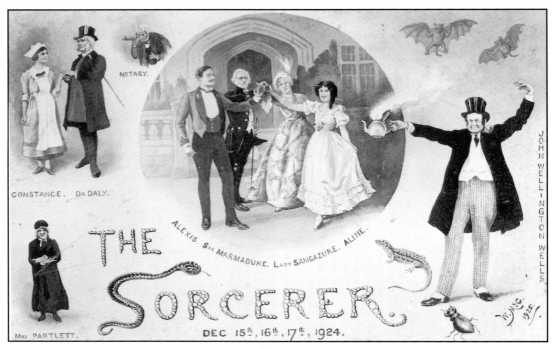

drawn by Walter McCowan

Strong is talking about the loss of 'qualitative judgement which had made the College prosper'. In three areas, Brighton College became vulnerable during the 1920s: the number of pupils, the financial obligations undertaken to service those numbers, and the academic quality of teaching staff as well as pupils. The exceptional influx of pupils–up to 601 in September 1927–has already been noted. At an absolute push, the College itself could in 1920 house 200 boarders and 65 dayboys. The new out-boarding houses extended that range and when in 1922 the last of those was opened, the Council declared 450 boys to be the ideal size–90 boys fewer than they then had and 151 less than they would end up with. Dawson's Second Master, who had to pick up the pieces as Headmaster in 1933, spoke of 'serious overcrowding' and 'numbers unduly swollen by the false vision of perpetual peace and prosperity'. The Board of Education Inspectors judged the College in January 1920 'full, and indeed overfull', a view echoed by the Chairman of the Council that March who 'confessed to considerable doubt as to the wisdom of increasing numbers'. Yet the roll careered ever upwards. Burstow described it as 'a disastrous megalomania'.

What was lacking was business acumen. Perpetual growth is not possible. Beyond a certain point, the diseconomies of scale undermine the whole edifice, especially if it is a boarding school trapped on a small urban site. True, the College spent virtually nothing on new boarding accommodation, but enlarged numbers required other and heavy capital expenditure:

sum £	year	purpose
900	1920	new sanatorium (15 College Terrace)
1,800	1920	School House overflow (13 & 14 College Terrace)
1,200	1920-1	new laboratories and classrooms
2,408	1922	new games pitches
17,057	1922-8	levelling new games pitches
5,677	1922-3	swimming pool
4,500	1926	new sanatorium (1 Bristol Gate)

In addition, they paid £500 per annum into the masters' pension scheme (established 1920) and £500 per annum capital repayment to the Phoenix. Then there was interest to be paid on the various loans which partially funded these projects—in 1923 amounting to £1,593 per annum. Belcher's reference to a 'false vision of perpetual peace and prosperity' is brought into sharp relief if we recall that, nationally, 1920-24 were years of post-war stringency. While government expenditure was being hacked back by 'Geddes Axe' and maintained schools were starved of funds, Brighton College sailed blithely forward, cocooned from retrenchment by comfortable annual surplusses.

One episode highlights what was wrong. By 1921, the 70 per cent increase in numbers of the previous five years had put enormous strain on games facilities, even with Manor Farm and Whitehawk. Negotiations were thus opened to buy nearly 21 acres less than three hundred yards further up Sutherland Road: the Craven Vale estate. The location was perfect and although the upper part of Bakers Bottom narrowed and had steep sides, engineers estimated levelling would cost around £8,000. The contract was signed in August 1922, but Brighton Borough Council objected because the estate was being used as allotments and it did not want them to be lost. Instead, the Corporation offered the College 25 acres just over one mile away in East Brighton Park, on a 99-year lease (rent £250 pa) if they would hand over Craven Vale for its purchase price. Initially the College agreed to entertain an exchange of freeholds, but that the Corporation rejected out of hand and then proceeded to threaten compulsory purchase. Even though the Borough was shown to possess no power to do that, the College Council gave up. In Dawson's own words, they did not want 'to incur unpopularity in the matter', so in July 1923 agreed to the Corporation's terms. Craven Vale's freehold was surrendered for leasehold land further away—which the College then discovered would cost £17,057 to level, divert the road and build a caretaker's cottage. To cap it all, the Borough Corporation itself subsequently evicted the allotment holders (1950) and turned Craven Vale into a housing estate. Of all Brighton College follies, none was greater than this. Such an excess of feebleness, of shortsightedness! What were they thinking about to surrender such patent benefits for the sake of appeasing a little odium?

When the College accounts for the year ending 31 August 1928 were presented, the accumulated capital liabilities totalled £27,490 18s.11d. (of which £14,890 6s. 8d. was the sum still owed to the Phoenix) and the current account showed a net deficit of £409 10s. 0d. Years of profit had built up a rolling credit of £17,466 2s. 9d. by 1924. All of that was now gone. On top of other expenditure, East Brighton Park

Brighton College - New Class Rooms and Library

North Elevation from Quad   Longitudinal Section looking North

F.T. Cawthorne's original design for the new classroom block, 1927 (unfortunately never built)

proved beyond the College's means. For the first time in 15 years, 1925 saw no operating profit and 1926 brought in a loss of £2,673 17s. 4d. As the cushion of past profits was consumed, the College's position became more fragile and in 1929 the Council decided to consolidate all the school's obligations in one new loan, for up to £20,000 at 5.25 per cent from the University Life Assurance Society. The Phoenix was paid off. So too were the first debenture holders (thereby ending their nomination of governors). At the same time, an appeal was launched to put up a new block of classrooms to the east of the entrance gateway. Designed, like the Hall, by F.T. Cawthorne, they were built most sympathetically to harmonise with Sir Thomas Jackson's Eastern Road buildings and cost £12,765 (of which £11,200 was received in donations). Much had been done to enhance facilities but, as the College moved towards the silver jubilee of Dawson's appointment, it was no longer a buoyant, thrusting institution. Above all, the College had become dangerously dependent on the recent very high rolls.

When the Board of Education inspectors reported in 1920, they suggested that 'now that the school is full (and indeed over-full), it should be possible to restrict the advantages it offers ... To this end, special attention should be paid to the age of entry and previous education'. Ten years later, their colleagues averred that 'This was an invitation to think of quality', an invitation which had been ignored at great cost.

The Council and Headmaster of Brighton College
request the pleasure of the Company

of _A. G. Jones Esq._

on Wednesday, October 29th, 1930.

Visit of H.R.H. The Prince George.

2.45 p.m.   His Royal Highness will open the New Building, and will
afterwards attend a Meeting in the School Hall in the interests
of the Brighton Boys' Club.

R. S. V. P. to THE WARDEN, *Brighton Boys' Club, Edward Street, Brighton.*

N.B.—This Invitation Card will admit to the Opening Ceremony only, and **must** be
presented at the College Entrance Gate.   When replying, please state whether
you wish for a ticket for the Meeting in the School Hall.

The boys perform for the camera after the opening ceremony

Scholarship was undervalued in Brighton College after the First World War. Led by
'HB' and Walter Hett, the Classical Side continued a bastion of excellence under men
who were well read and inspiring as well as demanding in the classroom; and in the
case of Hett, reinforced by 'a load of no.6 shot in the sleeve of his gown swung
shrewdly at the foolish ear' (L.A.G. Strong). The Classical Side was, however, a tiny
fraction of the school:

	Classical	*Modern*	*Total*
1920	36 (15.4%)	198	234
1925	69 (11.7%)	520	589
1930	77 (15.2%)	428	505

There was no problem with the amount of time given over to work:

Hours per week spent in lessons

	winter	*summer*
1906	25 hrs 50 mins	23 hrs 50 mins
1917	24 hrs 50 mins	23 hrs 15 mins
1925	27 hrs	27 hrs

on top of which the boys were given 30-minute preps in five subjects each night.
Neither was there much problem with the staff:pupil ratio which either equalled or
was more favourable than anything the College had known before:

pupils per assistant master

1907	11.1
1917	12.4
1927	14.9

Yet the academic standard was lower than it had ever been. Among the masters,
the critical deficiency was a dearth of first-rate men in the middle and lower parts of
the Modern Side, which in 1925 contained 66.4 per cent of the school (391 boys).
'Percy' Tollitt (1906-27), Head of the Modern Side with a triple first, the last College
master to wear a mortar board daily, did edifying work at the top. So too did 'Shotty'
Lister (1906-36) as, in his day, had Denys Bond (1908-13) who taught Lower French
and whom L.A.G. Strong described as 'a brilliant teacher of the second order', by
which he meant Bond had

> worked out methods of ramming down knowledge so securely that even the dullest can regurgitate
> most of it, devising fifty-two sentences embodying every rule of French construction, and a whole
> lexicon of catch phrases to illustrate each rule of grammar. This, combined with a vein of sarcasm,
> made his exam results excellent.

These men acted as tie rods holding together the academic life of the College. The
only other long-serving Modern teacher of academic account was William Bennett
(1906-30), known as 'the Buffer' or 'Fusty', who taught Science. To Kenneth Robertson,
he was 'a benign creature'. Burstow marked him down as 'baby-like in appearance

and squeaky in utterance'. Fusty was inefficient. He could be incompetent. At the same time, he was also a genius and, for all that they laughed at him, the boys knew it–for a long while they called him 'the seventh cleverest man in England'. Fusty was a wireless pioneer and was taken on by the Admiralty to do research work in 1914. He established the Engineering Class at the College which turned out everything from a model suspension bridge to parts for the school Carpenter's Shop to wireless sets to an electric trouser press. Strong assessed him as 'by far the best read and the most intelligent and cultured man on the staff'.

Several highly gifted young men stayed a short while, notably Christopher Butler (1927-28), subsequently Headmaster and then Abbot of Downside and later Auxiliary Bishop of Westminster. Another was Cecil Cullingford (1929-32), later Headmaster of Monmouth School. Both had a double first. Both would be ordained–Butler a Catholic, Cullingford an Evangelical Anglican. But such men were too few and their collective presence too fleeting to have much impact. Another judicious appointment of those last years, this time more lasting, was 'Teddy' Lester who arrived in 1927 with a good second in Mathematics and stayed on to inspire countless boys for 41 years. These were the exceptions. In part, the problem with the masters was that there were too many non-graduates, although that was a weakness eradicated in Dawson's last years:

full time assistant masters

	graduates	*non-graduates*	
1907	12	2	(14%)
1912	17	4	(19%)
1917	22	5	(18.5%)
1922	29	8	(22%)
1927	35	5	(12.5%)
1932	28	0	

In part, the problem with the masters was that most graduates had bad degrees—and that was a weakness which got worse. In 1911, the Oxford and Cambridge Board Inspectors observed that 'their qualifications, as measured by university degrees, are not so high as in the larger public schools'. By 1930, the Board of Education Inspectors found the situation had deteriorated drastically. While five of the 35 assistant masters (14 per cent) held first class honours degrees, no less than 23 (66 per cent) had a third or a fourth or a pass degree. Of course, as the Inspectors noted, 'the possession of a good degree is not in itself a guarantee of teaching ability, and a pass man may possess the flair for teaching and those personal qualities which count for much in a classroom or he may not'. Proof that their qualifying caution was not appropriate to Brighton College is to be found in College results for the Higher and the School Certificates. Entry of candidates ceased between 1915 and 1919 because of the war and concentration on preparation for the services. Thereafter, the record was terrible:

	pupils qualifying for		*total pupils*
	Higher Certificate	*School Certificate*	*in the College*
1920	0	31	483
1921	7	28	516
1922	0	36	540
1923	6	34	552
1924	2	30	564
1925	0	80	589
1926	0	52	597
1927	?	?	601
1928	6	64	571
1929	5	70	550
1930	6	77	562
1931	6	86	440
1932	6	80	402
1933	10	70	343

Reference back to the chart in Chapter 7 will show that, between 1875 and 1904, the number of boys gaining the Higher Certificate each year was never less than two, could be as high as 10, and averaged 6.3 (in a school never larger than 219 and more usually having 140-160 boys).

Hall interior in its original form, 1914

Hall exterior, before the ground-floor windows were inserted (1920) and the screen wall built (1926)

It is true that most pupils never had any intention of going to university and the Higher Certificate was irrelevant to their needs. Equally it is the case that many still left school at sixteen or seventeen, and that we are dealing here with a situation entirely different from anything experienced since the 1950s with the introduction of 'O' and 'A' levels, a massive expansion in higher education and the development of a culture demanding success measured by exams and paper qualifications. The purpose of education was judged very differently then and now. Admitting all of those extenuating facts, none will, however, explain away the dire position those results indicate. During these years, Rossall was a little smaller than Brighton (maximum 448) yet managed to average 42 Higher Certificates per year–Brighton averaged 4.1. Lancing never exceeded 383 boys, but its senior boys averaged 17 per year. Even allowing for distinct improvement from the mid-1920s, something was terribly wrong. The Rossall average in School Certificates in the 1920s was 63 boys per year; the Lancing average was 56. At Brighton it was only 47. As the schoolmaster Burstow commented, 'the lower forms were poorly taught and little attempt was made to ground them in the essentials'.

There is another test, more exclusive in measuring quality, but perhaps a better one because it was the one used during the 1920s. Prospectuses never listed results at Higher and School Certificate. The Headmaster's annual report on Speech Day often ignored them too (contrast that with the absolute need to publish detailed exam results today). But the prospectus and the Speech Day report took careful note of first-class honours degrees won by old boys. They were the blue ribbon league table of the day:

First-class honours degrees won by old boys

	Brighton	Lancing
1900-14	9	4
1919-33	10	37

However standards are measured, the College was not only far weaker than other public schools, but doing very considerably worse than its own performance in the 1890s or the 1930s. Dawson had appointed far too many masters by reference only to their qualities outside the classroom. Secondly, Dawson's free-for-all in pupil admissions led to a steep decline in academic quality. The emphasis was elsewhere, as Burstow noted: 'One hears [in the magazine] far more of the great 1925 Rugby side and Wilsons House than of scholarships and firsts'. In Sir Michael Hordern's opinion, 'there was no time for individual scholastic encouragement'. Even worse, the other OB actor of these years, George Sanders (1919-23), found 'an institution whose main purpose seemed to be that of convincing the boys that they were dunces. I myself was a poor student, partly because it was the fashion and partly because the efforts of the teachers to convince me that I was a dunce were highly successful'. A Brighton College education had ceased to address the whole man. As in academic standards so in financial probity, the drift of the 1920s led both to be sacrificed to the single god: expansion.

Defeat followed victory. The roll began to fall back and with it any hope of avoiding debt. Dawson's final years saw numbers drop by 43 per cent:

Numbers in College

Sept 1927	601
Sept 1928	571
Sept 1929	550
Sept 1930	505
Sept 1931	440
Sept 1932	398
Sept 1933	343

Dawson had begun in the high days of Edwardian confidence and was not used to set-backs. He did not expect failure. He did not know what was going on. His loyal lieutenant 'HB' tells us that these events 'took him by surprise and hit him very hard'. Back in 1916, a roll with 340 boys was excellent news. Seventeen years later, everyone could see only disaster.

In part, the decline must be linked to the lower birth rate of the war years. All schools were hit. But the major cause was the Depression which Brighton College entered in a vulnerable financial state, with an enfeebled Council woefully devoid of business experience, dependent for leadership and vision on a man no longer able to provide either. Eventually, even Dawson himself accepted that he was unable to cope and in December 1931 he offered to resign the following July. Sentiment made the Council reject his offer, a decision from which no one benefited.

Stenning House, 1933 (the matron is Dorothy Fenwick)

The Dawson family, 1933

Numbers started to drop before the world economic crash (that is a vital point to get clear). When the slump first hit Britain in 1930-31, however, the roll fell almost one quarter in 20 months. By coincidence, the Council met the day after Black Thursday (December 1929), the first stage in the Wall Street Crash. In the sobering reality of those events, the Chairman Frank Lingard (1875-80, Chairman of the Council 1910-32) warned that if numbers fell to 500 there would be a deficit of £1,880. Thus began a process of cutting budgets, reducing salaries by 10 per cent and making staff redundancies; seven posts were axed at the height of the troubles in 1930-31. The raising of tuition fees was considered several times, and mounting pressure eventually forced a £1 per term increase in January 1931. Whatever the Council did, any improvement in the College's financial situation could only be relative while the roll continued to fall and, even after borrowing a further £5,000 in the summer of 1930, the deficit on the revenue account stood at £4,137 in 1933.

An unrelenting new realism came upon the Council with the election of Wilfred Aldrich (1899-1903) as Chairman in December 1932. A local solicitor, he had only joined the Council in October 1929 (the year he was Mayor of Brighton), but instantly he had made his mark chairing a sub-committee on finances. He brought a no-nonsense approach badly needed. Tough times required tough decisions. Sentiment had its place but, to Aldrich, it was 'a dangerous commodity because it clouded judgement'. In the glimmer of the twilight, the Chairman advanced on three fronts. First he introduced the drawing up of draft budgets for the year ahead–the previous lack of which says much about the way things had been run. Second, he shut the weakest of the out-boarding houses, Stenning. Wilsons and Durnford were also well below strength and they could be propped up with the 31 boys left over when Stenning shut. There was, however, a particular reason why Stenning was sacrificed, even though Wilson's had fewer boys. Stenning was in debt to the tune of around £1,000. The Housemaster, Major Basil Tomlinson, had been in office for a year but curiously was not a member of the teaching staff. When Aldrich discovered that he had settled barely a single bill with any of his suppliers for the past year, he determined on pulling the plug to punish Tomlinson, not so much for his 'extravagance and mismanagement' but because 'the manner in which this House has been conducted has brought discredit on the College'. Third, Aldrich attacked 'the greatest part of annual expenditure': the salary bill. While an eighth master was given notice, he turned the Council's attention towards 'by far the most serious problem concerning this committee–the position of the Headmaster and the possibility of his early retirement'. From 1921, Dawson's method of payment by capitation had been altered to a fixed salary of £2,400 per annum. Even after recent cuts, his current pay of £1,866 was judged more than could be afforded and Aldrich reminded the Headmaster of his recent offer to resign. Taking the hint, Dawson 'expressed his desire to retire in July 1933'. But that was not good enough for Aldrich, who pressed harder and secured his agreement to go at Easter. There was more. Aldrich also arranged for Dawson to be succeeded by the Second Master for a three-year term *without* receiving the Headmaster's salary. Belcher's willingness to surrender £1,225 per annum was exceptionally generous. Just as remarkable, however, were the methods of Wilfred Aldrich. The once mighty Dawson had been purged by one as cunning and as ruthless as the old Chief in his prime. Dawson was Aldrich's first victim. He would not be his last.

Burstow's final judgement of William Rodgers Dawson was that

> it is less in his achievements than in his personality and leadership that he will always be memorable ... Dawson had many blind spots along with his brilliance. But he made Brighton College capable of great things at unpredictable moments.

Dawson is a first-rate example of what can be achieved by a man without great talent who yet acts with courage and determination. His horizon was limited and, in key respects, his tenure of office was far from distinguished. He was no scholar. Bishop Wand judged him 'theologically naif'. He was no manager of men or finances. Yet in Dawson there was the greatest of capacities to inspire, to guide, to lead. The effect he had on everyone who came under his influence was likely to be profound–Burstow called it 'being enlarged'. And the devotion he could engender was so great that it lasts for a lifetime.

Few indeed possess such a capacity. Both Strong and Burstow rooted it in Dawson's Celticness. They point out that everyone found him illogical, unpredictable and in-consistent because 'he lived outwards from his feelings in an impulsive, un-English way'. Without acknowledging that, Dawson will always remain an enigma. It is the key to his conduct and to his potency. Then if we add his sense of divine commission he starts to make sense. He had no formulated policies, only general aspirations. He was an opportunist, not a pragmatist. A manic optimist, he manipulated others with a caressing charm. He knew where he was headed, cared little how he got there and possessed the knack of convincing others that they were going there too. He was a stylish and accomplished performer.

His message was always simple, even simplistic. That in itself explains much. To leave in those around him the conviction that it was he who knew what was best for them was an exceptional gift. In the words of 'HB', all who had come under his influence came to value him 'as their own personal guide, philosopher and friend'. Many are the old boys who have testified that Dawson was the greatest influence on their lives. When they called him 'the Chief', this was what they meant.

Pupils at the naming of the Brighton College locomotive, 1933
(Schools Class 4-4-0 locomotive number 915)

Ten

1933-1944

The slow watches of the night

'The ensuing years brought little to the school save trouble and anxiety.' That was how Rev. Arthur Belcher summed up this part of the College's history, during which he was either Headmaster (1933-36) or a governor. The terms of Belcher's appointment have already been described. They were typical of the man, and saved the College over £4,000. His devotion to the school across 61 years cannot be exaggerated. Burstow describes him as 'the most solid, consistent and unchanging of men ... [a] cool, classical, slightly severe figure'. To new boys, HB 'sometimes seemed aloof', while to those 'who had no interest or ability in games' he came across as 'a little condescending'. For these reasons, HB 'was not universally popular'. But L.A.G. Strong goes on to declare:

> HB inspired in many of us a depth of trust which the Chief did not. Boys are suspicious of the incalculable. I loved the Chief, but I was at home with HB ... With HB one saw a steady table-land, which would always support one.

Belcher may have been 'steadier, less spectacular' than Dawson, but that was the precise requirement for 1933 (and it is tempting to speculate how far Dawson succeeded only because HB was his Second Master).

The worst of the Depression had passed by 1933. Registered unemployment peaked that January at 2.7 million.

Rev. Arthur Hayes Belcher

Between 1933 and 1937, the economy grew by 4 per cent each year. Interest rates were low (bank base rate 2 per cent). Salaries remained stable and, for those in work, real income rose by 19 per cent. A very considerable economic recovery carried production and employment to a then all-time high in late 1937. The British people spent their way out of the Slump, consumer expenditure being visible in the growing number of cars on the road and the boom in house building. But recovery passed Brighton College by. Whatever the school tried, the roll fell back and back:

Numbers in College

	total pupils	total dayboys	
Sept 1930	505	100	(20%)
Sept 1931	440	88	(20%)
Sept 1932	398	100	(25%)
Sept 1933	343	84	(24.5%)
Sept 1934	296	93	(31%)
Sept 1935	270	90	(33%)
Sept 1936	264	106	(40%)
Sept 1937	241	111	(46%)
Sept 1938	255	107	(42%)
Sept 1939	249	108	(44%)

'Teddy' Lester and senior boys from Wilsons House, c.1931

The school had been cut in half, almost all of the loss being boarders. The worst years were 1930-34 when numbers fell by 42 per cent. If by comparison the slippage thereafter seemed only as a trickle, the brittle state of College finances made net falls of 9 per cent in 1934-35 and 1936-37 exceedingly serious. To be economically viable, the school needed 350 pupils, but in the later '30s was around 100 short of that. Dawson's dream lay in tatters. Lopsided slump brought the dayboys back into prominence, just as they had been 40 years before (the closure of the Kemp Town branch line to passenger traffic in 1932 seems not to have dented demand). Once again, Brighton College was brutally reminded that its local market kept the school afloat. All of the 'new' boarding houses came under great pressure. Apart from Durnford, all closed between 1932 and 1935.

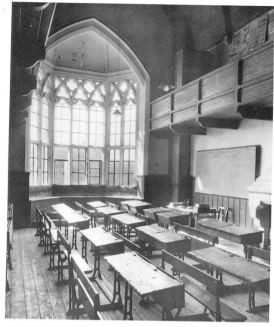

The VIth Form Room, *c.*1935

When Wilsons House closed in July 1935, many felt that a great era had ended. Under Rev. 'Bill' Williams, Housemaster from its inception in 1920, this House had carved for itself legendary status for sporting prowess, especially at its Housemaster's twin specialities, rugby and boxing. They were Cock House in seven of their 15 years, a feat without rival. Burstow judged the extinguishing of Wilsons' 'tremendous tradition ... the saddest blow inflicted by the Depression'. The appearance of Leconfield House in 1938 was not the creation of a new day House. Rather it was the substitution of a proper name for 'Hampden B', in existence since 1930.

The Depression hit Brighton College harder than most:

percentage fall in numbers

	1930-33	1933-39
Lancing	17%	23%
Malvern	19%	8%
Rossall	22%	38%
BRIGHTON	30%	27%

Retrenchment became an urgent priority, every year. In the phrase 'hard work, reduced fees, effective propaganda and efficient administration', Burstow summed up how Headmasters and Council sought to head off the disaster which always threatened. Since the 1930 Inspection, the raising of academic standards had stood a target priority. Several initiatives were pursued simultaneously: the recruiting of a more highly qualified staff, who would teach only their own speciality; the complete overhaul of the Modern Side; the development of clearly defined academic departments. Reduced numbers could so easily have been used to dismember the teaching staff. To everyone's credit, academic priorities were maintained:

Pupils per assistant master

Sept 1933	15.6
Sept 1936	12.6
Sept 1939	13.1

[the national average in grammar schools in 1938 was 19 : 1]

The management of staff reduction and the development of staff quality could go hand-in-hand because so many of Dawson's appointees were due for retirement (eight masters with over twenty years' service apiece, another four with more than fifteen); Belcher was a powerful but unsuccessful advocate of reducing the staff retirement age from 65 to 60. Here was the chance for new blood, for higher salaries to attract better qualified men and for vital savings still to be effected. Belcher and his successor Christopher Scott (1937-39) made a series of discerning appointments. Attention has always focused on six young masters brought in by Scott, dubbed from their average age of 21 'the creche'. Three had firsts, only one a third. Their specialisms ranged across the curriculum, and included a cricket blue and an Olympic sabreur. Under their guidance, classroom and sports field flourished. Because of all of that, and because two won the Military Cross and two were killed during the war, because one died still so young after becoming Housemaster of School House and because one went on to be College Headmaster, 'the creche' has gone down to immortality. In the process, their talents and tragedies have obscured Belcher's intake. The first was a Chemist, Dr. Robertson (1935-41). The others were a Classicist (John Bowes) and a Modern Linguist (Vaughan Harries). They were the first to invigorate school life and it was they, not 'the creche', who launched the renaissance of school societies. By 1937-38, these outshone anything for 50 years. But headmasters like to appoint their own men, and Scott gave Bowes and Harries summary notice the moment he arrived that they would not be required from the end of their probationary year.

When Second Master to the ailing Dawson, Belcher had restructured Higher Certificate teaching after the 1930 Inspection. In essence, what he did was to bring to Brighton College changes made elsewhere when Higher Certificate had been re-organised after the First World War. Thus 'VI Classical' and '6th Modern' were abolished (1930), to be replaced by four specialist VIth Form classes: Group I (Classics), Group II ('General Modern Subjects'), Group III (Maths & Physics), Group IV (Natural Science). Two years later, the ancient divide between the Classical and the Modern Side was removed from the rest of the school.

Structural reform was accompanied by changes to content fully in line with contemporary developments. Art was put back, in its own dedicated studio. Biology and Geography became fully-fledged subjects in 1934 and 1935 respectively. Economics was introduced to the VIth Form in 1936 (the first wholly new subject since Spanish started in 1919). Compulsory Latin was dropped gradually from the middle and lower forms. Greek was abandoned completely in 1940. None of this was revolutionary or progressive. Most public schools were making similar changes around the same time.

Chemistry laboratory, late 1930s

The area most difficult to tackle was the quality of the pupil intake. Only with strong numbers and a good waiting list could entrance standards have been raised. Very rarely has the College ever been in that most fortunate of positions. In July 1933, Belcher informed the Council that 'the Preparatory Schools are sending us in the main inferior material'. Of course they were. They knew the College took everyone's rejects. The Headmaster began to take steps. Belcher healed the ulcerated relationship with Brighton College Preparatory School. He began visiting others and inviting their headmasters to the College. Scott made a tour of the East Coast prep schools in 1937. He talked the governors into reinstating Council Scholarships and topping up the badly depleted endowed trust funds, pushing the value of entrance awards from £148 in 1933-34 to £900 in 1935-36. The national economic situation also worked in the school's favour. Parents paying fees began to put a hitherto unknown pressure on their sons to work harder and so justify the considerable cash outlay. School Certificate was coming to be seen as a basic requirement for any good job, while unemployment levels, which in 1933 stood at 19.8 per cent and which never dropped below one million (14 per cent), supplied an additional incentive to obtain qualifications. Belcher joined the College to the newly-formed Careers Advisory Bureau and appointed the College's first careers master.

Taken together, these developments wrought some improvement:

	pupils qualifying for		
	Higher Certificate	School Certificate	total pupils in the College
1932	6	80	402
1934	7	89	315
1936	6	68	264
1938	10	58	263
1939	20	34	254

Averages can conceal, but progress from the 1920s to the 1930s, especially in the new VIth Form, cannot be mistaken:

	Higher Certificates per year (average)	School Certificates per year (average)
1922-29	2.7	52.3
1932-39	9.4	64.4

especially when the size of the school is remembered.

Belcher's verdict on the financial situation he inherited was that 'we cannot entirely exonerate the great days of prosperity from the charge of making the difficult days that were to follow more difficult than they need have been'. Belcher and his two successors had to cope with the consequences of 15 years without strategic planning. The College's poverty of the 1930s was made worse by the debt burden inherited from the profligate 1920s. No boom can last for ever. No school knew that more painfully than Brighton College. But rarely are the lessons of history marked and learned. Planning and management were the greatest legacies of these years, virtually all of it the work of Wilfred Aldrich. This is what Burstow had in mind when he talked of 'efficient administration'. First to be purged was Dawson's extraordinary practice of negotiating fee levels with each parent. In September 1932, full fees were paid for only 42 per cent of pupils, which meant a revenue loss of almost £5,000 on a fee income that year of £16,590. Next to be transformed was the business side of the boarding houses, hitherto the private responsibility of individual housemasters. At Aldrich's suggestion, the financial conduct of each House was centralised in 1933 under the control of the Bursar.

Four years later came 'centralised feeding', which meant that every House was supplied with provisions bought by the College, and thus every House was eating the same menu. Since the Bursar had previously reported catering costs per head as varying from 11¼d. per month in School House to 1s. 2d. in Chichester and 1s. 3d. in Bristol, did a reduction in food quality accompany the efficiency of bulk buying? Finally, the College bought Durnford House in 1939, thereby acquiring the sole remaining privately owned House. Housemasters were now fully salaried employees. No longer was the running of a House a private business, from which a sharp-eyed man could earn an income substantially greater than his teaching salary. Given the economic climate, it is not difficult to imagine that the Housemasters were only too glad to be relieved of acute financial worries.

Centralised financing proved very cost effective, making a profit of £2,089 in 1934-35. Few public schools had taken the step before Brighton. Twenty-five years later, the practice was universal. There were other centrifugal reforms. Belcher had the Council sweep away the hotch-potch of private negotiations which formed the basis of staff pay to create a defined salary scale. His successor gingered up financial management by having detailed annual budgets drawn up for each House and Department, and by suggesting to the Council a permanent Finance Sub-Committee (which met for the first time in May 1937).

Between them, Aldrich, Belcher and Scott dismantled the College's Victorian financial systems and in their place put the basic structures we know today. Not that they always saw eye to eye. Belcher

The Museum in the Upper Corridor, c.1935

wanted fees cut to give the College a competitive edge. Regularly across the decade, Headmasters raised the subject, but the Council would not budge. At least Belcher managed to prevent fees being raised in 1934, but the longed-for cut came only in mid-1939 when boarding fees were reduced by ten guineas, to £139 10s. 0d. per annum. Since day place demand was resilient, day fees were simultaneously increased by two guineas to £64 10s. 0d. It was too late. Any advantage which might have been gained was more than lost by parents refusing to send their sons to the most likely site of German invasion.

Substantial capital projects were always out of the question. The tuck and uniform shop (1936) was paid for by a loan from the College outfitters, Frederick Gorringe Ltd. The squash courts (1937) were also funded by loan, from a governor (George Buxton 1936-63) and an old boy (Arthur Wilson 1906-11). Even more than usual, the College felt the want of the wealthy benefactors some schools have so prospered by. During the 1930s, the College received £2,475 in legacies and gifts. In itself a not inconsiderable sum (twice the Headmaster's salary in 1937), it pales before the £48,000 given to their school by Old Malvernians during the same period.

Aged 57, Belcher had been appointed for three years, and he stayed an additional two terms only to facilitate the transfer to his successor. He knew the College needed a younger man at the helm. Yet he never really retired. After a trip to India, he was a most active governor and President of the O.B.A. until his death in 1947. HB's headmastership was intended as a stop-gap and has always been seen as an interlude. That is a travesty. A lifetime associated with one school had not blinkered him to the need in any and every institution for change. This man whom Burstow suggests had 'the best claim of all to be thought of as the College incarnate' turned out to be most significant among its renewers.

The Tuck Shop, *c.*1930

The post was never advertised. Instead, at Belcher's own suggestion, the Council had been taking private soundings since December 1934. Eight names were put before the governors in May 1936. The only one identified, however, is the only one they decided to interview, Christopher Fairfax Scott, an old boy of Lancing aged 42, who for the past eight years had been Headmaster of Monmouth School. His subject was English and he had an impressive breadth of teaching experience, gathered from the Japanese Naval College, Radley, Kelvinside Academy and Cheltenham. He was also a layman, the requirement for a clerical Headmaster having been removed in 1909. Scott got the job, to commence in January 1937 at a salary of £1,200 per annum. Thus began the shortest and stormiest headmastership in College history. Burstow tells us that 'in his first term, Scott had not seen eye to eye with the Council on certain matters of financial control, particularly in regard to the Houses'. From the Council minutes, it is clear that those difficulties became so great so quickly that Scott asked (19 March 1937) to be released from his appointment at the end of the coming Summer Term. We know little of what was going on, and the mystery is compounded by the Council on 2 April agreeing apparently to all of Scott's requirements. Thereupon he withdrew his letter of resignation, declaring 'he would be happy to co-operate in every way possible'.

Menu cover from the dinner given to mark
'HB's retirement

Christopher Fairfax Scott

Scott's demands for greater financial planning have already been noted. The issues he raised, which Burstow says were unacceptable to the Council, were in fact admitted straight away. Burstow is right that there was trouble, but he missed its cause. Scott had requested 'a clear definition of the powers possessed by the Headmaster to authorise or veto expenditure'. Of his seven proposals, that was the only one not approved. Scott was trying to become his own Bursar and, as Dr. Bigg had discovered 60 years before, that shift in the balance of power the Council would not sanction. It is tempting to see the specific issues of a policy debate being transcended by a contest of wills between Scott and Aldrich.

The affair of memorandum and resignation must have raised among Council members disturbing thoughts about the wisdom of their choice of Headmaster. While again our lack of background makes it impossible to follow the nuances, the general drift is clear. Scott took up the reins in January 1937. Within a month he had developed proposals for financial reform which he put to his first Council and which the governors agreed to explore. Within another month, the Headmaster had drawn up further initiatives 'most of which' he put to a Council sub-committee on 15 March. There they were 'informally discussed' with Aldrich and the Bursar. Four days later, Scott sent to the full Council not only his proposals but also his resignation.

The Headmaster and his prefects, 1938

The critical information we lack in judging this affair is knowledge of how Aldrich reacted at that sub-committee. From Scott's behaviour, the obvious inference is that the Chairman slapped him down. Yet Aldrich stated at the next full Council (2 April) that 'as far as he was aware, there would be no opposition by the Council to the various points now submitted by the Headmaster'. While it is possible that Aldrich changed his tune upon receipt of the Headmaster's resignation, that seems the less likely explanation. On the motion of the Vicar of Brighton, the Council proposed that the Headmaster's letter should be withdrawn because it had been 'written under a misapprehension' that they would veto his suggestions. Further, the Vicar's reasoning rested on the premise that, when Scott put pen to paper, he 'was suffering from considerable stress and anxiety'.

Burstow locates the burden carried by Scott in the fact that 'the clouds of war were already gathering'. As we shall see, Scott's mind would indeed be tormented by the prospect of war. Were that true of the spring of 1937, however, he would have to have been even more of a hawk than Winston Churchill. No, the source of the strains on the Headmaster lay elsewhere and are now unknowable. Did he really want to go? His instant withdrawal of his letter suggests not. Was this brinkmanship? He did secure his objective and back down. Whatever afflicted him, his setting of the stakes so high so quickly in his very first disagreement with the Council shows, at the very least, a lack of prudence as well as of tactical skills. Was he not capable of negotiating? More to the point, could he not see that he was tilting against windmills? Alf Lester tells us that Headmaster and Chairman 'came out of this daggers drawn and, actually, had never got on from the day Scott found Aldrich inspecting the Houses unannounced, three weeks into Scott's first term'.

For almost a year that feud was contained. Then, from March 1938, Scott and Aldrich fell into a running battle, this time about the threat of war and the need to make contingency plans to evacuate the College. The Headmaster was one of the few not taken in by Chamberlain's guarantee of 'peace in our time'. Once Scott had seen newsreel of the destruction of Guernica by German bombers during the Spanish Civil War, he became convinced of the enormous threat posed by air power to civilian populations. As a preliminary precaution at the time of the Sudeten Crisis, Scott had slit trenches dug along the eastern side of the Home Ground and made exploratory contacts in the West Country to move the College; Westminster actually evacuated to Lancing. Presumably he kept Aldrich informed, but the signing of the Munich Agreement (29 September 1938) which lifted the prospect of imminent European war plunged Headmaster and Chairman into direct conflict. Aldrich declared his absolute opposition to the school leaving Brighton and ordered Scott to cancel his evacuation link. Indeed, when appointing Scott's successor, Aldrich extracted from Hett the guarantee that he would never seek to remove the College. In his *History*, Belcher toed the line and wrote in defence of Aldrich's stance. Burstow disagreed, describing Scott as 'a courageous realist'. Burstow is right. Aldrich's refusal to acknowledge the leaden gloom would bring Brighton College to its knees and endanger its very life. To argue that the Council's policy was correct because the school survived in Brighton is to ignore the enormous and wholly unnecessary risk Aldrich took. Both Belcher and Burstow explained Scott's departure by reference to the official statement. 'He had worked without sparing himself to cope with problems which seemed to have no solution' was how Belcher portrayed the collapse in Scott's health. Certainly he became seriously ill in December 1938. The College doctor ordered him away to convalesce and, just before the start of the Lent Term, Scott sent in his resignation. Belcher later told Vaughan Harries that 'when Scott threatened to resign, the Council was relieved to accept his resignation'. So it looks as if Scott was trying to repeat his tactics of 22 months earlier, only this time they called his bluff.

Tall and imposing, with a splendid speaking voice, Scott was a fine teacher with strong interests in medieval romances and Arthurian legend; at Cheltenham his firing of the young T.H. White proved the origin for his novel, *The Once and Future King*. But at Brighton he had little time to teach. Leslie Grose (Head of School 1937-38) states that:

the Juniors were overawed if not actually frightened, such was the overpowering presence of the H.M. As a senior I found it, at first, difficult to converse and confide in Scott, but when I had overcome this by standing up to him, I found I got on exceedingly well. He was a very strong character with fixed ideas which he would not change in any form. He was a handsome, well built man who was always well turned out, very articulate and with a direct method of expression.

We also know from 'Teddy' Lester that 'the older staff disliked him. He bossed them about far too much and they felt he allowed them no initiative'. In other words, Scott was a vigorous new broom. Bill Davidson (Head of Hampden 1938-39) describes him as 'a breath of fresh air ... His was a 'new look' Headmastership'. Obviously the staff found that as difficult to cope with as the Council. Scott's health recovered, but his career did not. First he went to Taunton School as Deputy Headmaster. Then in April 1940 he moved to Hereford Cathedral School as an ordinary master, becoming Headmaster that September. In 1945, however, he left and took an assistant master's post at Truro Grammar School. He died in January 1958 aged only sixty-three.

*   *   *

Throughout this period the OTC continued second only to games in significance. So highly regarded was the College contingent that an officer and four cadets were invited to parade with the Territorial Forces outside Buckingham Palace for the Coronation of George VI. War Office regulation in 1931 raised the minimum age for cadets to fifteen. At first, these were occupied with P.T., but Alf Lester felt that was 'a soul-destroying time-filler' and in 1932 started a scout troop, assisted by senior boys released from the OTC on passing 'Cert A'. Reminiscences speak unanimously of 'the fun' of College scouting, especially the annual camp.

Shooting maintained its triumphant run and, on top of competition successes every year, the VIII of 1936 won four trophies at Bisley, the Ashburton included. Cricket fared reasonably well, the College becoming known for the high quality of its fielding. Perhaps the XI of 1937 was the best, losing only one game. A number of individuals stand out: R.F.T. Paterson (1931-34) who later played for Essex and the MCC, A.K. Sharp (1933-37) who began playing for Sussex while still at school, W.W. Davidson (1934-39) who later played for Sussex and is (to date) the College's last Oxford cricket blue, and S.I. Phillips (1934-39) who scored five centuries for the XI and was recruited by Northamptonshire.

Rugby did less well. In Belcher's words, the XV were 'of average strength and capability'. Christ's Hospital and Dulwich were each beaten only three times:

	played	won	lost	drawn
1933-39	88	34	51	3
(1923-29	98	57	35	6)

But there were two blues (one more than cricket): R. Cooper (Oxford 1937) and L.E. Grose (Cambridge 1939). The opinion of the latter today confirms that of Belcher at the time. 'The standard of College sporting activities was reasonably high without being exceptional.' Can the difficulties of cricket and rugby be linked, as has often been tried, to the reduced average age of the school? Many pupils left earlier than they had done in the 1920s, in order to go out to work. Significantly fewer remained beyond 17, which meant that the XI and the XV were younger and less experienced. Surely all public schools were in the same position?

Fives was near to moribund among the boys (*not* the masters) and in 1937 the three courts abutting the dining hall were demolished. In their place came two courts for a game still new to public schools: squash. Malvern built its first squash courts in 1933, Lancing in 1929. With an Olympic fencer on the staff (Kenneth Campbell, 1937-51), that game took on a new dynamic; J.M. Bilimoria (1933-37) became the second College fencing half blue. Hockey proved a great success when introduced on an experimental basis in 1936 to take the place of cross-country running, which had been banned again in 1934 by the school doctor. Tennis finally took off when hard courts were laid out at the New Ground in 1934 and Ernest Hammett took on the coaching (as well as being an England rugby international, he played tennis for Wales). But Leslie Grose says tennis was 'the only sport not pushed'. Finally, there is record of a series of staff-pupil golf tournaments, and lessons were rearranged in 1937 so that the school could listen to the broadcast of the boat race.

P.T. in the Front Quad, 1933

BRIGHTON COLLEGE O.T.C. INSPECTION

GUN DRILL was included for the first time in the annual O.T.C. inspection at Brighton College, which was carried out in the College grounds yesterday by Lieut.-Colonel Villiers Smyth, D.S.O.

The College Scout troop, 1933 and 1936

As already noted, societies came out of the doldrums in the mid-1930s. New ventures were the Shakespeare Society, the Play Reading Society, the Geographical Society, the Film Society, the Music Society, the Gramophone Circle (joined later by the Photographic Society and the Model Aeronautical Club). When added to the surviving rump of Debating, Classical and Scientific Societies, the transformation in

Athletic Sports, *c.*1934

cultural and recreational life becomes immediately apparent. Such developments did not always wait on the masters. The reappearance of poetry in the magazine from 1929 was the consequence of a boy with literary ambition, Christopher Hassall (1926-30). Others similarly found the muse, including the future novelist Ian Serraillier (1926-30) who also also produced lino cuts to enliven the pages.

The Council and Headmaster of Brighton College

request the pleasure of your company

on

Monday, July 31st, 1939.

2.30 p.m. Distribution of Prizes by the Most Hon. the Marquis of
                Willingdon, P.C., G.C.S.I., G.C.M.G., G.C.I.E., G.B.E.

3.45 p.m. Tea and Physical Training Display.

4.30–5.15 p.m. Aeschylus–Agamemnon.

The Art Room and Model Aeroplanes will be on view during the afternoon.

It is regretted that owing to the limited accommodation in the Hall, this invitation can be for
two guests only.

                                                                              R.S.V.P.

Literary purchases by the Library reveal unimaginative and backward-looking tastes. Nearly all the new novels bought were the last efforts of old men whose best work was behind them—Arnold Bennett, E.F. Benson, Conan Doyle, Kipling, Galsworthy, H.G. Wells. Two items alone stand out, both plays. One is Strindberg's *The Father*, purchased in 1935, whose modernity (for all that it was written in 1887) and pessimism made it a rarity on the shelves. The other is *The Importance of Being Earnest* (1893), bought in 1937 to accompany the donation of *An Ideal Husband* (1895). This could have caused a rumpus for, 42 years after his trial, Oscar Wilde was a name still considered barely safe to mention.

As for contemporary poetry, the Library's stock offered nothing beyond de la Mare, Masefield and Alfred Noyes—hardly the names we would think of as the poets of the '30s. Contemporary novels and drama fared little better. The year 1930 saw the first purchases of J.B. Priestley, and Coward's new play *Private Lives*. Similarly rapid acquisitions were Sassoon's *Sherston's Progress*, Graves' *I Claudius* and Richard Llewellyn's *How Green Was My Valley*. But as one looks in vain for Auden, Eliot and MacNeice so there is no trace of Graham Greene, Hemingway, Orwell, Steinbeck or Evelyn Waugh. Did they even buy Agatha Christie, Leslie Charteris or Dorothy L. Sayers for boarding house libraries?

College music of the inter-war period always conjures up visions of the Gilbert and Sullivan productions staged from 1922 until discontinued as too expensive in 1939. But Charles Allen (Director of Music 1921-46) was much more versatile and ambitious than this annual jolly would suggest. He developed a series of choral groups: male voice quartets, the College Glee Singers and, in a brief throwback to concert parties on the prom around 1912, 'The Brighton College Nigger Minstrel Troupe'. He saw to it that a series of music practice rooms was created in 1930. From 1934, he pushed for music scholarships; by 1938 there were two, each worth £30 per annum plus free musical tuition. Outings to concerts at the Dome and visits by outside performers were begun. The Russian Choir which came in October 1938 must have made an intriguing contrast to the Barclays Bank Choir the following May.

Not least, Charles Allen used the orchestra to play a far broader repertoire than of old. He brought to College concerts a Baroque and Classical element rarely heard before 1914. That meant a little Mozart, Bach and Boccherini in the 1920s, some Handel and Haydn in the 1930s. He made standard much 19th-century Romantic music: primarily Wagner, Schubert, Beethoven, Brahms, Tchaikovsky and Grieg (in that order). Twice he played Sibelius, in 1922 and 1937. The backbone of his orchestral repertoire was, however, the music of English composers born between the 1850s and

'The Pirates of Penzance', 1936 (who would guess that the Major-General's beautiful daughters are all College boys?)

1870s. Elgar provided the core, around which he featured prominently Edward German and Percy Grainger, and gave occasional tasters of Walford Davies, Roger Quilter, Frank Bridge and John Ireland. For an English school of the 1930s, that was a very passable selection. Finally, we should not overlook less official music making. There is record of 'The Syncopated Trio' playing dance music at the Entertainment in July 1925. And Leslie Grose tells us in the later 1930s of 'numerous individually owned gramophones belting out the latest 78s of the day: Cab Calloway, Louis Armstrong and Harry Roy were the rage'. So the sound of jazz, so essential to the character of the inter-war world, was not absent either.

In a number of schools, drama took a new turn after languishing in the '20s. Beyond Gilbert and Sullivan, theatricals in the 1920s had been limited to the performance of a scene or two of a play within the concert each Commemoration Day. Full-blown theatre had, it seems, been stifled once again. From 1933, however, Walter Hett began to stage each Speech Day a complete Greek play in translation. Burstow describes 'their high seriousness, wit and poetry' as 'an essential complement to the light-hearted abandon of the G & S'. Certainly a greater contrast would not have been possible, right down to the home-made sets and costumes, and entirely pupil casts which made Hett's work true school theatre. For a school whose Group I

The Birds, 1935

was an endangered species, Athenian plays were a defiant swan song. Is it fanciful, however, to see the College stage being used to comment on contemporary politics? The play of July 1936 was an exception to Hett's usual series because it was the work of a living playwright, in itself very daring by College standards. To quote the magazine's review, John Drinkwater's *X=0; A Night of the Trojan War* 'is a poignant, unanswerable illustration of the futility of war and the senseless repetition of killing long after the cause that sounded the first call to arms has been forgotten'. Hitler had just marched into the Rhineland. Mussolini's forces had just completed their conquest of Abyssinia.

Some aver that politics was never discussed but, like so many things, enthusiasm was confined to a certain circle. The Debating Society organised mock general elections to coincide with the real things in 1931 and 1935, and a third in March 1939 which anticipated the contest due within a year:

College elections

1931	*1935*	*1939*	
Conservative won by 102	Conservative 82	National Government	109
Labour ⎫ no	Fascist 42	Fascist	37
Communist ⎭ details	Communist 26	Communist	27

Debates turned regularly to foreign affairs:

date	*subject*	*result*
March 1932	The powers should stop Japan landing troops in China	'lost by a large majority'
March 1933	'This house would in no circumstances fight for King and Country'	lost 40-6
November 1933	'This house deplores the policy of the German Government'	lost 14-20
March 1936	'This house admires the sporting spirit in which Italy is conducting her present campaign in Abyssinia'	lost 15-59
February 1938	'Ultimate victory for Franco would be disastrous for civilisation'	'carried by a considerable majority'

We do well to remember that the politics of the '30s had several faces. Some looked at the dictators and argued that Britain should watch from the touchline as they destroyed each other. Some judged Germany and Russia equally detestable. Others felt the need to choose. Speakers in these debates, like the candidates of the mock elections, reflected something of those various viewpoints. Nonetheless, the mock elections seem to conceal a subtle change in viewpoint. The 1938 debate turned into a consideration of the threats posed by fascism and communism, and victory went to 'the pinkoes'. Brighton was not unique; only by the narrowest of margins did Rossall vote to retain the British Empire. The 1936 College motion was framed to mock Mussolini. The 1933 debate on Nazi Germany was unusually close and speakers referred to Germany's legitimate grievances, a stance supported only by the Liberals and Labour. No OBs are known to have fought with the International Brigade in the Spanish Civil War, but it would seem that a soft left undertow developed within the school. As Auden wrote in 1937, 'now we are compelled to take sides'.

The King and Country debate stands by itself. It was held in response to the now legendary Oxford Union debate the previous month, about which the OB section of the magazine records C.F. Dimont, A.R. Serraillier and W.P. Wand as supporting 'the notorious pacifist motion', as did one of the new young masters (Vaughan Harries). To this day, this episode in misunderstood. It was not a rejection of patriotism and it was not an argument for pacifism. It was an attack on the evils of nationalism. It was a vote for collective security and for the League of Nations. But at the College, as across the country, supporters of the motion were branded cowards and traitors.

Can we view all of this as the frivolous antics of ignorant school boys? To some, the elections and the debates were no more than a bit of fun. That is not true of all.

THE COLLEGE, BRIGHTON.

DRESS REGULATIONS FOR BOYS ATTENDING BRIGHTON COLLEGE.

Each Boy must have :—
(a) One complete suit of dark grey tweed (coat, waistcoat and trousers) for Sundays.
(b) Two coats and waistcoats as above.   } for week
(c) At least two pairs of grey flannel trousers. } days.

There is only one pattern of cloth permitted, and only one pattern of grey flannel.

Samples of these can be obtained from the following firms :——

Messrs. Horton-Stephens, Ltd., 42 Western Road, Brighton.

Messrs. Jas. Shoolbred & Co., Ltd., Tottenham Court Road, London.

Messrs. Gieves, Ltd., Old Bond Street, London, and at Liverpool and Portsmouth, etc.

Messrs. Harrods, Ltd., Brompton Road, London.

Socks must be Dark Blue, Dark Grey, or Black.
Soft Collars may be worn on Week-days.
Stiff Collars must be worn on Sundays.

School Cap ...   .
Straw Hat with College Band | These are all obtainable at
Black or College Tie | the College Shop.
School Blazer   ...
Football Jerseys and Shorts

Parents are particularly requested to see that all clothes are clearly marked with the owner's name.

N.B.—All Trousers Pockets must be sewn up.

The Tory vote of 54.7 per cent in 1935 mirrored their real result (55.2 per cent). A Communist M.P. was returned at that same election, while one-eighth of Cambridge undergraduates in 1938 belonged to the Communist Party. For all the frivolity, no other period in College history displays such pupil interest in and awareness of outside realities, not even 1968-72.

Headmaster and Council found themselves in the middle of a fury in the summer of 1938 when they abolished the speckled boater (and the school prefects' bowler hat), and replaced it with a trilby. The wearing of boaters had ceased to be compulsory in 1937, but they still had to be carried. Nobody seemed to mind that pettifogging regulation or the introduction of a suit which Scott called 'more blithe and thrilling in pattern'. But the school did not want to look like Humphrey Bogart and erupted against 'that shapeless grey atrocity', as Burstow called it. Somehow, the affair became 'a story' and appeared in newspapers from California to Natal. On appointment, Hett exempted the prefects from having to wear it, and at the same time replaced the old plain black tie with the crimson and royal blue striped tie still worn today. The Headmaster of Malvern had almost as much trouble with the corduroy shorts he tried to introduce in 1941. Why should uniform changes so inflame pupils and old boys?

The crowd is fickle. These same boys rejoiced at the additional half holidays Scott introduced to celebrate OBs winning firsts and blues. Unlike the usual 'free half' which involved compulsory games or compulsory watching of the XV or XI, these offered genuinely free time to rest and relax. In all, his brief tenure saw six, the last of which appears decidedly odd. Quoting Shakespeare to the school, a free half was granted that 'Crispin Crispian shall ne'er go by, from this day to the ending of time, but we in it shall be remembered'. Given Scott's view of the European situation, his remembrance of the anniversary of Agincourt in the month after the Munich Agreement was unlikely to have been mere whimsy.

*   *   *

Judged in terms of pupils on the roll, the College had fallen back twenty years. Nobody thought that a bad thing. Judged by the range and quality of the education

The trophy guns went for scrap in 1940

offered, the College had made enormous strides forward. Had the 1920s been managed better, the 1930s give a good idea of what could have been. Had the '30s been even better managed ...

For all the retrenchment, the College continued to live beyond its means. Net fee income fell 18 per cent between 1934 and 1937 yet real costs were not reduced. The cost of salaries per pupil had risen 15 per cent. The cost of 'provisions and household expenses per pupil' went up 23 per cent. The bank overdraft which had stood at £10,000 in 1933 had risen to £17,430 in 1937 and £26,674 by 1939. When it is realised that those sums represented (respectively) two terms and then an entire year's fee income, the precariousness of the situation becomes apparent.

At the insistence of the bank, a report was commissioned from Price Waterhouse in October 1937. They could not but conclude that 'the present financial position threatens the existence of the College' and that substantial further credit was most unlikely. They therefore outlined five alternatives: (a) wait for more boarders; (b) exploit the area and increase day places 'so that the school should be considered mainly a school for day boys'; (c) sell the school and move to a suitable country house; (d) sell up and amalgamate with another school; (e) close the College.

Inevitably, the Council Minutes record no substance from what must have been a fascinating and historic meeting on 18 February 1938. All we are told is 'the general opinion being that suggestions (c), (d) and (e) could not be seriously entertained' whereas (a) and (b) 'dealing with the gradual growth in numbers ... were in accordance with the settled policy of the Council [and thus] provided the only possible method of improving the financial position'. Neither would be simple. The report argued that a boarding school with fees of £50 per term could not be run on less than

E & M Rayner

has leave to be absent from College

on *5 June 1938*

from *12* to *6.15*

to Brighton

will be grateful if

Mr & M Rayner

will fill in the following spaces :—

Time of arrival *12.*

Time of departure *6.10*

Signature *A. M. Rayner*

350 pupils. As for a day school, numbers would have to rise to around 300 to cover costs, which in turn would require capital expenditure of £3-5,000 for additional accommodation (which no institution would lend the College). Scott tried to prop up boarding numbers with Dawson Memorial Exhibitions and, as we have seen, the Council cut boarding fees in 1939. But option (a) was unattainable. Even after the war there were never more than 214 boarders (1960).

Given the stability in demand for day places, a reflection of the growth of Brighton and Hove's middle-class suburbs from 1920 (boosted by the electrification of the railway to London in 1932-33), option (b) looked far more feasible. The Council may have thought so too, for in December 1937 it made plans to double day places by building a block to hold 200 dayboys. The true level of local demand cannot be known because, from the 1920s to the 1960s, the College deliberately restricted day places. We cannot presume that the rise to 200 (1973), 300 (1984) and beyond was attainable in the 1940s.

If the Council was starting to think along these lines, their inability to raise the necessary capital impeded action. Indeed, the unpleasant reality was that Barclays refused any further credit, whereupon the minutes record 'it was very strongly urged by certain members that the future of the College could best be assured by removing the school to a site in a country district'. This was Price Waterhouse's option (c) and suggests that the Council had never turned fully to (b). When the bank softened its position, however, talk of removal evaporated and the scheme becomes no more than a tantalising might-have-been.

This saga of abortive strategic planning is instructive, for within lies the dilemma which Brighton College has faced since 1930. The Price Waterhouse Report should have provoked a defining moment in College history. The Council was told that it should stop muddling along and choose. Neither option guaranteed calm waters. Whatever they decided would determine the very nature of the school, but choose they should. Instead, they saw no vision, wobbled at the first obstacle and ended up doing nothing. Their post-war successors have done no better.

*   *   *

In 1939 as in 1933 and 1950, Aldrich arranged the replacement of the Headmaster by an internal candidate. Walter Hett had followed Dawson from Grantham in 1907. Since 1909 he had been Housemaster of Durnford. Belcher made him his Deputy. Known always as 'the Duke', Hett was a gentle, scholarly man, author of a biography of Alexander the Great and editor of several volumes of Aristotle in the Loeb series. In 1939 he was aged fifty-seven. L.A.G. Strong describes him as possessing a manner unfailingly suave and courteous. He had a real wit, which only turned sharp with the very idle or the very stupid ... I do not think that anyone on the staff had such natural charm, or treated boys with such courtesy.

Strong goes on to note that 'life for him was a code of rigid rules, and to those who kept them he was genial and delightful'. Hett was always immaculately dressed, a fact as much remembered as his gold pince-nez. He could come across as cold and stiff, to younger pupils (and masters) as remote, even terrifying. Of his talents as a housemaster, few would disagree with Lester's assessment that 'he was one of the very best ever'. And in Group I 'he was in his element, guiding, prompting, encouraging' (Edward Batt, Head of Hampden 1943-44). Both William Stewart and 'Teddy' Lester say that he did not want to be Headmaster and never enjoyed the post, taking it only out of duty.

War clouds gathered quickly. Parents were instructed to send their sons with their gas masks in April 1939. The following month the Chief Constable requested 'a list of aliens with their ages'. In September 1939, a (now unknown) College boy was interned in the camp on the racecourse. The immediate threat was that numbers would drop further, pushing the College into bankruptcy, so Hett

Walter Hett

worked harder than ever to maintain close associations with prep schools. The lease on part of Brighton College Prep School would expire in July 1940 and Hett managed to buy it back. Two-thirds of the boys went off with the old Headmaster to Berkhamsted School, but from August 1940 Brighton College again owned its own Junior School:

Numbers in College

	College dayboys	College boarders	Juniors	Total
Sept 1938	107	148	-	255
Sept 1939	108	141	-	249
Sept 1940	61	62	39	162
Sept 1941	69	69	51	189
Sept 1942	70	62	52	184
Sept 1943	64	58	72	194

Felling the diseased elms in the Front Quad, 1939

The contrast between 1914 and 1939 could not be greater. The College entered World War II in a parlous condition. Numbers held until the summer of 1940, buoyed up perhaps by the mini boom which accompanied rearmament. Even with the addition of the Juniors, the roll then dropped 29 per cent between July and September.

There was a bonus in all this, as Edward Batt recalls:

> One advantage of the small number was that you knew, and were known by, everyone. Another was that, if you were just moderately active, you could represent the College in several games! And, of course, the small size of classes meant you often received individual tuition.

But that was small comfort to Headmaster and Council as they saw the College slide towards insolvency. The problem was the school's location. As Belcher wrote in his *History*, 'few wise parents would send their sons to be educated on the South Coast'. Brighton's beaches had been closed on 2 July. Newspapers and the radio spoke repeatedly of the likelihood that the coast between Brighton and Worthing would be the centre of German landings. That August, the Home Office ordered the removal of all evacuees brought previously from London. The following March, Brighton was declared a 'Defence Zone', which meant that residents only were allowed in and the entire town was surrounded with barbed wire. Yet Brighton College was the only south-east coast public school not to evacuate or be requisitioned.

So bizarre was this that the school had to advertise in the national press from 1941 to 1943 to counter widespread assumption that it had moved away, or closed down. Between 1940 and 1943, Malvern suffered requisitioning twice and saw its numbers fall 19 per cent. Lancing evacuated and suffered a 24 per cent loss. Brighton stood fast and its roll plummeted 47 per cent (16 per cent if the Juniors are included). Hett refused to watch while what he termed 'the flight from the coast' drove the College under. Ignoring his condition of appointment, he took it upon himself to explore both evacuation and amalgamation, 'either temporarily or permanently'. Hurstpierpoint was approached, but they wanted to charge a rent the College could not afford. He tried again the following summer with Imperial Service College, Windsor (which in 1942 merged with Haileybury), but Aldrich was always there to stifle each initiative. Perversely, the College nearly became the host for another school. Terms were agreed with Malvern College in April 1942 to provide accommodation for one of their boarding houses when that school was requisitioned. At the last moment, however, Harrow undertook to house the whole of Malvern, so dismemberment was unnecessary.

As in 1914, a few Continental refugees were taken in. Five Norwegians are recorded in 1940; there were also some Belgians. But neither a handful of exiles nor the new Junior School could make up the shortfall, in income as well as in numbers. Neither for long could the personal guarantees for parts of the College overdraft most generously undertaken by several parents and friends:

	revenue account deficit	bank overdraft	mortgage indebtedness
July 1939	£2,795	£26,674	£31,754
July 1940	£5,043	£32,631	£37,853
July 1941	£8,008	£35,303	£41,579

Aware that a survey in 1938 had valued the College at only £61,740, the bank's growing unease was inevitable. The axe fell in December 1941 when Barclays told the Council they would close the account at Easter. At the same time, Hett's term of office was about to expire and he handed in his resignation to take effect at the end of March. Now was the College made to face the consequences of Aldrich's intransigence. His line was always that the College could not afford to evacuate. Rather, the reverse was true, and it may not be irrelevant that Aldrich was one of the Emergency Commissioners for Brighton, and Chairman of its Economic Committee. For Brighton College, of which he was Chairman of the Governors, to have pulled out of the town would have been very embarrassing for him. Whatever his reasons, they flew in the face of demand as well as the balance sheet. The bank was pulling out. No insurance company would give them further loans. Brighton College was bankrupt, and the staff were given notice that the school would close at the end of term.

William Aldrich

Salvation came from a parent, Mr. G. Rushton, who ran his own engineering works and (crucially) was a wartime government contractor. He was prepared to give high quality lathes and to place contracts for die cast and machine tooled components if the College would convert its workshops into a munitions factory. Thus was born 'the Engineering Scheme'. Rushton's machines were ready by March and work began that Easter holidays with 33 volunteer dayboys. To begin with, inevitable lack of skills led to reject rates of up to 90 per cent on orders.

At that point a Junior School parent, Mr. H. Upward of the local Reliance Motor Works, stepped in. He offered supervision, training and better quality tools. That did the trick. Machining to an accuracy of 2.5 thousandths of an inch in aluminium, brass and steel, reject rates thereafter were never greater than 3 per cent, even when the factory was turning out 25,000 items per month. Much was also due to 'Teddy' Lester, whom Hett seconded to run the factory. Throughout, munitions work remained voluntary, but Headmaster, staff, pupils and parents all joined in to take their turn on the rota of two-hour shifts. The timetable was reorganised in 1942-43 to allow a 12-hour day, six-day week to be worked in term time and holidays.

More than altruism was involved, as Thomas Churcher (1943-48) remembers: 'Many a double French for which one was ill-prepared was dodged by way of engineering!' Supervised, maintained and encouraged by Lester, that first year earned the school £2,109 16s. 3d. Only that saved the College from closing its doors leaving debts which guaranteed it could never have opened them again; Brighton College was on the Board of Education's list of public schools which would not survive the war. There is another fact to be understood. Regardless of the cash earned, the very presence of the factory determined the school's continuation. While output remained reasonable, a registered munitions factory could not be closed down.

THE OLD ENGINEERING WORKSHOPS, WHICH BECAME THE COLLEGE MUNITIONS FACTORY IN 1942

Staff losses to military service were heavy: one in 1939, six in 1940, three in 1941. Scientists proved especially difficult to replace and, in consequence, the College employed its first full-time female member of staff, Miss Aileen Browne (1940-41), a Biology graduate who had taught at St Mary's Hall. Ernest French (1939-44) also remembers 'an attractive American woman who taught Physics'. That could be either Dr. Semmens (Christmas Term 1942) or Miss Steck (Lent Term 1943). When the Junior School Science master was called up, Hett employed a school prefect (R.H. McMinn, 1937-41), who had already passed his first MB exam, to cover for the remainder of the term. The College was especially unlucky in having two bursars in succession recalled to active duty during 1939. At least the Headmaster could not be lost, a fate suffered by Harrow and Rossall.

The burden on some shoulders was enormous. Hett freely admitted to the Council that 'senior men [called out of retirement] have neither the enthusiasm nor probably the ability to run anything outside school hours'. He went on to make sure that the governors understood what was happening, testifying that

> Mr. Farnell, Mr. Williams, Mr. Hill and Mr. Langston, as well as Mr. Hough and Mr. Lester, have all done yeoman service with a cheerful readiness to do anything at any time by day or night, without which I could not have carried on the school. I stress this point because I feel that the staff would welcome an expression from the Council that they are to some extent aware of the amount of voluntary overtime which has been so generously given.

School life continued as normally as wartime constraints permitted. The making of blackout curtains or screens for almost the entire College proved quite a headache. Lessons were set permanently on the summer timetable so that classes ended at 3.30pm, allowing dayboys to get home before dark. Lessons also had to begin and end by each teacher's watch for only church bells could be rung, and then only as a danger signal. Air raids caused enormous disruption during Christmas Term 1940 but, thereafter, interruptions were never regarded as too serious. But Brighton continued to be bombed until March 1944 and air raid drills were rehearsed just as today we practise fire drill. For shelters, the various cellars were cleared and called into service, as was the Hall basement. Indeed, lessons were transferred there during the Battle of Britain. In addition, six Anderson shelters were dug into the bank of the Home Ground near the workshops for those on shift in the factory; each could hold around ten boys.

Most alarms proved false and by later 1942 were frequently ignored. From June

---

THE COLLEGE,
BRIGHTON 7.

Arrangements for the end of Term.

Saturday, Dec. 9th.	A musical and dramatic programme, 8 p.m.	
Thursday, Dec. 14th.	"The Crooked Billet,"	2 p.m.
Saturday, Dec. 16th.	"The Crooked Billet,"	7.45 p.m.
Sunday, Dec. 17th.	Service for last Sunday of term,	11 a.m.
	Carol Service,	6 p.m.
Monday, Dec. 18th.	Boarders return home.	

There is likely to be some difficulty about trains on this day. The Railway Company cannot guarantee taking many boys on the 8.0 a.m.

The Headmaster will be delighted to welcome parents to any of the above. No tickets will be issued, but it would be a great help if parents coming on December 9th, 14th or 16th would send a card to the Headmaster's Secretary with the number of their party.

The year was 1940

The Fordson, 1943

1944, that became official when the Headmaster ordered classes not to break unless gunfire was heard as well as the siren (of the 1,058 siren warnings in Brighton, just 56 heralded real attacks, mostly hit and run raids). One College boy, Peter Stuttaford, was among the six killed when the Odeon in St George's Road was bombed on 14 September 1940 during a matinee; he was fifteen. Beyond broken windows and lawns pitted by shrapnel and grenades, however, College premises remained undamaged throughout the war.

At the time of Dunkirk, star shells could be seen in the east and 'Ernie' Hammett, 'pausing whilst writing on the blackboard, crossed to the window saying—Hush, listen, gunfire'. But the Phoney War would seem to have lasted longer at Brighton College than elsewhere. Beyond a voluntary lecture to the boys on firefighting, a talk to the staff and prefects on first aid to bomb casualties (both June 1940) and putting some buckets in the corridors, fire-watching and fire-fighting procedures were not in place until January 1941, seven months after the bombing of Brighton began. Membership of the splendidly titled Brighton College Fire Guard, which provided night-time cover in term time and holidays, was popular with senior boys. As Tony Worth (1941-45) recalls, 'to carry a fire bucket was almost a passport to walk anywhere!' In case the College received a direct hit, a second entrance to the Front Quad was created to improve access for fire engines and ambulances. During the Easter holiday of 1941 a roadway was thus prepared across the Headmaster's garden and a gateway knocked through the front wall.

College boys did their bit for the national war effort beyond munitions making. Part of the Home Ground was dug up to grow vegetables, and at least one boy kept rabbits there. With Varndean Grammar School, pupils attended fruit-picking camps at Horsted Keynes in 1941 and 1942, and a farm camp at Mayfield in 1943. Some were drafted off school for entire days to pick sugar beet or plant potatoes at Ovingdean Farm. Digging for victory never became an official activity, however, organised alongside games as at Cheltenham and Malvern. But it did have its bonuses. Besides access to off-ration food and the chance to smoke, senior boys could join the Ministry of Agriculture scheme to train tractor drivers. The College was sent a Fordson in June 1941 and, by the end of term, 26 had passed the test and went off to help harvest in various parts of England. When Brighton held a 'War Weapons Week' in February

1942, some boys were equipped with 'stop me and buy one' ice cream tricycles to tour the town selling war savings stamps. They collected £271.

The New Ground became a major burden. There was too much space. Pitches could no longer be maintained. During Christmas Term 1940 at least, it was abandoned completely because there were no air-raid shelters. In the end, parts were sub-let to sheep pasture and some pitches were simply given up, while the few maintained were (as often as not) rented out to local service and ARP sports teams. So too sometimes was the swimming pool.

What of the OTC, renamed the Junior Training Corps in a War Office reorganisation of 1941? Call-ups left Hough and Bill Williams to run it on their own for most of 1941-43, with occasional help from a sergeant or two borrowed from regiments stationed around the town. For nearly two years, the Corps also had to operate with virtually no weapons, their armoury having been taken in 1940 for use in coastal defence. With invasion imminent, the government appealed for the formation of Local Defence Volunteers. All College boys over seventeen were organised into an LDV section, which from 1942 was officially classified as 30th Platoon, 10th Sussex Home Guard. Throughout the war, they paraded and drilled with other Brighton platoons. During the Battle of Britain, the College unit was given the job of guarding the pumping station at Balsdean Reservoir each night, against saboteurs or German paratroops. Each cadet carried 10 rounds of live ammunition. These were the days of 'we shall fight in the fields and in the streets'. If the Germans landed, Churchill told the LDV to 'take one with you'.

The ATC's Avro

With a little pressure on the Air Ministry, Hett was able to secure the College a place in 1941 among the first schools permitted an Air Training Corps. Available to boys over sixteen, this was run with enormous success (and popularity) by 'Teddy' Lester. He made a flight simulator powered by a gramophone motor and, from early 1943, they even had their own Avro bi-plane parked in the Back Quad. How did 'the Weed' (a reference to his pipe, not his physique) find the time, the stamina and the enthusiasm to teach, to run the ATC, to be part-time Bursar, to be Housemaster of Leconfield and to run the munitions factory?

Academically, the College maintained the progress made in the '30s. Given the many and constant problems which undermined work, the achievement was remarkable:

	pupils qualifying for		total pupils in the College
	Higher Certificate	*School Certificate*	
1939	20	51	254
1940	3	44	227
1941	6	29	138
1942	6	22	139
1943	9	23	122
1944	6	21	143
1945	8	17	243

The war reduced candidates for Highers because, as Ernest French explains, 'most of us were keen to get into the armed forces as soon as we could'.

With East Brighton Park largely abandoned, part of the Home Ground under cultivation and a total absence of young masters, the trials suffered by sport were every bit as difficult as those endured within class. Travel and petrol restrictions left little scope for matches with other schools. The only regular Rugby and Cricket fixtures were with Emanuel and Hurstpierpoint. Instead, contests were arranged (as in the First War) with scratch sides from military units and the police. In such circumstances, school sport turned in on itself. Swimming, boxing, cross-country running and squash were all pursued with vigour and, to provide competitive games for all, athletics standards were started. Fives and fencing, however, died out.

Proof that the corner had been turned came when the accounts for the Summer Term 1942 showed a small surplus. This was the first time any term had not shown a loss since 1933. Two years later, the deficit had been cut to under £2,500, a reserve fund of £2,608 had been accumulated and interest payments on the mortgages had been resumed. Economies were always being looked for, but the Council never dared to put up the fees, even though they discussed it at almost every meeting. Numbers were too weak to take the risk:

average numbers in College (all three terms)

1941	135
1942	136
1943	120

From January 1943 to March 1944, the roll stood between 117 and 122 boys.

In 1943, the ban on non-residents entering Brighton was lifted. The tide of war was turning. Parents again were prepared to consider Brighton as a good place to educate their sons. Confidence turned into actual registrations from March 1944 and the school began that September with 143 boys, a 20 per cent increase on the previous term. That was Hett's parting legacy. In December 1943 he had given notice that he wished to resign the following April, but would stay on 'if the Council deemed it necessary' until July. Burstow tells of his determination 'to relinquish his post in order that a new, young and permanent Headmaster might have as long as possible to prepare for the vast problems of a post-war existence'.

Hett's had been an interim appointment, initially for three years, thereafter for the duration. The explanation Burstow offers, however, mixes rationalised hindsight with gentle discretion. Thoughts were indeed turning to the challenges of the post-war world, as the 1942 Beveridge Report illustrates. In his termly letter of April 1944, Hett himself talked of his successor having the chance 'to get to know all the internal conditions before he is confronted with the many difficult problems which the post war situation must inevitably bring'. But Hett was going early, some two or three years before the war was thought likely to end. The minutes tell us that he 'indicated in some detail the reasons for his decision' and the Council 'felt in the circumstances it had no option but to endeavour to give effect to [his] wishes'. The meaning of those cryptic phrases has been explained by 'Teddy' Lester. Strictly speaking, his resignation was entirely his own act. But it followed a rising tide of criticism and dissatisfaction from within the Common Room. Lester says that his staff found him 'too imperious, too inflexible' and that 'there was lasting resentment of a 30 per cent pay cut in the summer of 1940, imposed without warning or consultation'. They too were looking to the future and it was they who asked him to resign. He was 62 and exhausted by the ceaseless burden of keeping the College open. The strain had been enormous, heightened by his own puritanical sense of duty. As the staff found him grow more difficult so to the pupils he became a remote, even terrifying figure, described by one as 'a sarcastic chain-smoker never known to smile'. Lester says he went very willingly, but Burstow relates how Judge Pugh persuaded him: 'Walter, you have given us your all. There is no need for you to play Leonidas. The worst is already past–and it is you who have borne us through. Take the chance. Go home to your Greeks. Another year here will kill you'. Hett went to Cyprus as Chief Representative of the British Council and died there four years later.

June 1934: 'three boys borrowed dresses from a sister and paraded on the main drive for
15 minutes until spotted by a master, when they fled. They were never discovered.'
(Gwyn Griffiths, 1931-34)

Part V

Headmasters

Arthur Stuart-Clark	September 1944
Roland 'Teddy' Lester	January 1950 (acting)
William Stewart	May 1950
Henry Christie	September 1963
William Blackshaw	September 1971
John Leach	September 1987

[Photo: David Hollinshead]

Eleven

1944-1963

The flags of dawn

Hett's successor would be the fourth new Headmaster in 11 years. There must be no more *pro tem* appointments, no more fleeting shades. The Council was looking for a young, experienced schoolmaster in hope and expectation that he would spearhead post-war renaissance. These were the heady days of 'New Jerusalem' politics. As Attlee's government, elected under similar euphoria in 1945, would discover, earnest reality in post-war Britain burst all such dreams, leaving the bitter after-taste of disappointment.

Behind the scenes, soundings produced a list of names laid before the Council in February 1944. Unimpressed, the governors pushed all to one side and advertised the post, still at a salary of £1,000 per annum. From an unknown number of applicants, a short-list of three was prepared: Mr. E.W. Davies (Headmaster of King's School Rochester), Mr. Arthur Campbell Stuart-Clark (Headmaster of Steyning Grammar School) and a Mr. R.W. Kirkman. Davies subsequently withdrew and, for the first time, the Council interviewed more than one candidate.

Recommended by the Chairman of the Steyning governors as 'extremely congenial to deal with ... His genius lies along the lines of organisation and adaptation ... He is not afraid to try experiments', Stuart-Clark got the job. Aged 38 and educated at Tonbridge and Cambridge, he had taught in Switzerland and then at Weymouth College, where he had run the rugby and been a Housemaster. Only in time of need has Brighton College Council selected a serving Headmaster, so we must presume that his successful tenure at Steyning since 1937 won him the post. Certainly he was not appointed for his third in

Arthur Stuart-Clark

Brighton College
Centenary Celebrations, 1946

Set out hereunder are the details of the proposed Centenary Celebrations :—

FRIDAY, 21st JUNE—

OLD BRIGHTONIAN DINNER IN LONDON.

Full details as to location and times, etc., have yet to be completed.

In view of the existing conditions, it is regretted that it will be necessary to ask Old Brightonians to pay £1 1s. towards the cost thereof.

THURSDAY, 27th JUNE—

CRICKET MATCH. The College v. Lancing College.
On the College Ground. Play begins at about 12 noon. Teas will be provided on the Ground.

FRIDAY, 28th JUNE—

CRICKET MATCH. The College v. Old Brightonians
(One-day Match). Play begins at 11.30 a.m. Teas will be provided on the Ground.

SATURDAY, 29th JUNE—

CRICKET MATCH. The College v. Old Brightonians
(Another One-day Match). Play begins at 11.30 a.m. Teas will be provided on the Ground.

DANCE in the SCHOOL HALL.
Admission will be by ticket.

History. Tony Worth (Head of School House 1945) remembers well his arrival as 'a breath of fresh air. [He] was keen to get to know the boys and was always trying to do things that were not always popular with other staff'. Peter la Touche (1942-46) confirms that he 'brought a newer and fresher approach to the running of the school' and tells of a sight unfamiliar to any boy then in College— a Headmaster 'in rugby gear and refereeing some matches'. Opinion among the staff was less sanguine, as Tony Worth had noticed. In the opinion of David Dykes (1945-81), 'he was not a leader. He failed to force the pace'. 'Teddy' Lester put it slightly differently: 'After the war, the College needed lots of 'go'. So much needed doing. The staff were pretty good, but not electric. That was where S-C let us down. He was not a strong enough character'. Stuart-Clark is more than difficult to assess. His treatment at the hands of the Chairman of the Council won him enduring sympathy, while appraisal since 1950 has always (and inevitably) involved unfavourable comparison with his successor. Both colour all judgements of this Headmaster. The record of Stuart-Clark's years must be allowed to speak for itself.

In the Headmaster's order book for 7 May 1945, Stuart-Clark told the school

> if the announcement of V.E. Day is made after school hours, dayboys will not be expected to come to school on the two days following. If the announcement is made during school hours, the school will be given the news in the Hall, and the rest of that day and the next will be a holiday

and added for the masters, 'I have told Smart to ring the school bell for a longer time than usual'. The nation allowed itself only a brief period of rejoicing. Post-war reality sank in very quickly, as the magazine editorial for November 1945 illustrates: 'We are told with wearisome regularity that we have fought to win the war and that we must now fight to win the peace. It is a depressing truth to a war-weary world, but it is a truth that must nevertheless be faced. We must not let the reaction of relief turn into indolent stagnation'. Toil, deprivation and monotony characterised life in Britain during the first seven years of peace. Continued shortages and rationing undermined spirits. While the 1951 Festival of Britain provided a desperately needed tonic, most questioned what the nation had to celebrate and how the expense could be justified.

The centenary of the College was marked rather than celebrated. At the conclusion of the anniversary in 1946, Commemoration honoured the school's war dead. The vellum memorial book contains the names of four masters, 163 old boys and one pupil:

British units		Colonial units	
Army	54	Australian Army	2
RN/RM	21	Australian Air Force	1
RAF	69	Canadian Air Force	1
Merchant Navy	2	Indian Army	8
Kings Messenger	1	Malay States Forces	1
A.R.P.	1	New Zealand Air Force	1
civilian air-raid victim	1	Sarawak Govt. Service	1
unknown	1	Sudan Defence Force	1
		Straits Settlements Volunteers	2

We now know also of Gunter Guhl (1935-39) who was killed in France in 1944 serving with the German Army. No definitive list of old boys who had served was ever published. But, then, the war dead of 1939-45 have never held the imagination as, uniquely, did those of 1914-19.

Because they are so unfamiliar, it is instructive to pause and notice several characteristic features. First, conscription from 1939 meant there could be no rush of under-age men to the colours, as in 1914-15. Except in the RAF, fresh-faced schoolboys were not nearly so vulnerable as they had been in the trenches. Thus, whereas 60 per cent of the College's First War dead were aged 25 or under, the proportion from the Second was 43 per cent (71); only one was aged under twenty. Similarly, the number who were killed within five years of leaving the College was 43 per cent in the First and 24 per cent in the Second War. Two other components are noteworthy. First, eleven of the British and Indian Army officers killed (21 per cent of that group) were colonels and brigadiers. Second, the number of school prefects among the dead was also disproportionately high. Some 33 fell (20 per cent of all fatal casualties), including two Heads of School and 18 Heads of Houses.

Stuart-Clark's first job was to ensure that the rise in numbers proved no false blip:

Numbers in College

	total pupils	boarders	dayboys		plus Junior School
Sept 1943	122	58	64	(52.5%)	72
Sept 1944	143	65	78	(54.5%)	77
Sept 1945	243	136	107	(44%)	
Sept 1946	288	184	104	(36%)	
Sept 1947	305	188	117	(38%)	
Sept 1948	315	186	129	(41%)	
Sept 1949	332	178	154	(47%)	

The school grew by 53 per cent in 1945, and by another 22 per cent during 1946-47, creeping thereafter towards the Council's target of 340 boys (reached in

PHILIP EVELYN GIBBS,
Pilot Officer, Royal Air Force
Volunteer Reserve.
Killed on Active Service,
January, 1941.

IAN ROBERT MACKINTOSH
(1932-36)
Sergeant Pilot, Royal Air Force.
Killed on Active Service.

JOHN BERNARD WILLIAM HUMPHERSON,
D.F.C.
Flying Officer, Royal Air Force.
Killed on Active Service, June, 1941.

ERNEST RENE DAVIS
(1929-31)
Pilot Officer, Royal Air Force.
Killed on Active Service,
August, 1941.

DENNIS HUGHES JACKSON
(1932-6).
Paymaster Sub-Lieutenant,
Royal Navy.
Killed on Active Service, May, 1940.

ALBERT JOHN OETTLE, D.F.C.
(1930-33).
Flight Lieut., Royal Air Force.
Killed on Active Service,
November, 1941.

KENNETH HUGHES JACKSON
(1934-37),
Sub-Lieutenant, Royal Navy.
Missing, believed Killed.

GEORGE RONALD WATSON
(1935-38).
Acting Leading Airman,
Fleet Air Arm.
Killed on Active Service.

1952), with 170 in the Junior School (achieved in 1954). The later slow-down is not surprising. The economy from 1947 showed ever worsening signs of dislocation. Food rationing was increased in August 1947. The pound was devalued in September 1949. Wags said the government had no economic policy beyond 'hope of manna from America'.

Governors who had endured the anxieties of the 1930s now claimed to behave with a model prudence. In Burstow's words, 'periodic increases of fees were not as unpleasant as overcrowding, over-investment and disorganisation would have been', but it is far from clear that potential pupils were actually turned away before the mid-1950s. We should not take at face value the claim to a managed post-war expansion. Further, while it is the case that prep schools were cultivated carefully, it is more important to recognise that the Attlee Labour Government was good news for private education. The south east was the centre of a particular economic boom. Despite rising prices and high levels of direct taxation, the middle classes enjoyed a new prosperity, their ranks swollen by a significant injection of new families with new money. What is more, the continuation of an austerity economy meant post-war consumption was so depressed that private education was one of the few commodities still freely available for people to spend their money on.

Often overlooked is the surge in demand for private schooling created by the 1944 Education Act. This had nothing to do with the raising of the school-leaving age to fifteen (April 1947). When fee-paying places at the grammar schools were abolished,

The Headmaster's Study, *c.*1956

not a few felt keenly that these schools had been deprived of all cachet. Snobbery has long been a characteristic of the English middle classes and, from 1944, pushed many towards the only remaining fee-paying sector. Stuart-Clark was thus working to ensure that Brighton College secured a good share of the potential market. He did well:

percentage growth, 1944-50

Cranleigh	46%
Malvern	87%
BRIGHTON	124%
Lancing	125%
Eastbourne	156%

More difficult to meet were the quotas the Council set him. One was to keep the number of Jewish boys below 9 per cent. The other was to preserve the boarders in the majority. Given the strength of local demand, neither task was easy, and the Council reprimanded him for allowing non-Christian pupils to reach 16 per cent.

Bristol and Durnford Houses were brought out of abeyance in 1945 and 1946 respectively, which meant that the Junior School would have to move yet again. Opposite the College, the buildings of the former Deaf and Dumb Asylum were then available. Bought on mortgage for £10,500, these dingy and totally decrepit premises provided a home to the Juniors for 27 years, virtually all of them under the accomplished ornithologist Stanley Bayliss Smith who had come to the College to be Housemaster of Leconfield but found himself almost immediately appointed Headmaster of the Juniors (1945-70). But this was not 1921 all over again. Now the College possessed the wisdom to keep hold of its own prep school, and grant it home rule.

The wartime dayboy majority may have been destroyed rapidly but, even so, day numbers doubled under Stuart-Clark. Wisely, it was decided to start the long-needed third day house. Named after the Chairman to honour what Stewart called 'his signal role in keeping the College alive in dark days', Aldrich House opened in September 1945. Folly had by then been turned into a virtue and a great myth fabricated. The College trumpeted its steadfastness, its vision in never having evacuated. Hindsight is always twenty-twenty. Aldrich's labours on behalf of the school were indeed many. His devotion cannot be questioned. In 1938-42, however, he alone had brought Brighton College to the edge of extinction. The naming of Aldrich House in 1945 enshrined a fable and perpetuates a falsehood.

Financially, the school remained weak, a truth similarly concealed most carefully. On Speech Day 1946, Aldrich declared that the College entered its second century 'in the happy position of being entirely free from debt'. The accounts told a different story:

	revenue account deficit	bank overdraft	mortgage indebtedness
July 1946	£2,902	£48,608	£73,580
July 1949	£3,433	£14,675	£80,649

Speech Day 1946 (note the painted proscenium arch in the style of Michelangelo). Alderman Aldrich is speaking.

The bridge connecting the College to the Deaf and Dumb Asylum, bought for the Junior School in 1945 (the bridge was only in use for about two years in the very early 1970s).

Since the 1930s, almost no private school has been able to live free from debt, an uncomfortable truth requiring considerable mental (and moral) adjustment from governors and headmasters. Into the 1950s, the College Council still entertained notions that capital debts could be paid off.

Buoyant demand in the late 1940s enabled the College to service those obligations and even to build up reserves. The market was strong enough to weather four fee increases which together raised boarding charges by 40 per cent (to £195) and day costs by 17 per cent (to £75 12s. 6d.) between 1946 and 1949. With revenue predictable, College finances were restructured by Aldrich in 1946 in deals somewhat reminiscent of that struck with the Phoenix in 1909: Barclays accepted £25,000 as full payment for a total debt of £48,608, while the Eagle Star took £29,295 instead of the £39,407 actually owed. Both were paid off by a single new mortgage from the Regency Building Society (£60,000 at 4.5 per cent for 21 years). Debt rescheduling had removed £28,000 from the College's burden. The new loan nonetheless consumed £4,500 in annual charges which alone precluded any large capital expenditure from ordinary funds.

Instead, the enlarging and modernising of the central kitchen, a project which incorporated a flat for the Housemaster of School House and cost £9,757, was financed by the Centenary and War Memorial Fund. Launched in 1939, this had raised only £26,357 by 1953. The scale of its failure becomes apparent with the knowledge that £18,000 (68.3 per cent) had been given by HB and his sisters. The least successful of all College appeals, it says little for the efficacy of the Old Boys' Association between the wars.

The survivors of 'the creche' and a flush of new men appointed to the staff reinvigorated school life. The JTC came back into its own under a retired regular officer (Lt. Col. Villiers Smyth, 1945-57), and provided a much praised guard of honour when the Duchess of Kent visited the town in 1947. Two years later when the new Bursar (Cdr. John Head, 1949-63) organised a Naval section, the College could form a combined cadet force. Most games similarly exhibited new vitality, but none proved more successful than squash. Fixture lists were long and impressive, but rarely was the V beaten. Barrington (1942-47) won the public schools tournament in 1946 and 1947, when he also won the Drysdale Cup. He later played for England. David Owen (1945-48) reached the Drysdale final in 1948. The Headmaster took a keen interest in tennis and the first courts were laid out on the Home Ground. Cross-country was permitted to return in 1949.

With a College maximum set at 340, East Brighton Park remained unmanageable, so the southern part was surrendered to the Borough in 1946. Of rugby, Burstow declared that it 'did not generally attain its pre-war excellence, although in 1948 and 1949 there were many great struggles'. Cricket too made a shaky start but, coached by Bill Stewart and the Sussex and England wicket-keeper 'Tich' Cornford, the XI was showing some signs of promise by 1950.

Burstow is quite correct in asserting that 'educational standards were rising with numbers, although they did not yet attain to anything remarkable':

| | pupils qualifying for | | total pupils in |
	Higher Certificate	School Certificate	the College
1945	8	22	243
1946	9	33	288
1947	6	56	305
1948	9	58	315
1949	20	54	332
1950	23	43	330

Certificate results could not match those of the 1930s, because the intake remained non-selective and Stuart-Clark's staff were academically weak. Of the 17 full-time masters he appointed, 15 were graduates but nine held a third or a pass degree, and only one a first. This slippage from the requirements of Belcher and Scott was observed by the Ministry inspectors in February 1951. Their report noted also that 'few masters have substantial experience in other schools or have had any professional training' and concluded 'on the whole, their teaching skill is rather below the average, and too many of them fall back on dull and out-moded methods'. No area was weaker than the VIth Form:

	total pupils	pupils in the VIth Form
Sept 1935	270	53 (19.7%)
Sept 1940	123	29 (23.6%)
Sept 1945	243	26 (10.7%)
Sept 1950	320	41 (12.8%)

If his own appointments had in no way helped the academic life of the school, Stuart-Clark nonetheless gave it a profile badly needed. Boys were left in no doubt that the classroom mattered and, in a much criticised move, he asserted that by making a scholar Head of School in April 1945 (David Humphreys, 1940-46, staff 1958-62). Stewart and Lester, the two VIth Form masters, did what they could but, as in the 1920s, were hampered by a shortage of very bright boys and undermined by weak teaching lower down the school. Group I had merged with Group II in

September 1939, Group IV with Group III in September 1941. The old four-part VIth Form did not return, but none could mistake the bias towards Science and Maths which was developing:

Pupils in the Remove and VIth Form

	Group II	Group III
Sept 1945	18	25
Sept 1947	27	37
Sept 1949	26	43

Careers advice was strengthened (1947) by the establishing of an interview panel through which boys could talk with somebody working in one of thirty professions. Another notable innovation was the foundation of the 'manual class' in 1945. Reminiscent of the 'new school movement' begun 50 years earlier at Abbotsholme and Bedales, College boys were taught plumbing, electrical wiring, decorating and glazing (as well as carpentry and metalwork); practical experience was gained by working around the College. Craft skills were valued by Stuart-Clark. So too were the arts which he had fostered at Steyning. The orchestra and the House Music Competition

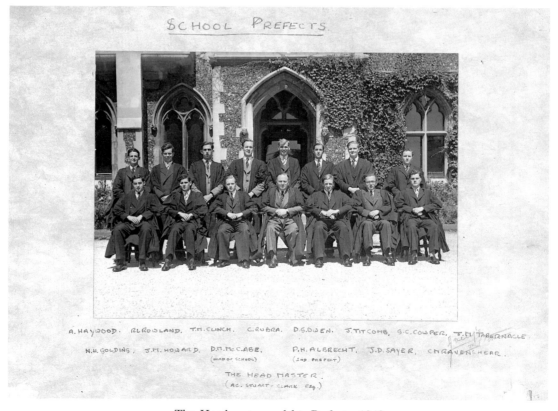

The Headmaster and his Prefects, 1948

The Carol Service, 1949

were revived. The Leonardo Cup (1948) encouraged creativity by offering prizes in 'craft, literature, art and music'; one by-product was the return of essays and poems to the magazine. Finally, Stuart-Clark improved communication with parents by replacing the single sheet report with a booklet in which each teacher could write a substantial paragraph.

Stuart-Clark's fresh approach also removed physical drill as a school punishment, oversaw the appearance of a half-term holiday and brought the Festival of Nine Lessons and Carols to the College (1944, with a Christmas tree in chapel from 1947). On Speech Day 1948, Lt. General Sir Francis Tuker (1907-12) heartily endorsed the Headmaster's moves to 'maintain that vital spirit of individual creativeness without which life is all drabness and ugliness'. Others did not. Every school and Old Boys' Association contains a group of permanently fixated men, filled with longing and nostalgia for the certainties and successes of adolescence. At Brighton College in 1947-50, these hardened opponents of change, orchestrated by Charles Hough (1897-1902, master 1908-12 and 1919-48) and Bill Williams (master 1919-45), began what

Lester described as 'a systematic campaign to get rid of a Headmaster they saw as undermining the old school'. The school song had been allowed to die. School prefects had been enfeebled by the ending of punishment drill, and their stature undermined by the removal of Hett's restoration to them of the boater. Above all, the attention paid to what Bill Williams called 'the useless arts' and the encouragement given to non-team games (especially squash), were judged to threaten College rugby; the Junior School had even been allowed to convert back to soccer.

Normally, these permanent schoolboys are no more than an irritant, but one of their number was Chairman of the Council. Silently, Aldrich spent two years gathering a dossier which, seizing the opportunity of the Headmaster's absence through illness with angina, he put before the full Council on 17 February 1950. Charged with 'lack of leadership', Stuart-Clark was accused of having lost the confidence of the Common Room, of the parents, of the pupils and of the old boys. According to the Council minutes, 'the Chairman expressed the opinion that in all probability the most serious of these complaints were those emanating from the staff'. The harpies knew precisely how to strike. In the words of the Council minutes, Aldrich told his colleagues that three senior masters

> had sought interviews with him, and claimed to be speaking on behalf of the staff generally, and they had expressed the opinion that the School had never been at such a low ebb in relation to teaching staff and morale of staff.

Reg Henderson (staff 1946-73) described Stuart-Clark as 'somewhat reserved'. Burstow reported, 'He was considered by many people either very conceited or very shy'. Is this the key to difficulties with some of the staff? Burstow's view is especially intriguing because, associated with the coterie of disgruntled old boys, his diary nonetheless reveals a certain objectivity:

> He was quite a good Headmaster who was unwise in antagonising his staff ... He did not seem to fit in with the College traditions ... I have always said that, at the price of two cups of coffee per head per term, he could have had a cooperative staff ... Some of his dislike, particularly among the lesser men, was jealousy or self-importance: was I one?

Furthermore, Lester and Peter Gough (master 1946-66) deny that the deputation of three spoke formally on behalf of the Common Room, or after consultation within it.

One month later, the Headmaster presented his reply (which does not survive) and resigned. He was actually getting better, but he saw the impossibility of his position. Like Scott, he had found Aldrich's domineering manner hard to take—within weeks of appointment they had crossed swords when the Chairman was allegedly discovered wandering around the Headmaster's house, uninvited and unannounced. Subsequently, Stuart-Clark served as Senior Tutor and Registrar of the Hospital Administrative Staff College, and later as Bursar of Darwin College Cambridge. He died in 1973. Stuart-Clark had been deposed. By his own admission, Aldrich had known of various criticisms for up to two years. Yet never before drafting his bill of indictment had he raised any of these matters. If there really was a mounting tide of complaint, he as Chairman was obliged to investigate and take remedial action. A co-conspirator, Aldrich did nothing and thus failed lamentably in his prime responsibility, to Brighton College.

Always well informed, Burstow knew something of dirty work:

I expect he [Stewart-Clark] has quite a case against the Chairman who apparently attacked him violently at a Council meeting on points not on the agenda. I cannot understand how the other members let him get away with it. It seems that, despite opposition, the Chairman carried the day ... I wonder how much longer we shall have the same Chairman?

The Council minutes show that the Bishop of Peterborough and the Bishop of Lewes insisted that the record state, 'that they were not satisfied, on the papers before the Council, that a case has been made out against the Headmaster'.

So there was another side, and the Bishop of Peterborough and Professor Gilbert Ryle (1910-19) resigned. Years later, Ryle told Alf Lester, 'both of us went in protest at these grubby proceedings. Aldrich was a swine'. The Chairman's grip on the Council guaranteed his own position, but his power was no longer absolute. Burstow's *History* talks vaguely of 'long deliberations' to find a successor. In fact, something of a running battle developed within the Council. At the very meeting where Stuart-Clark tendered his resignation, Aldrich had pressed hard for the immediate appointment of William Stewart, one of Scott's creche who returned from the war with the Military Cross and in 1950 was Head of History, Housemaster of Chichester and master in charge of cricket. But the Council, disturbed by the recent coup, would not be bamboozled into election by acclamation. They insisted that a dozen headmasters be asked for suitable names. In due course, the post was advertised, at a salary of £1,000 per annum with annual increments of £100 rising to a maximum of £2,000. (In 1950, a Principal in the Civil Service earned between £800 and £1,100, a County Court judge £2,000 and a Cabinet Minister £5,000 per annum.)

From eight applicants, three men were short-listed and interviewed: Robert Dahl (who in 1952 became Headmaster of Wrekin College), Alfred Doulton (who in 1955 was appointed Headmaster of Highgate School, later serving as Treasurer of HMC) and Stewart. The selection sub-committee favoured Doulton, but when the three appeared again before the full Council, Stewart won through to become the fourth internally appointed College Headmaster. Then aged 34, he shares with Dawson the distinction of being the youngest College Headmaster this century. Like Dawson, Stewart cut an impressive figure and became a legend within his own lifetime. A man of massive energy and apparently tireless enthusiasm, his voice and his physique gave him a commanding presence he had learned to exploit. He behaved as a man in authority—within two hours of appointment, he had called the staff together for a meeting. The Ministry inspectors in 1961 judged that 'his vitality, good sense and understanding

William Stewart, *c.*1943

have given the school all that was most needed at a time of rapid development'. Burstow talks of his 'dynamic and attractive personality', Norman Frith (staff 1950-87) recalled how 'his laughter rang round the Common Room; his roar after the wayward shook the fabric; his melodious voice filled the Chapel'. William Stewart put the school back on the map and in the process, as any good Headmaster should, he became Brighton College.

In the 'you've never had it so good' 1950s, the post-war renaissance in private education became a bonanza. The Conservative election victory of 1951 unleashed a slow but uncontrolled economic boom which, with occasional blips, outlasted the decade and created a wage-price spiral. Under the slogan, 'a little of what you fancy does you good', Britain turned from war-economy austerity to embrace an indulgent, self-centred consumerist society. Despite the accompanying wage and price inflation, a slump in 1955-56 and deflation in 1961-63, middle England felt prosperous on the neo-Keynesian post-war consensus of full employment and rising incomes. Affluence thus accompanied 'the bulge', the post-war jump in the birth rate, which by 1955-57 began to fuel renewed demand for Common Entrance and scholarship places. Another factor not to be overlooked was the growing significance of paper qualifications which induced parents to keep their sons longer in school. The proportion of boys leaving under the age of 17 had fallen from 30 per cent in 1950 to 20 per cent by 1960. At the same time, 40 per cent of all leavers in 1960 took 'A' level, compared with 12 per cent who tried Higher Certificate in 1950.

Numbers in College

	total pupils	boarders	dayboys
Sept 1950	320	177	143 (45%)
Sept 1951	338	185	153 (45%)
Sept 1952	339	192	147 (43%)
Sept 1953	347	193	154 (44%)
Sept 1954	338	192	146 (43%)
Sept 1955	340	189	151 (44%)
Sept 1956	346	184	162 (47%)
Sept 1957	363	194	169 (47%)
Sept 1958	372	197	175 (47%)
Sept 1959	367	203	164 (45%)
Sept 1960	383	203	180 (47%)
Sept 1961	369	191	178 (48%)
Sept 1962	378	200	178 (47%)
Sept 1963	378	208	170 (45%)

The College felt itself to be full and was not going to slip into a Dawsonian explosion. From 340 boys in 1952 to 365 in 1959 and then 384 in 1963, each maximum size set by the Council was exceeded with care. Across the Stewart years, boarding numbers grew by 17.5 per cent and dayboys by 19 per cent (26 per cent

Room E (Archibald Hill's class), *c.*1955 ('Tubby' Hill taught at the College 1920-58)

to 1960). Stewart became famous for his contacts with prep schools. He needed to recruit to compensate for a fall-off in supply from the Junior School (76 per cent of their leavers came to the College in 1960, as opposed to 90 per cent in 1950). Primarily he was working to fill boarding places. He told the Chairman in 1953 that 'without having to lift a finger, the school could have 250 dayboys'. Brighton College had, of course, always been atypical in its mix of dayboys and boarders. But when they looked at fellow Victorian HMC schools and saw dayboys making up just 1.4 per cent of Malvern, 2.5 per cent of Rossall, 9.5 per cent of Cranleigh and 11 per cent of Cheltenham, both Headmaster and Chairman could only sigh.

Neither Council nor Headmaster had yet come to terms with the inevitability of a dayboy majority, continuing to see the boarders as 'the nucleus of the College, from which it draws its continuity, its character and its ethos'. When in 1961 the Ministry inspectors wrote that old College prejudices against dayboys had now 'virtually died out', they exaggerated the rate of change. Three times Stewart pushed an eligible

Tom Smart, Head Porter 1925-64

candidate into becoming a boarder before he would appoint him as Head of School. Only under considerable pressure was Stewart persuaded, most reluctantly, to appoint dayboys to lead the school in 1954 and 1956. *The Brightonian*'s claim in 1963 that the dayboy was 'on an equal par with the boarder' was true only in the minds of a minority of the staff. Geoff Lees (1948-1963) was the prime mover. His championing of the dayboys directly challenged Stewart's prejudices. Uniquely, he refused to accept the 'normal' housemasterly progression from Day to Boarding House, asking instead for a second term in Aldrich. Stewart was dumbfounded, but agreed.

Price sensitivity was another concern always on the Council's mind. Between 1950 and 1960, the rise in the retail price index (49 per cent) outstripped that in real earnings (30 per cent). Despite very significant increases in personal savings, inflation was eating away at apparent prosperity. College fees had to be raised 10 times during Stewart's reign:

Annual fees

	dayboy	*boarder*
1951	£105	£210
1962	£234	£414

Three times the Bursar was instructed to collect information about 'comparable schools':

Annual fees at 'comparable schools'

	dayboy			*boarder*		
	1953	*1958*	*% increase*	*1953*	*1958*	*% increase*
Eastbourne	£120	£175	46	£270	£355	32
Cheltenham	£116	£184	59	£296	£397	34
BRIGHTON	£120	£171	42.5	£240	£324	35
Malvern	£132	£189	43	£276	£375	36
Lancing	-	-	-	£255	£354	39

Because Brighton's fee increases were neither exceptional nor excessive, it is odd that the Council did not use price to suppress day numbers or to subsidise the boarders.

New buildings always impress and Stewart's reign saw desperately needed action taken to replace the worst of the College's facilities: a new Science block (1957-8, costing £49,160), workshops and two day Houses, together with the relocation of the third (1959, costing £42,000). Regular deficits in the later 1940s had been turned into a surplus every year between 1950 and 1958, the revenue account showing an average profit of £3,824. This was an extraordinary achievement. No governor and few masters

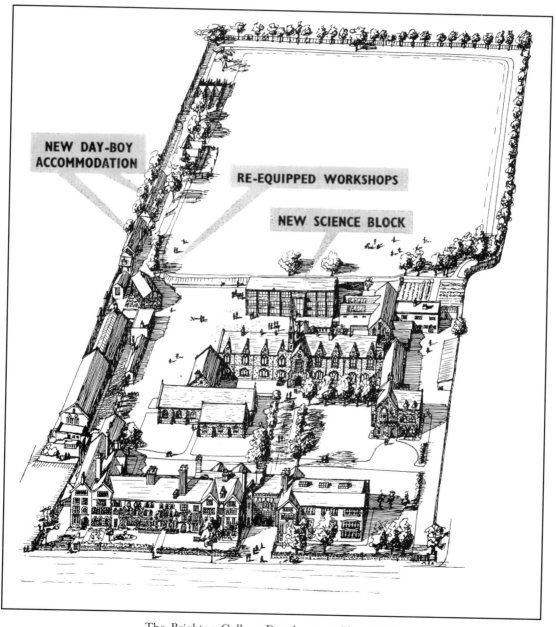

The Brighton College Development Plan, 1955

The Science Building (second and unexecuted design)

could remember a situation so healthy, but new buildings would have to be funded from an appeal (for £100,000). By 1961 this had produced some £85,000 gross, of which £25,300 came from the Industrial Fund (set up to make grants to public schools building Chemistry and Physics laboratories) and another £12,500 came as an interest-free loan from the Dyers' Company (whose then Prime Warden was a College parent).

In the space which became available, a fine new library was created in the Main Building, while the old Chemistry labs and part of the upper corridor formed part of the newly-housed Aldrich. There might have been much more. A new assembly hall was mooted and development plans looked for a classroom block, a central dining hall capable of holding the entire College at one sitting, a third squash court, a self-contained Music School and a new Art Department. But the College was hit by a financial crisis which came without warning in 1959. The accounts for 1958-59 showed a wholly unexpected deficit (£3,938) while the overdraft jumped £14,962 to £26,433. The appeal shortfall had necessitated borrowing £23,000 at the very moment when interest rates stood at their highest point since the 1920s. On top of that, the Regency Building Society announced it must recall its mortgage, the Registrar of Friendly Societies having judged the College to be commercial property—which left the Regency over permitted limits for commercial loans. A flurry of activity succeeded in refinancing the College with a 25-year debenture for £100,000 at 5.5 per cent with the Royal Insurance Company.

The Council judged that they would need a minimum annual surplus of £10,000, but the deflation of 1961 which followed a pre-election consumer spree ruined all calculations. 'A touch on the brake', Macmillan called it, but the raising of the bank rate to 7 per cent and a 10 per cent increase in consumer taxes ushered in two years of industrial stagnation and produced the spectacular Orpington by-election in March 1962. Brighton College endured the roller-coaster with a regimen of even stricter budgetary controls and four fee increases in three years. From these troubles dates the requirement on pupils to buy their own textbooks.

College finances were, of course, always a matter of faith and hope. Sir Alun Pugh (Chairman 1955-66) described Council policy as 'nervous'.

> We lived in dread of deficit. When Alderman Aldrich was Chairman, he would not countenance even talk of new buildings. The Headmaster and the Bursar [Commander Head, 1949-63] were not financial managers. Neither was I. After the Alderman died, we relied on Reggie Green [1921-24; Treasurer 1950-57], Harold Elliott [1919-23; Chairman of the Council 1974-78] and Ronnie Pickering [1926-28]. The last two I recruited, not because they were loyal OBs–the traditional criterion–but because they were sound and experienced businessmen. The Council needed badly men with specific talents to bring to its deliberations. It was, I think, the most significant thing I ever did as Chairman.

Brighton College was not alone in regretting the decision of Attlee's government not to incorporate the 1942 Fleming Report into the 1944 Education Act, and thereby fund 25 per cent of the places at selected public schools for children from maintained primary schools. Local authorities were, however, permitted to make their own arrangements and the College had at once negotiated with Brighton Borough to take

The new Library, *c.*1960

four 'day scholars' per year—increased to six in 1948 when similar arrangements were made with East Sussex to take two boys. The Council saw a possible lifeline. Just as they had explored grant-aided status in 1932, so in 1958 and again in 1959 they proposed an 11-plus entry to the Borough. From 1957 to 1959 they tried to interest education authorities in Surrey, Kent and Hampshire, as well as Sussex, in taking up 'reserved assisted places' so that, in Stewart's words, the College 'should have something to offer to the parent of modest means, but of the right type'. Such offers came too late. The bulge was past and, with grammar school places to spare, no L.E.A. showed the slightest interest in teaming up with any of the public schools then proposing such schemes. More practical was the consideration given in 1957 to joining the newly re-opened direct grant list. This too came to nothing but, taken together, these ideas show that Burstow was wrong to claim that, in response to the 1944 Act, the Council insisted that 'the College should remain free and independent'. Stewart himself seems to have been the originator of all these propositions. His thoughts are most revealing:

> We should lose some independence—and we should lose some prestige; we should gain a considerable measure of security in a world in which it is to be expected that the unendowed independent school

The new Art Room (top floor of the Dawson Building), 1956

(*above*) 'Dixon of Dock Green' opening the fête, 1960

(*left*) R. Green

will find it increasingly difficult to pay its way ... The competition for entry (and therefore the academic standard) would be raised still further ... The luxury of independence may be too expensive when we pass the bulge, or if ever the country has to face inflation.

Some 51 of the 193 HMC schools were already on the direct grant list. Another 25 took this opportunity to join. The Council's reasons for deciding not to be among them were never recorded, but their decision was a defining moment. Sir Sydney Roberts, who as governor of Framlingham College had experience of the grant, felt the College had 'thrown away the chance to exploit the growth of modern Brighton and become the great grammar school of Sussex'.

Confidence returned in 1960-62 with financial recovery. The roles of Harold

Lord Woolton

The Royal Visit, 1962

Elliott and Ronnie Pickering have already been noted. The work of one other needs specific mention: the President, Lord Woolton. As Minister of Food and then of Reconstruction in the wartime government, 'Uncle Fred' became known for his organisational skills. Previous College Presidents had been no more than figureheads, but Woolton did far more than secure eminent guests of honour for Speech Day and the visit of the Queen. He attended the Council regularly, taking a particular interest in finance. He overhauled the College kitchens. He led the discussions with the Industrial Fund. He it was who negotiated the 1960 debenture.

*   *   *

Solid academic achievement has long been acknowledged as a cardinal feature of the College in the 1950s:

	'O' level passes	'A' level passes	pupils in the College
1952	379	64	340
1954	438	50	339
1956	462	101	347
1958	473	83	372
1960	625	114	383
1962	619	135	379

Whereas just two Oxbridge open awards were won in 1950-54, 11 were brought home in 1955-59 and 10 in 1960-64.

Seminal was the re-emergence of the VIth Form. Before Dawson, the VIth had been the intellectual powerhouse of the College, valued for its scholarship and the prestige it brought. But it had always been very small. Now, even though only four 'O' levels were required for admittance, its stature grew with its size as much as its distinction:

	total pupils	pupils in VIth Form	
Sept 1950	320	41	(12.8%)
Sept 1955	340	60	(17.6%)
Sept 1960	383	118	(30.8%)

Between 1954 and 1957, the proportion of the College in the VIth Form doubled, and Stewart bequeathed to his successor a school where 41.5 per cent of pupils (157 boys) were VIth Formers. By contrast, the largest it had been in the 1920s was 31 boys (5.2 per cent).

Lancing secured 52 Oxbridge open awards between 1950 and 1964, compared with Brighton's 23—or Malvern's 112 and Marlborough's 147. Much more comparative evidence is required before the academic renaissance can be truly gauged. Internal

David Allen (1926-32, staff 1946-78), in the old Physics lab, c.1955

reference provides only a limited answer, but nonetheless testified to the absolute improvement. How was it achieved? Mention is often made of the raising in 1954 of the Common Entrance pass mark to 55 per cent. Yet in 1961 some 93 boys within the College (25 per cent) had failed the exam. The introduction of internal half-term reports (1957) and a tutorial system (1960) definitely helped. The broadening of feeder prep schools played a vital part. Nothing, however, must overshadow the improvement wrought among the masters. In the words of the 1961 Ministry Report, teaching skill

is well up to the standard found in comparable schools ... This is a hardworking and keen staff, a good team to whose members, during term, the usual distinction between work and leisure can seldom apply. They have the satisfaction of men with a deep sense of vocation.

In his own notes, the Chief Inspector wrote, 'As a whole, a fine team (with one exception). We are struck by the general quality of HM's recent appointments. Some need still for high academic quality, but he has picked consistently well'. The inspectors singled out the Science and Geography Departments as particularly strong, English as outstanding. As for the individual masters, 10 were judged of average competence, only three as unsatisfactory and 14 as above average—the most highly rated being Dr. John Hall (Chemistry 1960-63) and Geoff Lees, the Head of English. These judgements are of the utmost significance, for no inspection since 1911 had praised the academic staff.

Intriguingly, the immediate post-war bias towards Maths and Science failed to develop, despite the school's own expectations (and hopes, perhaps). At Speech Day 1960, Stewart declared that there would soon be five scientists to every three on the Arts side. Some public schools indeed witnessed the triumph of the Sciences; the proportion of VIth Formers at Malvern studying 'A' level Science rose from 40 per cent to 60 per cent in the ten years from 1948. Not so at Brighton College, despite a surge in the later '50s, stimulated (presumably) by the new laboratories:

	VIth Formers in		'A' levels gained	
	Group II	Group III	Arts	Maths/Science
Sept 1954	27	19	32	18
Sept 1958	44	54	49	28
Sept 1962	83	60	71	53

What else would follow when Physics and Chemistry ceased to be compulsory 'O' levels after 1954?

Masters on Speech Day, 1952

Philip Dore (1953-58), Peter Gough and Bill Lloyd (1945-60, 1964-68, governor 1973-78)
[cartoon from *The Brightonian*, May 1956]

Exceptionally few took an 'A' level language (French, German, Spanish). There was not a single Higher Certificate or 'A' level pass in Latin between 1945 and 1954. A Modern Languages trip to Paris in 1948 was not followed up. No French exchange was set up. Greek made a small come-back from 1953, while Russian was introduced in 1959. These were not the only newcomers. Geology was added in 1958 to the diet of separate 'A' level Sciences–which since the war had included Botany and Zoology. Economics and British Constitution AO became Lower VIth options in 1960, Economics becoming an 'A' level subject two years later. As an academic subject, Music failed to get off the ground (one 'O' level and three 'A' level candidates 1951-62), unlike Art which at last took wing. An Art Scholarship had been established in 1950, but the real elevation of painting, drawing and graphics was due to Gordon Taylor, an inspiring and a much underrated Director of Art (1954-69). By 1960 he had 36 boys taking 'O' level, and 9 taking 'A' level.

The '50s were thus a time of significant curriculum expansion. Less obvious, but equally important, were the first steps beyond 'chalk and talk' in the classroom, perhaps made easier after hosting, in 1951, a conference on visual aids in education, opened by J. Arthur Rank. Vth Form visits to the theatre and the cinema to see their 'O' level set texts were highly novel departures in 1955. Hard as it is for us to imagine now, Modern Languages had no tape recorder before 1961 (14 years after they first went on sale), the Art Department no slide projector until 1963. The Junior School was watching schools' TV from its inception in 1957. When did the College start?

Much had been achieved. Yet in some respects nothing had altered. Like many headmasters of the time, Stewart had to be pushed hard to elevate the academic side even to parity with character-building in his priorities for the school. The Vth Form in 1961 still contained nine boys (11 per cent) taking 'O' levels at the age of 17 or even

18–which represented a reduction of only 3 per cent in ten years. Some 25 VIth Formers leaving in 1952 went to University. Despite significant expansion in the number of universities and the total places available, and marked growth in the VIth Form, only 30 went up in 1962. The recent introduction of grades at 'A' level had made life much tougher. The inspectors in 1961 put it thus: 'By running hard, the school has just held its ground'. In the magazine in May 1962, Mark Ellis (1958-63, School Prefect and Captain of Squash) added,

In this school, far too little encouragement is given to work ... He who shines at games is a hero: he can flaunt five or six different ties, pretend to be one of the most valuable boys in the College, and yet be no more intelligent than the average Fourth Former.

We must be careful not to transfer the academic rat-race of the 1990s back 30 years. For parents and masters in Macmillan's Britain, to have 17.6 per cent of College leavers going to university was considered good; both retained strong prejudice against the redbrick universities. At the same time, competition for university places was becoming ferocious as the baby boom and the 1944 Education Act produced more highly qualified candidates which university expansion had only partly met. Brighton College's problem was one faced by all the public schools from the later 1950s. The loss of their monopoly in academic secondary education had deprived them of their reversion on university places.

In spotlighting the lack of a cutting edge in much College teaching, the 1961 Inspection showed the way forward. Too much was prosaic. There was 'too much emphasis on knowledge, too little on method'. College boys were 'overtaught, the learning process being almost entirely passive'. And like Ellis, some were starting to call for 'a change in attitude towards the importance of work by everybody concerned'.

Inside the new Biology lab, c.1960.

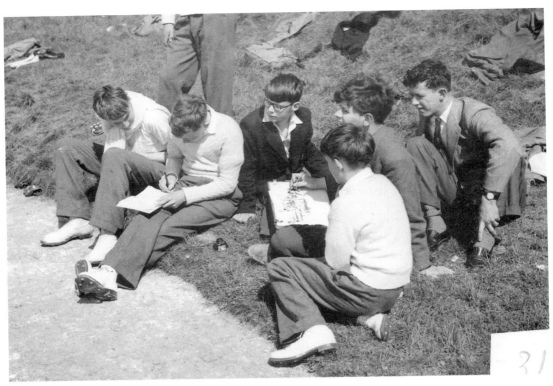

Sketching on the Home Ground

The new Engineering workshops (in the white coat is David Hollinshead whose appointment in 1962 as the first professionally qualified technical studies master represented a marked improvement in the status of his subject)

*   *   *

Beyond the classroom, the whirl of incessant activity continued oblivious to the stirrings of an academic revolution. The corps provided a broadening programme of activities. The Army had Signals, R.A., R.E. and R.E.M.E. sections, from 1961 a Band and from 1962 a Civil Defence Unit. Alternatively, on passing Cert. A, cadets could opt to join the RN or RAF sections. For a while, the latter built and flew its own Eon glider on the New Ground. A permanent assault course was built (by the cadets) in 1958. Arduous Training Expeditions to North Wales began the following Easter.

Games prospered with Stewart at the helm. Some even talked of 'the silver age of College sport'. At the front of their mind was cricket. On Tich Cornford's 'sleek and indestructible wickets' (Burstow), coached by Geoff Lees and then Gordon Smith (1946-52; staff 1959-67; Headmaster of the Junior School 1970-80), College cricket matured to such a degree that in 1963 the Sussex County Club asked for the Brighton-Lancing match to return to the County Ground after a 32-year absence; Lancing refused.

Farewell to Colonel Smyth, 1957

1st XI	played	won	drew	lost	abandoned
1946-51	90	32	17	41	-
1952-57	77	40	25	12	-
1958-63	84	37	28	17	2

In 1952, 1956 and 1959 the XI was unbeaten (for the first time since 1885). Often overlooked, the XI of 1960 won 11 of its 14 matches—the highest number of victories in one College season since records began. Four batsmen scored over 500 runs in each of two or more seasons (A.B.D. Parsons, D.I. Stewart, J.A. Lush and R.W. Lewis). Lewis amassed 2,413 runs in his career with the XI. Parsons scored 2,703 and went on to win the College's first Cambridge cricket blue since 1914.

The situation with rugby could not have been more different. Many noted that, while Stewart appointed to the staff two soccer blues (a game the College did not play), he omitted to select a fine rugby-playing master until 1958. When finally he did so, it made little difference:

CCF inspection, 1960 (note the Brighton College film unit in action). The inspecting officer is General Sir Cecil Sugden (1916-19), Master General of the Ordnance.

1st XV	*played*	*won*	*drew*	*lost*
1946-51	71	27	4	40
1952-57	67	18	5	44
1958-63	69	17	8	44

Against Christ's Hospital, Dulwich, Mill Hill and Whitgift, College XVs could garner only two victories apiece between 1951 and 1963. In the words of Stewart himself, 'College rugby was sluggish'.

These were the two 'major' sports, compulsory for all on four afternoons each week. Such was the norm in the public schools of the '50s. Every other game, the 'minor sports', operated for small groups of selected boys as additional activities twice a week, after lunch and one evening. Fives enjoyed something of a renaissance and, with alteration to the rules, the first ever inter-school matches were played from 1954, with St. John's Leatherhead. Swimming, water polo, fencing, tennis and boxing enjoyed regular success, unlike shooting, which seemed to be in terminal decline until, out of

In the Cricket nets, 1956

Getting ready for Water Polo, *c.*1955

the blue, the VIII scored 512 in the 1960 Ashburton. That result represented the highest total any College VIII ever reached, although in 1960 it was good enough only to secure 11th place. The third College game continued, however, to be squash, of which Stewart argued regularly that the College possessed 'the best school team in the country'–a claim perhaps true from 1954 when Lancing was beaten for the first time since the war.

As in the classroom, there was a broadening of sporting activities. Sailing came first, in 1952. Basketball was introduced to P.T. in 1958 (which was cut down from five to two lessons per week). Golf was added in 1959, as was riding, after seven years in abeyance. Ski trips in the Christmas holiday began in 1958. But that ancient problem of what to do in the Easter Term remained unresolved. Soccer and hockey were both suggested as replacements for the compulsory-but-loathed athletics stand-ards competition; the magazine in 1960 called it 'that most malignant of all tyrannies'.

*   *   *

With a solitary exception, College cultural life was vibrant for a public school in the 1950s. The weak area was music. True the revived Choral Society performed the Mozart Requiem in 1949, but after that its record was feeble. Unlike Lancing, the College made no contribution to Brighton's Festival of Britain programme. In Stewart's own judgement, 'this Department has no ambitions', and he sacked two successive Directors of Music (1953, 1958). Not that there was a dearth of talent, or interest. From 1955, the Jazz Appreciation Society, that touchstone of the modern, organised a vibrant programme promoting the contemporary: Dave Brubeck, Duke Ellington, Benny Goodman. And the new dynamic at work from 1959 can be seen in the Gramophone Society's sudden turn to Mahler and Richard Strauss, Bartok, Prokofiev and Shostakovich as much as in the recommencement of great concerts by the Choral Society.

The contrast with drama is extraordinary. Stuart-Clark had decided that true theatre must be restored, so there would be no revival of Gilbert & Sullivan (another 'sin' the OBs held against him). Rev. J.F. Dobson (1944-48) brought the College stage to life with his *Captain Brassbound's Conversion*, *The Silver Box* and *I Killed the Count*. From that base, Peter Gough

BRIGHTON COLLEGE
DRAMATIC SOCIETY

presents

Captain Brassbound's Conversion

BY

BERNARD SHAW,

ON

THURSDAY, FRIDAY, SATURDAY,
December 13, 14, 15, 1945.

The Silent Woman, 1951

The Hypochondriac, 1956 (the lead was played by
Stephen Cockburn)

launched a grand experiment in the theatre of the unfamiliar, centred on the 16th and 17th centuries. There was Kyd and Massinger, Vanbrugh and Farquhar. A single foray beyond 1750 saw him employ the chapel to stage Eliot's *Murder in the Cathedral* within a cocoon of shadows, as much expressionist as medieval. He also put on single plays by Plautus, Seneca and Sophocles (the last two in masks). Three times he put on Molière, once using the newly adapted texts by Miles Malleson (1898-1908) who himself came to help, and twice using his own translations. In 1956 he included a short play from Richard Buxton (1950-56). The sumptuous 'look' of Gough productions was due entirely to the stunning costumes conjured out of so little by his wife Daphne. The professionalisation of College drama was noticed by the London press, whose critics came down and wrote of 'a quality above anything the term school play can conjure' (*The Daily Telegraph*, 1958).

Visiting lecturers came three or four times a year. Dame Sybil Thorndike and 'Tubby' Clayton (1946), Sir Adrian Boult (1947), the cricketer and future bishop David Sheppard (1953) were imaginative choices. But the visit of four principals from the London Festival Ballet to give a lecture-demonstration in place of afternoon rugby was, in 1957, truly bold. Of the various school societies, the most stimulating was The Humanist Society, 'generally based on the Arts and the Humanities', founded in 1957. Their range of activities indicates a vitality and an enquiring spirit second to none. Members read papers on existentialism, on James Joyce, on Pushkin and on Verdi. They watched Eisenstein's *Battleship Potemkin* (only granted a British certificate in 1954). They went to the Royal Academy, the Old Vic and the Royal Opera House.

The genesis of Art has already been noted. In all probability, its origins lay in the Leonardo Competition, begun in 1948 to foster literary composition, painting, draw-

BRIGHTON COLLEGE PRESENTS

A NEW WAY TO PAY OLD DEBTS

A PLAY BY PHILIP MASSINGER

Two performances to be presented on Friday and Saturday 14 and 15 of December 1962 at 7.30 p.m.

The Brighton College Press: their logo and a specimen of their work

ing and sculpture. Other sources (and reflections) were the Photographic Society, the 3As Society and the vigorous little College Press. Burstow talks of 'boldness and novelty in the artistic products of pupils'. He could also have noted the reawakening of The Play Reading Society. After years consuming only comedies, it suddenly turned its attention to the contemporary theatre, tackling *Waiting for Godot, Look Back in Anger, A Taste of Honey, A Man for All Seasons* and *Luther* when all were new plays. Literary endeavours also played a significant part in the cultural renaissance. The content and style (as well as the cover) of *The Brightonian* became less turgid after 1958. Pupils' poetry reappeared and in 1963 an editorial even announced the intention to become a publication 'of artistic and literary merit'.

Talents were directed primarily, however, into pupil-produced papers and magazines. Like *Gamut* (1960-61), *Wallpaper* (1962) and *Satire* (1962), most were experimental and ephemeral. Not so *The Pelican*, a newspaper which appeared weekly between February 1954 and December 1955. *Gamut* defined itself as 'an intelligent literary magazine', declaring that

> our editorial policy amounts to this: an encouragement of the arts, a fostering of interest in affairs in and around Brighton College with emphasis on politics, and unbiased criticism of whatever is going on. Briefly, our main intention is to reduce the apathy at present abundant in the school.

True to its word, it surveyed C.N.D., attacked the Labour Party for having lost its radical edge and investigated the 1960 U.S. Presidential election. There were articles discussing jazz and the origins of the universe. A 'Gamut poll' of school opinion demonstrated that the change most desired by pupils was the installation of a juke box in the Tuck Shop.

By contrast, *The Pelican* was a very staid publication, devoting its columns to recounting day-to-day happenings within the school. That said, it was a campaigning broadsheet, setting up a tennis tournament and an inter-House table tennis competition. The single great issue it ran with was the introduction of ballroom dancing lessons. First the editors built up a head of steam for the cause. Then they put the proposition to the Headmaster and, when he rejected it, *The Pelican* lobbied successfully for his veto to be rescinded. Such was Brighton College radicalism in the era of the coffee bar, the Lambretta and Teddyboys.

Stuart-Clark had encouraged his pupils to interest themselves in current affairs. Stewart did not, which may explain the Librarian's statement in 1956 that daily

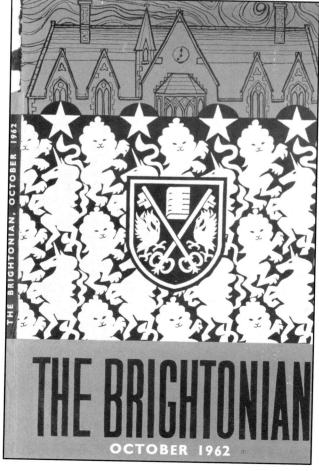

One of a number of imaginative magazine covers produced under the influence of Gordon Taylor

Salad Days, 1954 (the leading man was played by John Warner, 1937-40). The College revived this classic '50s musical in 1990

newspapers were 'not desirable'. In reaction against the 1930s, commitment of any kind was considered dubious in '50s Britain, the era of *Lucky Jim* and the pursuit of mediocrity. The Debating Society wasted its time on frivolities. If the country at large took minimal interest in the end of the Empire, silence on Mau-Mau or Suez is understandable. Occasionally, the Cold War did register, but talks on 'Life in East Berlin' (1959) and 'Red China' (1960) were exercises in propaganda, not discussions of world affairs. In 1961, some VIth Formers attended a debate between Canon Keeling and Vanessa Redgrave on nuclear disarmament. But that was the exception. Even allowing for the absence in Britain of U.S.-style Cold War paranoia, the view from Brighton College, contrasting the '50s with the '30s, was very circumscribed.

*   *   *

Superficially, Britain in the 1950s represented a high tide of continuity. Within the public schools, glorious summers of cricket and schoolboys wearing boaters spun the deceptive impression of a serene stability. For boys as well as masters, these could be capital days. 'A' levels were often taken early, leaving the final year to be filled with acting, rugby and being a school prefect. 'My last year was so valuable', writes Gordon Smith (Head of School, 1951-2). 'I learned an enormous amount about man-management and administration. I was over nineteen when I left, and that was by no means unusual.' With far less exam pressure, the pace of school life was as slow as it had been in 1870 or 1920. Whole days off for shooting or cricket caused no anxieties.

But these years have been invested with a certainty they never possessed. At Speech Day 1962, the Headmaster 'concluded by pointing out that young people are more complicated than they used to be, chiefly because their society is in a state of moral upheaval'. In his farewell letter to parents (July 1963), Stewart reflected bitterly, 'We must accept the fact that the prevailing cynicism, materialism, insecurity, early maturity and commercial exploitation have created many new problems for the adolescent'. Some housemasters had, Canute-like, attempted to keep the world outside College walls. But the agents of change were films, television and rock music which together fed into an unprecedented cultural and intellectual exchange. Wartime dreams of liberation and reconstruction, dashed by post-war austerity, were finally released by economic growth and a thaw in the Cold War. A mixture of hope deferred and pent-up frustration, the bubbling mix spread everywhere. Progress was no longer taken for granted. Inherited assumptions were questioned. 'The Establishment' (a phrase coined in 1955) was put under scrutiny.

The Dining Hall, 1955

At the same time, masters coming back from the war had brought to the public schools an openness never possible in the days when, man and boy, they knew of no other world. Men like Peter Gough, Geoff Lees and Gordon Taylor set out to make the boys think. Their impact, on Brighton and every other public school, cannot be overstated. In the words of Mark Andrews (1957-62, governor 1991-94),

> here was a breath of fresh air in an era which was still largely dominated by sport and fairly meaningless ritual. Some of the petty rules and regulations of the time remind me very much of the opening chapters of *Gormenghast!*

Before long, younger masters, themselves influenced by such men, reinforced the bridgehead (Nigel Jacques, 1958-61; Tim Pearce, 1961-62, 64-72).

The world was indeed changing, but what worried people was not change itself so much as the speed and scale of change. At a specially summoned assembly in November 1960, the Headmaster warned of the corruption inherent in the novel by D.H. Lawrence which Penguin was about to publish. 'Sewers are very necessary, but you don't want them in the drawing room', he told the school. No boy must purchase a copy of *Lady Chatterley*, which of course many, hitherto ignorant of Lawrence and (despite a sensational trial) unaware of the book, instantly proceeded to do—and then found the forbidden fruit distinctly disappointing.

Stewart's 1962 Speech Day remarks are the authentic voice of a generation alarmed by 'the new morality':

> Failure alone will result if we do not impose a code of absolute truths.

The Tuck Shop, 1956 (now part of the Art School)

In 1962, two school prefects were demoted—the first time any had been removed since 1939. On 16 May 1961, Stewart called an assembly described in some detail in the diary kept by Maurice Root-Reed (1958-61):

> The Duke then talked about the bounce in the school and the general apathy—especially the attitude in Chapel yesterday. He threatened to have a four day half holiday [sic] and he said he wished somebody could tell him what the matter was. I can—No Sunday leave, (town leave).

Over the following days, groups of boys responded to the appeal and, two weeks later, Stewart called separate assemblies for the dayboys and the boarders. Root-Reed's diary takes up the story thus:

> The dayboys came out and told us they have only to come to 4 [Sunday] mattins per term, instead of the whole term. After a long preamble ... he got down to business and said 1) Bicycles for boarders next term 2) 6 Sunday social leave outs.

This was not 1972 or 1969, but 1961. Five years on from the premier of *Look Back in Anger*, more than a few (in the nation as well as in the College) were becoming conscious of the need for change, and the undertow from the past which held them back. Back in 1951, strictly enforced bounds and town leave of 1.5 hours per week were acceptable. Ten years later, the same restrictive framework was not. 'Headmastering had been such fun in the '50s', Stewart wistfully admitted many years later. Critical opinion was being voiced in the magazine from 1956. Burstow tells us that *Gamut* was 'permitted in response to rebellious comment in *The Brightonian*'. A letter in *The Pelican* (10/vi/1955) talked of the corps as 'something so widely disliked'. Without doubt, the CCF was the most hated part of the College life, just as it had been in the 1920s. *The Brightonian* carried detail of an opinion poll carried out in Christmas Term 1957 showing that, whereas only 6 per cent would not go to Chapel if services became voluntary, two-thirds would not join the corps if they had the choice.

That poll is instructive. Complaints about fagging or the power of prefects to beat or cold dormitories–the staples of modern critiques of the public schools in all times past–barely register as concerns. Neither did Chapel or hair, the great issues still to rise. While the Headmaster worried about the need for heating in the dormitories and the provision of more studies, his pupils' restlessness began with the desire to get out of school–does that explain the popularity of sailing, golf and riding?

Bullying and beatings, inexorable rugby and the dread of being late were all likely to fill life in the IIIrd and IVth with too many moments of very hell. Burstow states that the food was 'very monotonous'. The key problem was the lack of a heated trolley for moving food to the boarding houses. The Inspectors in 1961 reported that the tomato on fried bread served for breakfast in Bristol was 'stone cold, congealed to the plate'. The restaurateur Neville Abraham (1950-55) remembers 'meat which sat in grease. Rarely did the meat have any meat on it'. The need to accept the lowest

A dormitory in Durnford, 1956

(*above*) In the College kitchens, 1955

tender (from the local butcher) explains much.

A substantial number understand precisely the description by Peter Mayle (1953-56) of his College days as 'a great period of terror'. On the other hand, a substantial number enjoyed themselves and cannot recognise the brutal and petty school he describes. The same is true everywhere. In some ways Brighton College lagged behind. Personal fagging had been abolished at Marlborough in 1938. Prefects at Cheltenham lost the power to beat in 1942. Boarding houses at Lancing had TV sets from 1948. On the other hand, Brighton boys suffered none of the almost numberless and pettifogging customs and privileges by which Malvern boys maintained hierarchy among themselves.

(*left*) 'The Corn Huskers', 1951

BRIGHTON COLLEGE

1963

Stewart was no slave of tradition. Neither was he unbending. His abolition in 1957 of the prefectorial privilege allowing them to smoke in their studies was deeply unpopular. So too had been his forbidding in 1950 of fags being sent shopping into 'the village'—a school term for the local shops. In contrast to later régimes, he was quite happy with unsupervised fireworks and snowballing on the Home Ground. VIth Form boarders were permitted from 1955 to miss House roll and allowed not to go to bed until 10.15pm. From 1959, dayboys were allowed to come to school by scooter. *The Brightonian* not infrequently carried criticisms of the school. And, as we have seen, the reforms of 1961 were guided by pupil advice.

The most urgent problem never addressed was an overly competitive House system which, as *The Brightonian* of September 1963 explained, 'at the moment tends to deeply divide the school into seven small, isolated groups'. Stewart was not unaware of the problem, and several times suggestions from the Houses for their own ties and colours were vetoed. But he took no steps to cut House pretentions down to size. Alf Lester's description of his tenure in Bristol illustrates what was wrong: 'I separated my boys from all the rest and kept them apart. Only if their entire world revolved around the House would they live and fight for it'. Richard Buxton (1950-56) was his Head of House and explains just how perverse the consequences could be:

> The grip of the House system, and the insistence that everyone of whatever age or inclination should participate in it, ensured that one hardly saw anyone else out of class. A man came up to my Oxford college from Brighton in the year after me, on the Arts side moreover, to whom I spoke for the first time in my life when I met him in Hall on his first evening in Oxford—and that from a school of less than 350 boys!

Stewart's failure here lays bare his fundamental shortcoming. As Peter Gough observes, 'Stewart had no awareness of the need for change. He accepted new ideas. He even welcomed them. But rarely did he generate them'. The reforms of Stewart's

'I had taken in an pair of plastic specatacles with false nose attached. Norman Frith, a young man with a sense of humour so unlike many of his colleagues who ruled by fear alone, donned them for the cameraman' (John Miles, 1949-52).

era were engendered by a group of Housemasters: John Page (1954-85), Norman Frith, Geoff Lees, Peter Gough and Dick Crossley-Holland (1950-82). The last named draws the contrast between 'the strong autocrat, which everyone took Stewart to be, and the Headmaster who in reality was manipulated by skilful work behind the scenes'. Parochialism rather than a lack of money hemmed in Brighton College during the 1950s. The staff were too few, and overworked. Both chairmen of the governors were old boys, while the Headmaster had spent his entire teaching career within the school. In fast-shifting sands, the inability to imagine that there could be an alternative, or that it might be possible to do even better proved a terrible handicap (suffered by virtually all the public schools). Stewart's regimen, outwardly so self-possessed and solid, masked a desperate need for certainty. Because reality was confusing, even incomprehensible, it bred a nostalgic emphasis on the formalism and cohesion of the past. The targets of the 'Angry Young Men' and of *Brideshead Revisited* were one and the same.

Twelve

1963 -1995

Songs of expectation

William Stewart bestrode his world, incapable of operating at less than full steam. A traditionalist to the core, he belonged absolutely to that school of English thought which favours character over intelligence. He was no theorist, no pioneer. As Stuart-Clark fell because he was inventive, so Stewart had been brought in to reassert the old. Yet his statement, 'I think we'll start a new tradition and let prefects walk across the grass' was typical of the man. He was responsible for the abolition of compulsory Latin and a curtailment of personal fagging. At Haileybury, he would later admit girls. The puzzle of the autocrat manoeuvred by his housemasters has already been noted. Norman Frith crystallised another apparent contradiction: 'You always felt he wanted to control everything but, once he had appointed you to a post, he left you completely to your own devices. While he was a good motivator, you knew he had only the haziest idea of what you were doing'. He was respected (and popular) with staff and boys alike. Most pupils were afraid of him, at least to begin with. His steely-blue eyes could flash with a disabling glare. Against the Lady Chatterley assembly must, however, be set the school prefects' dinner of 1952 when, Gordon Smith recalls, 'very polished in our prefectorial blue suits, he took us to a show at the Hippodrome after dinner, and laughed uproariously when one scene included tableaux of topless girls'. School approved of a Head who joined in their cricket and who knew their birthdays. For all the enigmas, Bill Stewart was a fine 'hands on' Headmaster. For all his brisk paternalism, his snobbery and his lack of a vision, he was open, direct and uncomplicated. And he put Brighton College back on the map as a school of some repute.

Within the classroom, the 1961 Inspectors judged him 'often too vigorous and overpowering; he almost bullies the boys along'. Outside, they could see that 'his leadership has taken the school a long

William Stewart

Henry Christie

way'. Others saw it too. He was elected Chairman of HMC's Eastern Division, chosen a member of the Common Entrance Board and of the Court of Sussex University. He was also ambitious, looking to move on and up, something only two of his predecessors had ever done. In 1958, he was invited to apply for the Headship of Stowe. He came close to several plums, in 1961 being runner-up for Repton, before being selected two years later as Master of Haileybury, where he died in 1975 playing soccer with the boys.

From an unknown number of applicants and a shortlist of four, Guy Willatt (later Headmaster of Pocklington) was beaten to the vacant headmastership by the 38-year-old Henry Christie, Under Master and Master of the Queen's Scholars at Westminster. His starting salary would be £2,500 per annum and he would earn every penny of it, for his reign coincided with the best of times, or the worst of times, depending on your point of view. They were certainly the liveliest of times.

The academic continued its inexorable drive to dominate life within the public schools. In the 1960s, that principally meant the rise in significance of 'A' levels. Even with the Robbins Report (1963) and the opening of its seven new universities in 1964-65, which increased the total number of places by 25 per cent, demand outstripped supply. The introduction of grades and the universities rapidly attached to them were not the only problem. Unless you were the Prince of Wales, two 'A' levels would no longer be sufficient for a university place. Brighton College academic standards had to advance, and they did. The 16 open Oxbridge awards won from 1966 to 1970, when set against this background, represent an even more substantial improvement on the 12 gained in 1961-65 than at first sight appears.

Whether standards were good and teaching was dynamic in the Lower School is uncertain (and the extraordinary failure to keep 'O' level records makes judgement almost impossible). Academic progress was certainly to be found throughout the VIth Form, which boasted a range of subjects impressive for so small a school. Economics, English and Politics were particularly well taught and popular too. By the margin, compulsory General Studies (1964) added further breadth, and deliberately cut 'free periods' by five. The results are clear. In 1968, some 57 per cent of public schoolboys leaving with 'A' levels went to university, as compared with 60 per cent from direct

The Masters, 1969

grant schools and 46 per cent from maintained grammar schools. Brighton College beat them all, with 61 per cent.

'A' levels and university entrance

	total pupils in College	successful candidates	total passes	boys taking 3 at one sitting	university entrants
1962	379	61	135	19 (31%)	21 (34%)
1964	387	70	138	24 (34%)	24 (34%)
1966	371	73	165	34 (46.6%)	30 (41%)
1968	369	75	164	37 (49%)	46 (61%)

Since the war, College pupils going to university had almost all been steered to Oxbridge or London, or nowhere. Rodney Fox (1955-60, staff 1968-88) remembers 'the powerful snobbery [among parents as much as masters] dismissing anywhere not Oxbridge ... Other universities were scarcely mentioned. Even to get advice about what other universities existed was quite difficult'. That changed. By 1970, OBs had gone to most 'red bricks', all of the new Robbins universities bar York (Warwick was the favourite), and seven of the eight colleges of advanced technology turned into universities (Bath was the exception, Loughborough the most popular). In five years, these new institutions were taking 23 per cent of university entrants from the College— the same proportion as Oxbridge.

Some of the Masters, 1969 (*The Brightonian*'s view)

The rise in the roll which had so characterised the latter 1950s peaked at 384 boys in April 1961. Across the next 10 years, the College shrank by 12 per cent:

Numbers in College (September)

	dayboys	VIth Form	total
1963	170 (45%)	157 (41.5%)	378
1964	177 (47%)	155 (41%)	378
1965	178 (48%)	158 (43%)	371
1966	187 (50%)	173 (46%)	373
1967	178 (49%)	172 (47%)	363
1968	175 (50%)	148 (42%)	353
1969	165 (49%)	114 (34%)	335
1970	187 (54%)	112 (32%)	345
1971	193 (57%)	105 (31%)	338

What was going on? The figures show three salient points. First, numbers were slipping even in Stewart's latter days. Second, dayboy demand remained so solid that their numbers rose marginally. Third, the decline was entirely confined to the boarding houses. Boarding numbers fell some 30 per cent. Taken together, these facts disprove the received wisdom that, as one master of the era alleges, 'the place was falling apart under a weak Headmaster who could not cope with rebellious schoolboys. Our reputation sank as a consequence and prospective parents voted with their feet'. Had that been true, demand for dayboy places would have slumped even faster than for boarding. Instead, cultivation of the prep schools led to the College exploiting the post-war adoption of the private car to draw dayboys, for the very first time, from the Sussex hinterlands. At the same time, Christie's introduction of a Jewish Religious Instruction class in 1964 served to strengthen the College's local appeal. In consequence, the dayboys became the majority of the College, by accident. Christie was more comfortable with a 50:50 situation than Stewart, but he never advocated a dayboy majority.

Tickets are now available

for

BRIGHTON COLLEGE
Son et Lumière

an adaptation of the history of the College for voices and lighting effects.

The part of the Chairman of the Council through the years will be spoken by

MICHAEL HORDERN (O.B.)

The Headmaster, The Chaplain, Mr. William Stewart, Mr. Peter Gough, and others, including Tom Smart, will also take part.

The script is by
Mr. GORDON SMITH, assisted by Mr. BURSTOW

Performances are on . . .
Friday, 21st July, until **Tuesday, 25th July**
. . . at 9.45 p.m.

The performances on Friday and Saturday (Speech Day) are reserved for Parents and Old Boys.

Please apply for tickets, at **10/- each,** to
N. J. FRITH, The College, Brighton 7.

Son et Lumière, written and produced by Gordon Smith, 1967

Pupil admissions: catchment areas (i)

	1967-70	1947-50
Brighton & Hove	140 (41%)	119 (37%)
rest of Sussex	117 (34%)	73 (23%)
rest of S.E.	49 (14%)	96 (30%)
total admissions	344	320
total day admissions	179	155

The first peak of the post-war baby boom reached their 13th birthdays between 1956 and 1962. Brighton College was bound to be affected. The disparity between day and boarding numbers shows, however, that something else was at work. While the College was well placed to exploit the on-going expansion of greater Brighton and commuter-orientated mid-Sussex, and thus increase dayboy numbers against a shrinking total market, it fell victim to the first signs of a middle-class rejection of boarding as, *de rigueur*, the right form of education for their sons.

This began to manifest itself surreptitiously. Christie took over at the absolute peak of Brighton College's post-war boarding strength: 208 in September 1963. Five years later, there were 185, a drop of 11 per cent. Another five years on, there were only 145, and most of that 22 per cent fall occurred during 1970 and 1971. The sole remaining out-boarding house (Durnford) was sold, re-opening in September 1971 within the College full of dayboys.

In an adverse climate, the College's ever-narrowing geographical base could only count against boarding. Before 1900, between 50 per cent and 60 per cent of pupils came from homes outside Sussex. At the height of the Dawson bonanza, that proportion was 67.5 per cent. In the last years of the 1960s, however, only 25 per cent of the school was being drawn from beyond the home county:

Pupil admissions: catchment areas (ii)

	1967-70		1947-50	
rest of S.E.	49	(14%)	96	(30%)
rest of England	6	(2%)	8	(2.5%)
rest of UK	1		2	
continental Europe	5		3	
Commonwealth	14	(4%)	12	(4%)
rest of world	12	(3.5%)	7	(2%)
total admissions	344		320	
total boarding admissions	165		165	
total non-Sussex admissions	87	(25%)	128	(40%)

Price had little to do with it. Boarding fees rose less steeply than day fees (was that deliberate?), and by significantly less than during the previous equivalent period:

Annual College fees

	1963	1971	% increase	1953	1961	% increase
dayboy	£271	£411	52%	£138	£234	70%
boarder	£429	£627	46%	£242	£414	71%

During those same years, net middle-class taxation fell because of the massive reduction in surtax in 1961 and, although price as well as income controls were abandoned (1969), real incomes surged ahead. Perceived prosperity was strong.

Few today recognise any College buildings as having been put up during the 1960s. This is not simply the consequence of their insipid architecture which makes them indistinguishable from the aweless works of the 1970s also designed by John Daviel. These buildings occupy secluded sites and, deprived of advantageous vistas, their externals are rarely noticed. Chronologically first was the new School House,

(*above left*) "Tin Pan Alley' after the fire, June 1965

(*left*) Norman Frith (Housemaster of School) inside the burnt-out shell. He had slept through the fire, while his House Tutor had problems calling the fire brigade (repeatedly dialling 000)

(*above*) School House, the architect's vision, 1965

built in 1966-67 on the site of the old study block known as 'Tin Pan Alley', burnt out in the fire of June 1965. Next came two small adjuncts to the Dining Hall (1969), a block of studies attached to Chichester and the refurbishment of Bristol (1970), and finally the Woolton Block of classrooms, lecture theatre and squash court (1971-72).

The new School House cost £62,562. Under insurance meant that the school had to find all but £10,170 of that sum. Arnold Bartlett (1925-28, College Treasurer 1957-67), Aldrich's partner both as a solicitor and in the running of the College, covered that shortfall by a new loan of £70,000 at 8.5 per cent from the Royal. The works of 1969-70 cost some £68,500, the Woolton Quad £95,500 on top of the £20,000 needed to buy the site (which, like Small Field and Cooper's Land, the inaugural Council had been unable to secure). At the same time, four houses (in Walpole Road and Clarendon Place) were bought, as were two schools in 1971. These last were a Sussex prep school (Hawkhurst Court, costing £35,000 plus £11,500 on improvements)

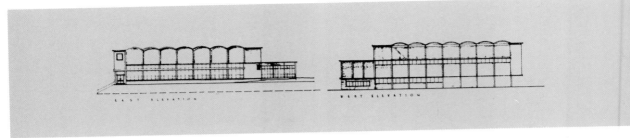

Proposed Dining Hall on the Home Ground, 1964 (it would have occupied the site where the Sports Hall now stands. Designed by Clayton, Black and Daviel, this is *far* better architecture than anything they actually built for us).

and a Brighton pre-prep (Kingscliffe, at £10,500). To complete this impressive catalogue, the Junior School was rehoused in the former Convent of the Blessed Sacrament (which cost £100,000).

Against a falling roll, the Council thus laid out £408,141 between 1966 and 1972. Ever poor, the College's finances were, however, nothing like the web of shreds of the 1890s. Insurance, a loan from the College scholarship trustees (at 8 per cent), the sale of Durnford, an appeal and the opportune compulsory purchase of the old Junior School (for road widening which never occurred) together brought in 73 per cent of that sum. The additional loan from the Royal brought it up to 90 per cent, leaving £40,971 to be found over seven years. Stringent economies were made. For the first time, classrooms were let during the holidays. Rents charged to the masters in school accommodation were raised. So too, of course, were the fees.

The Woolton Quad, first design, 1969

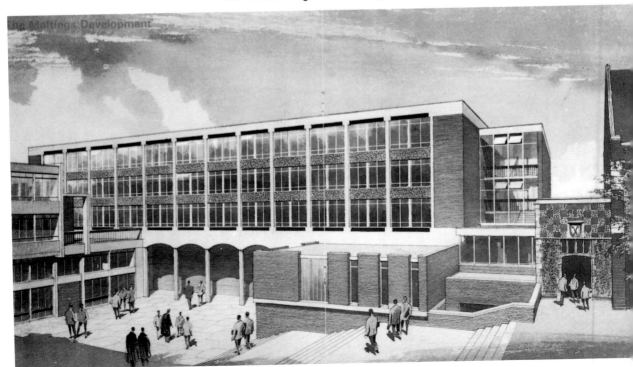

School House JCR, 1968

The job was not made any easier by the universal and simultaneous increase in costs. Bank rate from 1966 was never less than 6 per cent, and by the end of 1967 stood at 8 per cent. When Selective Employment Tax was introduced (1966), that alone created an additional burden of £7,200 per annum. The balancing act required (and sustained) bears testimony to the skills of Harold Elliott and Ronny Pickering, supplemented by Harold Myerscough who joined the Council in 1965 at the Head-master's suggestion. Recently retired as Brighton manager of the District Bank (and thus as the College's banker), he changed sides to fill the critical post of Treasurer from 1967 to 1978. He it was also who gingered up the ailing appeal, by bypassing what he termed 'those apathetic old boys' to bring in a total of £94,000, mostly from the parents of current pupils. But it was not enough. Inflation had pushed building costs up by 15 per cent. The professional fundraisers initially employed had used up £12,000 in costs and fees. So the original scheme for the Woolton Quad had to be scaled down and ideas for a Sports Hall on the Home Ground postponed. Was it cost or old-fashioned thinking which put into the new School House facilities of the most basic kind? Martin Smith (1967-72) gives us a picture of B dorm on the top floor:

It was a dismal place. The only heating was a hot water pipe running around the edge of the room, the floor consisted of cold tiles and there were no curtains to cover the dozen or so large windows. It was bare, spartan, and very cold in winter.

*   *   *

Bill Peters (right), Jack Hindmarsh (left) and the Choir sing 'The Epilogue' for Southern TV, 1965

A rehearsal for the Television Broadcast in St Peter's Church, Brighton, 1964

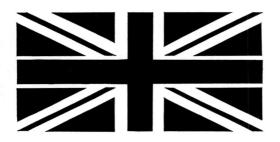

Published in conjunction with Arts Festival Week, 1965

The winning entries in a Notice Design Competition by Miles Hutchins (top) and N.J. Rumley Dawson (bottom), 1964

These years were distinguished by the rise and rise of the cultural within College life. To the creative energies of Peter Gough and Tim Pearce must primarily be added those of Jack Hindmarsh (Director of Music 1962-66). These three were the true apostles, and the renaissance they fostered cannot be exaggerated, in scope or in significance. Three times during 1964 Brighton College singers were to be seen on Southern Television. The Choral Society, in regular collaboration with St Mary's Hall and Roedean, delighted and impressed audiences with a rich feast: Britten's *St Nicolas*, Vivaldi's *Gloria*, Rossini's *Petite Messe Solonelle*. Hitherto, College music had always meant song. No longer. Supported stoutly by the Headmaster (who himself played the clarinet), Hindmarsh so promoted instrumental music that by 1967 the school possessed its very first true, all-pupil orchestra. Alas it did not last; by 1971, there were but six pupil members of the college orchestra. Stronger proofs are to be found in the explosion of House-based and pupil-organised culture. In 1965, Aldrich set things moving with a concert whose programme ranged from Bach to Kabalevsky. Hampden began musical evenings. Bristol gave play readings of Camus (1965) and Ionesco (1966). Chichester staged Arthur Miller (1969) and Harold Pinter (1970); Hampden followed with Max Frisch in 1971. Pupil journalism maintained its sporadic but intensive enthusiasms. *Wallpaper*

Poster for Arts Week, 1968

returned in 1967. Four Houses were producing magazines in 1968. Some boys were making films, and that same year saw three distinct film societies—one to watch 'ordinary' films, one to watch and discuss 'art' films and one to produce films.

It's All Life Really, an arts magazine, appeared in 1965. A group of musicians formed their own wind quartet, the Duholenspiegel Concertante. Other pupils (and staff) combined in 1970 and 1971 to give lunchtime recitals, drawing audiences of around fifty to each. Overarching this vibrancy was the Arts Festival, a week of 'music, art, film and literary activities' first organised in 1965 and the brainchild of Gavin Henderson (1961-65), later to be Artistic Director of the Brighton Festival. Subsequently called Arts Week, this gala produced by VIth Formers ran for five years. The proposal made in *The Brightonian* editorial of May 1964 for 'one afternoon a week of enforced artistic activity' might not have been acted upon, but talent, confidence and ambition abounded.

*   *   *

Brighton College is in an extraordinary state. Revolution has set in. It may in the long run produce something all right, but it is well away from anything we have had before ... It is purely rebellious and very unpleasant. The teacher's bluff has been called and he has been shown to have feet of clay ... Something will happen soon. I feel the rumbling of an explosion and I should not be surprised to find Christie engulfed.

Thus Philip Burstow wrote in his journal on 23 February 1969. Analysis of the College during the 'sickly sixties' inevitably involves judgement on Henry Christie. Opinion is divided, now as then. Burstow's depressed outpouring gives us the thinking of the old guard, whose confidant he was. The College was falling apart. Morale could not have been lower. Nemesis loomed. Others saw a very different Brighton College. One VIth Former wrote in November 1969,

Revolution is underway. Pharoah's army will be swamped. The old order cannot last. We think for ourselves now. Brighton College is coming to life. Bliss is it in this dawn to be alive. To be young is bloody marvellous.

Some on the staff agreed (and would have been impressed by his reference to *Exodus* and to the apposite adaptation of Wordsworth).

Not quite the Beatles, 1966

If we are to understand what was going on, it is essential to set the years 1968-71 within a wider framework, remembering that challenge to authority and received values which had been building, slowly at first, from the mid-1950s. Stewart had faced awkward College boys, and was not at all certain how to respond. Western society was in flux. For the first time since being written, Tennyson's couplet, 'Theirs not to reason why, Theirs but to do or die', was thought an attitude more stupid than praiseworthy. The Victorian age was finally being snuffed out.

Remember too that because for so long so few masters had had experience of other schools, Brighton College in 1963 was among the most traditionalist of public schools. Games for VIth Formers had been voluntary at Stowe from its inception in 1923, and Marlborough made cricket optional in the 1930s. Cheltenham abolished the right of prefects to beat in 1942. If there were to be explosions, Brighton College was thus a more likely site than many. On the other hand, the College's urban setting reduced very substantially pupil frustrations. They could (and did) escape to local cafes and pubs. Contrary to the official view of the time, Kemp Town saved Brighton College when the troubles came. It is no accident that the public schools most disturbed were rural or small town boarding schools.

What actually happened? One thing cannot be disputed. Christie surrendered none of the totems of the public school world, then so much under attack: the corps, the chapel and cricket. None was abolished. None became voluntary, unlike say Cheltenham, where CCF and weekday chapel both became discretionary. The regular corporate life of the school continued unbroken. Formal Speech Day was retained, as was the wearing of gowns by masters and prefects. School prefects continued to beat (a power ended at Marlborough in 1965). The Council rejected a Junior School proposal that the staff should elect one of their number to be a governor. Contrary to many an assertion, Christie never sold the pass.

His *Times* obituary described him as 'neither a hasty innovator nor a strict traditionalist'. According to *The Daily Telegraph*, 'he was firm, but not inflexible'. Both give the measure of Henry Christie, but leave unresolved a mystery. By conviction a pragmatist and adept at calming the infuriated, was he at heart a conservative or a liberal? That those who knew him so well can disagree on something so fundamental says much about this urbane English gentleman. In his politics, he was never a party man, sitting as an Independent on Eton District Council and preferring to vote for a good candidate, regardless of label. Thus he supported Fenner Brockway while a young master at Eton and, impressed by Dennis Hobden, voted Labour in the 1966 general election; wags in 1964 had noted that Hobden's majority of seven equalled the Headmaster's household. Pragmatism guided by intelligence and experience was Christie's greatest virtue–but, to those who felt he would not march toward the sound of gunfire, his fatal weak point.

As a reformer, Christie was a gradualist. Coming from Trinity Cambridge and two of the great schools, his view was broader than most of his senior staff. With Peter Gough and then Peter Points (1963-69) as his Second Masters, however, such a view could be sustained. Caricatured by one master as 'the sphinx running first with a leopard, then a fox', they made first-rate teams. The capacity to see beyond the village pump would never be more vital than in the 1960s. This was seen first in little things of profound significance, given the temper of the age. Stewart had left Brighton College in what was now seen as a strait-jacket and the astute way to manage the years 1963-67 was to take it off.

In Christie's first term, Stewart's veto on elastic-sided shoes or boots was scrapped. 'Cleanliness and tidiness of dress is just as important–if not more so–as the style', Christie told the Housemasters: 'Polished Chelsea boots are, to my mind, vastly preferable to scuffed and grubby conventional lace-up shoes.' College boys were still to be smart. The old ban on winkle-pickers remained. But latitude was not the tune College Housemasters were used to. The second alteration to uniform was the removal of the boater, which became optional for VIth Formers in 1966 and was done away with completely three years later. This was hardly aggressive radicalism. Malvern got rid of its mortar boards in 1965, Cheltenham its boaters in 1966. But it removed a real grievance, and served a practical need too. As Martin

In the early days of the Voluntary Service Unit, *c.*1972

Smith found out, the boater 'was such a badge of privilege that it was a red rag to the local yobbery, who would jeer and hoot (and on one occasion, gave chase—but with games three times a week, we outpaced them)'. The abolition of the boater had taken 30 years. That tells us something essential about Brighton College.

Genuinely amazed by a regimen so restrictive of boys' leisure time, Christie loosened leave-outs. He extended Stewart's concession on boarders' exeats to every Sunday after chapel. He permitted boarders access to the village between 8.30am and 5.30pm, when not involved in a school activity. With the same proviso, the Upper Sixth were allowed into 'any part of Brighton' between 7.45am and 5.30pm. What most in Brighton thought to be a drastic relaxation of discipline, Henry Christie had known as normal all his school life. The ways of Eton and Westminster were very different, and in the 1960s Brighton College badly needed their more relaxed and gentlemanly approach (it is not irrelevant here to note also that his new staff could not believe that their new Headmaster had never once played cricket). These chapters have chronicled the erosion of a liberty for pupils the high Victorians judged essential to make the man. By the age of angry young men, those restraints were at their most extensive. The two cannot be coincidental.

Symbols are more important than the 20th century usually accepts. More redolent even than boaters was fagging and its associate, the position and power of prefects. Brighton College had, of course, been founded with specific bans on fagging and corporal punishment (by masters, let alone boys), and without prefects. 'Fagging is not allowed in any form here', the Secretary wrote to a prospective parent in 1850 and the scant surviving references indicate that, while general fagging existed from the 1870s, personal fagging seems to have arrived with Dawson (the same is probably true of prefectorial power to beat). The fundamental which Housemasters thus worked themselves up about was at most two generations old. In the tradition of College housemastering, which evolved in the 'out-houses' under Dawson and ended with the centralising reign of Bill Blackshaw, Houses were self-governing dominions. That was a pattern Christie himself took for granted from Eton and Westminster. Housemasters and Headmaster were thus in harmony. But whereas Brighton College Housemasters knew only the operation of a common system, with peripheral variations, their Headmaster knew of a world in which Housemasters created houses of considerable individuality. Thus when John Rolland (1955-65) drastically cut back personal fagging in Chichester in 1964, and his successor John Page removed all that remained (took away his Head of House's cane and very soon superannuated his own), there were grumbles from the other boarding Housemasters who had no intention of following suit.

A similar dichotomy existed in the day Houses where Aldrich alone operated personal fagging. Its Housemaster, Gordon Smith explains:

> I had been given a House in 1963 and over the next four years I felt myself becoming more and more out of step with what was going on. I had always been a traditionalist, and I could not shake off Lester's upbringing [Smith had been Head of Bristol], so that Aldrich and its Housemaster became known as the awkward House ... It seemed to me that my colleagues had got it wrong, in that personal fagging provided so many benefits while community fagging was the responsibility of all members of the community and not just the youngest.

Tension was building between the Housemasters and between some Housemasters and the Headmaster. The Housemasters who wanted the errant brought back into line interpreted Christie's big school style of headmastering (which would not dream of interfering with the professional judgement of his Housemasters) as a failure of leadership and as proof of weakness.

Needless to say, they would have been the first to complain had Christie exercised the small school style and clipped their wings. More to the point, Christie's policy of unity without uniformity, permitting initiative to reform-minded Housemasters like John Page, Peter Points and Fred Hankins (1964-82), was the only ethos which could have kept Brighton College on a reasonably even keel in 1968-71. These dissensions were, however, to play a significant rôle in shaping attitudes and postures when 'the troubles' began in 1968-69. The pupils could not present a united front, but neither could the staff. Norman Frith later referred with distaste to those years as 'the days of the *sans culottes*' (note this second reference to the French Revolution). Chichester's 'House Notes' of April 1969 declare, 'It has been a somewhat restless term in which Chapel and Hair seem to have featured too prominently'. Boys were starting to remain silent in chapel and, a Chichester speciality, stand outside until the very last moment. They began walking out of the meals, in protest at poor food. Boarders spread across the Kemp Town pubs on Saturday (and other) evenings. Hair grew longer. Rules were questioned and boys began not merely to demand 'Why?', but to say 'No!'. Behaviour deteriorated; some was exceedingly bad.

Everything was changed by perceptions of the summer of 1968. Bewildered and feeling beleaguered, schoolmasters saw campus unrest from Berkeley to Berlin and presumed their difficult pupils to be revolutionary students. Some of the schoolboys

Part of a Sussex University demo, staged to coincide with the CCF Inspection, 1970

'For the times they are a-changing'; Chichester House on the building site of the new study block, 1970

dreamt that they were, but there the connections end. Particular analogy was made with the street-battles of Paris and the fall of de Gaulle. This was nonsense. The joy of a revolutionary moment does not make for a revolution. Chichester House was not the Sorbonne. Schoolboy rebellion was parochial and non-political. At Brighton College there were no walk-outs from chapel. There was no bonfire of textbooks, as at Sherborne. The cricket square was not painted white, as at Dulwich. 'White Boot', the anti-CCF protest of 4 May 1970 was spontaneous and involved no more than three-quarters of the cadets turning up for parade minus *one* item of uniform. When six boys were suspended, nobody organised a sit-in (which would have been the crucial fracture). English public schoolboys had not read Trotsky, had never heard of Marcuse or the liberating function of negation.

Burstow and the unknown VIth Former quoted at the start of this section would not have used the word 'revolution' before mid-1968. Both had failed to spot those quieter revolutions which started with wartime anxieties, with John Osborne in 1956 and with the Beatles in 1963. As Peter Points observes, 'the gradual swell in dayboy ranks meant that housemasters were less able to keep the school ring fenced'. And the

College dayboy was much more sophisticated than the country-based boarder. The word did not exist then, but they were 'streetwise'.

If there was a catalyst, it came not from Paris but Massachusetts. Into a well-prepared seed bed came Patrick Lydon, the E.S.U. exchange scholar for 1968-69. American schools had experienced pupil troubles several years ahead of England. College boys did not need a Lydon to see the way things were going, but he was very articulate, even messianic. Finding a ready audience, first in Chichester and then the whole school, he informed Brighton College pupils that 'there are 300 of us, and only 30 of them. There is nothing they can do'. Dining Hall walk-outs were the prime result. In an effective variation, which made *The Evening Argus*, Bristol staged a hunger strike on 4 March 1971, attending meals but refusing to eat.

Faces became longer and longer. There was an air of expectancy on both sides. Burstow tells us that the Housemasters of School, Bristol and Durnford saw them-selves as 'the only island in an ocean of chaos'. That sense of isolation, and fear, reveals a dimension critical to any understanding of the forces of conservatism within Brighton College during these mercurial days. After listing 'far too many good men' who had moved to other appointments (in fact, only three or four), Burstow went on to lament that 'all those who would have helped a strong H.M. have gone, and there are very few men of any calibre left'. The weakness pinpointed by the keepers of the flame was thus the majority of their colleagues (especially the other Housemasters), but this analysis will not do for it suggests there were two distinct camps. That there were not is well illustrated by Norman Frith, titular leader of what one young master termed 'the patriarchs'. As Housemaster of School, he allowed the VIth Form to drink beer or cider with Sunday lunch, he legalised VIth Form smoking (1971) by setting aside one room within the House for that purpose, and he even allowed personal fagging to virtually die out. 'Sixth Formers have to be treated more like undergraduates' was one of the last suggestions Stewart made to the Council.

Here is another clue. Agitation was not confined to the VIth Form and by 1970 was rooted elsewhere. 'White Boot' is described as 'a movement of fifteen and sixteen year olds'. In *The Brightonian* of April 1970, Christopher Terleski (Head of School 1970-71) noted that 'the Lower Sixth is pink about the edges ... [while] the juniors are positively radical'. Latitude with VIth Formers was one thing. Hierarchy is always prepared to grant privileges, to the few. But change must never be asked for, novelty must be understated and the implications for change inherent in any decision must not be exploited. The Lower School had to be kept in check. So too must young masters who allowed boys in class to sit on desks and windowsills, who

Fred Hankins

drank in pubs with VIth Formers and who openly sympathised with pupil grievances. Discipline was at stake. So too was the hierarchy. The whole school could unravel.

In an atmosphere of illusion, everyone became too intense. Masters and boys lost their sense of proportion. Peter Points contends that, above all, 'both sides lacked a sense of humour'. Had Burstow been writing a little later, he would surely have had Fred Hankins in his sights. Appointed Housemaster of Hampden in September 1969, Fred launched what he himself terms 'a Day House experiment ... an attempt to meet new needs whilst enabling the House to sustain its position within the College system'. Beating and fagging were already gone. Now, house prefects were done away with and replaced by the entire Upper VIth, who were held responsible for supervising the House. Drill was abolished, and replaced with house punishments which were 'socially useful'. In inter-House competitions, Hampden VIth Form participation became voluntary. And, to the disbelief of all, they won the Senior Cross Country in 1972.

Many thought him mad, and the rest knew the tremendous risk he was taking. But this was not playing with tokens. An enterprising Housemaster was setting out to tackle what he saw as that 'huge gap between official school policy and what happened in practice, with Housemasters in many instances turning a blind eye'. Boys were to be challenged to take the individualism they so trumpeted and put it to use. Fred was tackling head on the self-centredness and laziness which accompanied rampant individualism. He might be redefining the community, but he was insisting on a sense of responsibility and duty. It met school needs as well as pupil complaints. That was statecraft.

In the late afternoon when dayboys were still required to be at school after games, but there was no adequate activity programme, heels were kicked and resentment festered. In Hampden, that time was put to use. The old boxing ring was cut up to help divide the senior common room into four studies. An obstacle course was built for a local school for handicapped children; one boy persuaded the police to donate an old police car. Fred explains 'I did a deal with my Upper VI ... Provided they did something sensible, I let them go after games on one day, with their contribution being ensured on the other ... My Upper VI liked this: it was fair, and open'.

Launched at the very moment when housemasters began to confess doubts about their ability to motivate the boys, and when pupils were at their least willing to assume responsibilities, the Hampden initiative showed there was a way forward. From that soil came their pupil-produced production of *The Fire Raisers* (1971) and the first of those prodigious annual pupil-organised galas dubbed 'Hampden at Home' (1973). All schools were overtaken by events. All were out of their depth. But those who floated were the ones who could see that the world had changed. Because Brighton town could not be kept at arm's length from its College; because the law had turned VIth Formers into adults who could marry and vote; because they enjoyed an independence which came from money in their pockets and a mobility from borrowing mum's car, senior boys had to be treated differently.

If what I have termed Christie's 'big school' approach worked better in 1964 than 1969, that was a reflection on the times, not the man. With his staff he should perhaps have been stricter. The nude bathing parties organised by one housemaster were a liberty too far. But he sacked two masters and in 1966 had the courage as well as foresight to pick Peter Points, the newest and youngest Housemaster, to be Second Master when John Page turned the job down. As for the boys, he expelled eleven,

Peter Points

CCF farewell to Henry Christie, *The Brightonian,*
September 1971, drawn by Nick Bremer (Director of A
since 1969)

six of them in 1969-70. His critics wanted him to be tougher but, while he showed scant sympathy for his troublesome charges, he saw that to draw a line in the sand would in such times turn something innocuous into something fundamentally dangerous. He understood about inessentials and the need for pressure valves. And he could be confident in the darkest moments because admissions were rising from 1969.

Henry Christie may not have reacted too well to the mass. At a one-to-one level, however, he was a past master. He was so approachable. The door to the Headmaster's house was as wide open to the staff as that of his study was to the boys. The hospitality of Henry and his wife Naida is still talked of, as is their warmth, their genuineness, their skill at promoting Collegiate feeling. Naida 'pulled in everyone and was quite extraordinary in creating a friendly, relaxed atmosphere' (Fred Hankins). The Scout Award Society expedition up a Welsh mountain, to find Henry and Naida at the cairn at the top waiting to distribute Easter eggs, encapsulates the splendour of this delightful couple.

After eight years, however, they were gone–to St Edward's Oxford, where Henry had been elected Warden. Seven years later he went to be Director of Studies at Dartmouth. Later still, he was Visiting Professor of Mathematics at Annapolis Naval Academy. He died in 1992. Such an easy man to work for, some were fooled by his gentle manner. Beneath was a man of shrewd, even acute judgement. The shallow and the specious rarely deceived him. Burstow's judgement was that, 'I would sooner work under this Headmaster as any I have known' (and, when he wrote that, he had worked for twelve). When many all around were losing their heads, and blaming it on him, the wisdom of Henry Christie carried Brighton College safely through. In the words of Peter Gough, 'he managed the '60s bloody well'.

*   *   *

William Blackshaw, 1971

School Fête, 1980 (note the T-shirt design)

From a field of 55 applicants and a first short-list of seven, which included Hubert Doggart (soon appointed Headmaster of King's Bruton, and Treasurer of MCC), Guy Wilkin (a Cheltenham Housemaster) was runner-up to William Blackshaw, aged 40, a Modern Linguist and for the previous five years a Housemaster at Repton. His starting salary was £3,400.

'Steady as she goes' is never for long the policy of a wise Council. What turned out to be the most important legacy of 1968-70 was the reaction provoked by those seekers after liberation. Outside the sciences, every action generates a disproportionate reaction. Across the West, the student riots and sit-ins of 1968-70 implanted fear of disorder and kindled desires for top-down authority. Electorates embraced Ronald Reagan, Helmut Kohl and Margaret Thatcher. These would be years when hopes were lowered and hearts hardened.

The College Council made their shift to bolster the body politic in 1971. As Harold Elliott explained,

> when the Council picked Bill Blackshaw, it was looking for someone who would take the school by the scruff of the neck. Dear Henry had navigated treacherous waters with a fine skill, but the past three years had been hell and we would have taken on less water if the new Second Master [Norman Frith] had put the stick about. That was to be Blackshaw's task. He had held a firm line in his House at Repton. Four of his boys had been expelled—we liked the sound of that.

The old order changeth, yielding place to new. Here was the origin of 'Bill the Beater', a Headmaster who, like Cotterill 120 years earlier, used stern discipline to revive the corporate, to re-emphasise the collegiate and thus to remake Brighton College. During his first ten days, three housemasters found a group of boys taking LSD. The four pushers were expelled and six juniors were beaten. Clear and decisive action like this did wonders for the school's image. Applications took a marked up-turn. As Blackshaw himself remembers, 'it did us a power of good'. That went on being true, for the crack-down was no flash in the pan. Blackshaw puts it thus: 'My generation of Headmasters were determined to turn the clock back and have a bit more discipline'.

Hand-to-mouth expedients there were, but an era of purposeful direction had begun. Approachable (some say 'clubbable') and always prepared to listen, this was nonetheless a Headmaster with little time for committees. He knew his mind and, a man of double vigour, always led from the front. Never afraid to be unpopular, if necessary, some found him astringent. But, as one master put it, 'even if [you] did not agree, even if you were furious, you always knew where you stood and you couldn't but respect the man'. His staff found him supportive, and they prized a Headmaster willing to give 'lame dogs' a chance, or those who had made mistakes a second chance. Liberal in their hospitality and unreserved in their care for staff families, Bill and his wife Elizabeth proved another first-rate couple in the Headmaster's house. In

In the Pottery on Open Day, 1977

a telling comparison, Harold Elliott confessed that 'we were rather worried that
the new rigour might provoke a staff exodus. Nine masters had left Lancing after
one year of Dancy [1953]. We lost only
three!'. When Blackshaw retired in 1987,
the Council picked John Leach, aged 48,
a housemaster and Director of Studies at
St Edward's Oxford (out of 52 applicants
and two shortlists, where all but one candidate soon got a headship). Inflation had
pushed his starting salary to £25,000.

The present is an interlude whose
measurement must be as experimental as
it is conditional. Dispassionate analysis of
these our most recent years must await the
next College History. The final pages can
do no more than attempt an impressionis-
tic (and preliminary) assessment of one part
of that story: the many developments and
innovations which have so changed the
face of Brighton College that they will

John Leach

surely come to be seen as occupying a cardinal place in the history of the school.

New buildings and the refurbishment of old ones have transformed the face and
facilities of the school. Numbers have risen significantly, while the pattern of demand

'The New Building' under construction, 1979

PERSPECTIVE VIEWS
PROPOSED MATHS BLOCK, BRIGHTON COLLEGE
THE MILLER BOURNE PARTNERSHIP

The Lester Building (first design), 1985

has shifted the balance sharply away from boarding. Equally fundamental has been the admission of girls, first to the VIth Form (1973) and then after 15 years to the Lower School as well. Simultaneously, the College has endured the ravages of inflation, the threat of political assault and the roller-coaster of a 'boom and bust' economy.

Blackshaw has already gone down to posterity as 'Bill the Builder'. He arrived as the Woolton Quad was being completed and left shortly after the Lester Building had been opened. In between, the lack of indoor sports facilities was addressed by the erection of the Sports Hall (1972-73) out of a munificent gift by his mother and stepfather, Sir Thomas and Lady McAlpine. The Junior School took occupation of Walpole Lodge (1973). Art was relocated to better premises in 1974, complete with a pottery room. Next door, the Music School was enlarged and refitted three years later. The foyer to the Hall was transformed (1978) into an exhibition space, the Burstow Gallery. The Woolton block eased the pressure on classrooms but, as the College continued to grow, the problem did not go away. Temporary huts provided four extra classrooms (1976) and the New Building (1978-80) added seven more, as well as a new pavilion and an on-campus home for Kingscliffe.

But these were not additions. Rather they were replacements for those classrooms on the top floor of the Dawson Building lost when it was turned into a new dayboy House, named after the philosopher Gilbert Ryle (1910-19). Extra classrooms, together with an electronics laboratory and two computer rooms, came only in 1985-86 with

Bert Swarbrook, Head Porter 1964-88

The restored gates being rehung, 1989

the Lester Building (named for Teddy, in his last years known as Alf), raised on arches in unconscious imitation of Gilbert Scott's Big School which, if built, it would have abutted. Less visible but no less valuable, the dining hall was civilised. The modernisation of boarding houses continued. At last, headmasters and governors had accepted that communal living need not be 24 hours a day, that provision for privacy was necessary, that comfort was not incompatible with masculinity and that the views of mothers counted.

Beyond refurbishment of science laboratories and the organ, and a host of 'minor' building works, there also began the first attempt to restore the College's historic buildings (listed as Grade II in 1972). Chief among the projects undertaken have been the putting back of diamond-paned leaded lights to the Front Quad facades of Scott's buildings, the renovation and re-hanging of Jackson's entrance gates, the rebuilding of his Home Ground gate and railings (now partially completed) and the repair of the chapel's Morris & Co. glass. Of what remains to be done, the most valuable will be the renewal of badly weathered terracotta blocks along Eastern Road, the removal of cables, which disfigure every building, and the replacing of the Tower battlements and gargoyles.

*   *   *

At 20 boys below viability in 1971, Blackshaw was also brought in to increase numbers. Throughout his years, there would be a need for what the Bursar in 1977 termed 'expansion to contain unit costs'. Blackshaw inherited a school with 338 boys and left one with 486 boys and girls, an increase of 44 per cent on the roll. Growth did not stop there. Numbers continued rising until a total of 498 was reached in 1990,

but the recession has pushed them down to 471 (in 1994). As incomes are squeezed by rising taxes and high interest rates, and as real wage growth is at best minimal across the Home Counties, Brighton College's urban setting has, not for the first time, helped enormously.

The decline of 1961-71 was reversed, and rapidly. After only two years, the roll had jumped by 82 and the College had over 400 pupils (for the first time since 1932). Only the reigns of Stuart-Clark and Dawson had seen mightier growth than Blackshaw's. Apart from Dawson's 1920s' aggrandisement, Brighton College had never been so full. How was it achieved? The slow death of Brighton Grammar School helped. So too did the federation of two prep and one pre-prep school which

(left) Latin in Room D, 1979

(below) Mendelssohn's *Elijah*, 1972

the College now owned. The second (and greater) peak in the post-war baby boom lent a strong tail wind. Against these aids worked the recession which began in 1971 and, from 1978, a fall in the secondary school age population. As the mini recession in 1981 struck hard into that shrinking market, the roll dropped 31 and Blackshaw confessed to the Council 'the strain of striving for the figures is immense'. Recovery from 1985-86 received a kick-start from maintained school teachers' strikes and moved almost in tandem with house prices–until the crash. Neither Headmaster has been able to sit back. Expansion has come as the result of hard work:

Numbers in College (September)

	total pupils	boarders	day pupils	girls	VIth Form
1971[a]	338	145	193 (57%)	-	105
1972	340	142	198	-	107
1973	389	171	218	7	150
1974	420	189	231	21	159
1975	427	179	248	27	164
1976	439	180	259	28	165
1977	457	190	267	27	174
1978	466	175	291 (62%)	36	178
1979	487	167	320	34	187
1980	477	165	312	35	178
1981	483	165	318	43	183
1982	470	167	303	41	189
1983	452	166	286	41	183
1984	459	150	309 (67%)	44	188
1985	468	148	320	45	192
1986	488	168	320	50 (10%)	195
1987[b]	486	156	330	50	194
1988[c]	498	151	347	55	197
1989	495	137	358 (72%)	76 (15%)	194
1990	498	121	377	93	194
1991	484	104	380 (78%)	105 (22%)	199
1992	479	110	369	114	193
1993	476	102	374	118	178
1994	471	101	370 (79%)	119 (25%)	170

notes: a= Blackshaw became Headmaster
b= Leach became Headmaster
c= full co-education began

The massive and unchecked expansion in day pupils (71 per cent increase 1971-87; 92 per cent 1971-94) is unprecedented in College history. Having taken 28 years (1945-73) for day numbers to rise from 100 to 200, the leap from 200 to 300 occurred in only six (1973-79). The old prejudice finally died out in the 1960s–Centenary Scholarships were opened to dayboys in 1965–and Brighton College has been well placed to profit by the onward march of parental rejection of boarding. For the first time, more than half of College pupils now live in Brighton and Hove.

Bill Blackshaw singles out another reason for growth: the establishment in 1976 of Foundation Scholarships. These offered three completely free places per year to pupils aged 11

> and anticipated Assisted Places ... My gosh, I had to fight to get the Council to accept the cost. But look what a difference they made. We had 60 to 80 candidates putting in each year.

The Assisted Places Scheme, which the College joined at its inauguration in 1981, has also been a help. The story of vicissitudes in the roll must, however, concentrate on the closely related issues of boarders and girls.

The decay in boarding is complex. Boarding numbers had fallen by 32 per cent in the eight years before Blackshaw's appointment. Throughout his period in office, he worked desperately hard to shore-up boarding, standing four square on the axiom that 'boarding is fundamental to the current ethos of the place'. Fortnightly and then weekly boarding were both his initiatives (in 1972 and 1977 respectively). For five years, vigorous marketing brought a 25 per cent turnaround. But the market was not to be bucked, especially when only 7 per cent of pupils were recruited from beyond Sussex. Boarding numbers fell back and Blackshaw's reign saw an overall increase of 0.76 per cent—quite a feat, given the circumstances.

Within the College, this decay led to the conversion of Durnford to a dayboy House in 1970, the closure of Bristol in 1983 and the forthcoming merger of Chichester and School. Since 1987, boarding numbers have dropped 65 per cent. It might have been worse. Blackshaw had estimated there would be 88 boarders in 1985-86, and none by the end of the century.

Two schemes of these years are of some interest. One proposal was the idea in 1976 to open a feeder prep school in Brussels for the sons of an expatriot community then expanding fast. Feasibility studies killed off the idea very quickly—very fortunately because the market for English private schooling there slumped badly soon afterwards. A red herring, it nonetheless shows how seriously the boarding problem was taken. More feasible was a proposed link-up with St Mary's Hall in 1972. Joint musical activities between the two schools had been taking place since 1964. St Mary's girls began attending College Sunday chapel in 1968, provoking what *The Brightonian* editorial termed 'some thoughts about the future of educational co-operation'. From 1970, pupils from St Mary's replaced boys for the female rôles in College plays.

The election of St Mary's Chairman of Governors to the College Council in 1968 was the clearest sign that increased co-operation was on the agenda, and in 1971 the two schools began discussing 'shared facilities' for the VIth Form. Intended to ward off the perceived threat of the new VIth Form colleges, nothing developed beyond shared VIth Form R.E. lessons because of the College's admission of girls after 'O' level in September 1973.

Four years later, there were tentative talks on 'a closer working relationship', but serious discussions resumed only in 1980. Dubbed 'co-instruction', the idea being explored was a merger at VIth Form level. Details were agreed for 'a joint curriculum' from September 1980. In the Headmaster's words:

> It got to the Saturday before it was going to be announced. We had letters of intent ready to release on the Monday. Out of the blue, however, their Chairman rang ours saying they were pulling out because their Headmistress had cold feet.

Fenwick House, 1979

A fascinating might-have-been, Blackshaw is absolutely right in saying that

the whole history of the College (and St Mary's) would have been completely different. Boarding might have been sustained and, after about 10 years, one fully integrated co-educational school would have emerged.

Brighton College was going to admit girls. Marlborough and Cheltenham, founded just before Brighton, were the first HMC schools to admit girls to their VIth Forms (1969). Brighton followed suit in September 1973, very much at the Headmaster's request. He had seen it succeed at Repton, albeit in very limited form, and demand was already there to make it work at the College. A 10 per cent straw poll he conducted among parents showed almost unanimous approval; the Common Room was much more divided.

Although the great majority of early girls were boarders, Blackshaw's prime objective lay elsewhere. 'What I was really trying to do', he says, 'was to boost VIth Form numbers. Along the way, I also wanted to improve music and drama.' The presence of girls would also serve to guarantee that the liberalisation of the 1960s could never be undone. Perhaps 'Bill the Beater' knew that. A self-confessed 'pragmatist who tried to engineer quiet evolution over a period', he was far from reluctant to admit girls and his reforms did much to continue the development of a softer atmosphere within the College (some will gasp at that self-assessment!).

VIth Form girls, a cartoon by Nick Allen, 1974   A Fenwick study bedroom, 1979

Co-education began in the Junior School in 1983 and in 1985 the College Council decided to admit girls at 13 from September 1988. Now they were operating from a position of strength, numerical and financial. Again, the decision met parental demand and, this time, the Common Room was much happier (resistance being confined almost entirely to a part of the most senior ranks). But the early stages of this story show that, this time, it was the Headmaster who was uneasy. F&GP recommended to the Council in October 1981 that the College go co-ed. 'By the time the Council met in November, I was the one with cold feet', Blackshaw confesses.

> The plan was almost an emotional response to the St Mary's thing and something in my guts said 'no', so I told the Council 'I'm sorry, I'm not prepared to do it. I'll try to get more boy boarders. If I fail, then we'll go co-ed'

That created a pause in the debate but the Junior School changes had altered the landscape. Blackshaw takes up the story thus:

the plan had been co-ed 8-11, but somehow that got changed to 8-13. The Junior School was very keen, but there were considerable implications for the College. The alteration rushed it, without looking at the whole.

When, therefore, he was unable to find an alternative source of boy boarders and the parents of Junior School girls were planning their daughters' secondary schooling, the subject had to come back to the Council table. In the words of the Headmaster's final Report to the Council (June 1987), 'the tail has in fact wagged the dog'.

The Headmaster had come around, but he would not stay to oversee the change.

> I had no doubt it was the right decision for the College, but it was not the right thing for me to implement. Either I stayed to '89-90 to see through something I knew nothing about, or I got out and handed over to someone who knew all about these things. In a sense, my hand had been forced and I was not the right man.

That was sad because the decision taken in 1985 was his last great contribution to the cause of boarding. Boarding and co-education can never be separated in Blackshaw's reign. As he told the Council in March 1985, the decision to admit girls at 13 represented

> the best chance for slowing down the decline in boarding. It would also buy time and provide a ten year term in which to strengthen our image as a co-educational GRAMMAR school with a good academic reputation. By this means, the change of ethos would be organic and progressive; evolution rather than revolution.

*   *   *

The most recent phase in the academic revolution has finally cured the public schools of residual ambivalence to intellectual attainment. Parental expectations, retrenchment in higher education and the prospect of graduate unemployment have combined to force a reassessment of priorities. As demand for university places again outstrips supply and the attainment of specific 'A' level grades becomes ever more critical, schools like Brighton College have taken over the ground unwillingly vacated by the grammar schools. Despite the cost, the maintenance of low pupil:teacher ratios becomes ever more vital (1953 = 15.1:1; 1973 = 13.3:1; 1993 = 9.7:1).

As the changeover in Headmasters in 1971 allowed the Council to shift emphasis, so too did Blackshaw's retirement in 1987. The Council now looked primarily for a Headmaster who would push forward academic standards. It was thus no accident that, in John Leach, they picked the first Headmaster since Dr. Bigg (1871) with a first-class honours degree. In one intriguing way, the teaching staff have changed too. Until 1914, virtually all full-time masters were Oxbridge graduates. Between the Wars, around 20 per cent held degrees from other universities. During Stewart's years, that dropped to an average of 13.6 per cent; the HMC average in 1963 was 17 per cent. Today, 26 per cent of the teaching staff are Oxbridge graduates and the employment of non-graduates has become unthinkable. Yet the mirror has not cracked from side to side. Academic standards have never been higher.

Simultaneously, the quality of pupils has been boosted thanks to Blackshaw's other campaign cause: scholarship provision. Foundation Scholarships have already been referred to. Another venture was the introduction of VIth Form Scholarships in 1973. New endowments have been received, most notably the bequest in 1992 of £850,000

The Common Room, 1972

by Francis Cooke (1926-29) which stands with the gifts of the Soames and Belcher families as our most bountiful benefactions. Equally important has been the trustees' policy of investment for capital growth, which allowed the Headmaster to push the Council to increase the number and value of scholarships. By the early 1980s, the trustees managed a capital of £250,000–which Blackshaw describes as 'a very good sum for Brighton College'.

Business Studies (1973), Computing (1974), Electronics (1982), Home Economics (1988) and Theatre Studies (1994) have been added to broaden the VIth Form curriculum, but nothing has been taken out. The gentle pace of the old has gone in the stampede for grades and league table position. Coursework and modules have changed what happens in the classroom more than overhead projectors and video recorders (the College's first VCR was bought in 1976, and cost £1,600). Pupils are kept incredibly busy and competition thrives. Pretensions have gone and performance is up.

*   *   *

Troublesome pupils were replaced by troublesome politicians who threatened a financial squeeze if not outright abolition. Brighton College has monitored Labour thinking since 1958. Their policy commitment 'to reduce and eventually to abolish private education' (1973), followed by the pledge to end 'all forms of tax relief and charitable status' (1974), made the governments of 1974-79 far more menacing than anything in the 1960s; as General Elections approached, Blackshaw would make plain at parents' evenings the danger of voting anything but Conservative. Now the issue is Assisted Places, the policy which more than any other broke the post-war bipartisan consensus on education. Desirable or not, the scheme has left participating schools mortgaged dangerously to the fortunes of one political party.

Thus far, passion has never been translated into action and the most publicised threat has turned out to be the least dangerous. Rather, the great challenge was inflation which came far closer than the Labour Party to destroying independent education. A simple chart says it all:

Annual College fees (September)

	Day	Boarding (full)	Boarding (weekly)
1965	£298	£480	-
1970	£411	£627	-
1975	£915	£1,320	-
1980	£1,800	£2,730	£2,475
1985	£3,015	£4,635	£4,155
1990	£5,715	£8,685	£7,800
(1994	£7,854	£11,940	£10,680)

Inflation worried the public schools in the 1950s but, to our jaundiced eyes, the rising costs they fretted over were as nothing compared with what was to come:

College fees (% increase)

	Day	Boarding (full)
1950-60	91%	95%
1960-70	93%	63%
1970-80	438%	435%
1980-90	317%	318%
(1990-95	37%	37%)

The very worst years were the early 1970s when the combined effects of 'the Barber Boom', massive increases in oil prices and the Houghton pay award for teachers destroyed any possibility of order. During the school year 1974-75, the peak in the inflationary hurricane when average prices rose by 27 per cent and wages by 25 per cent, the governors had to make *four* separate increases in fees. The anti-inflationary

(left) Open Day, 1977

The cover of *The Brightonian*, October 197?

Thatcher years brought little more comfort and only very recently has stability returned.

One final table permits us to gauge more clearly what has happened to prices, and values:

Annual College fees (£)

	Day	Boarding (full)
1847	25	70
1895	33	105
1947	61	157
(1995	7,854	11,940)

How did the College survive? In the 1970s as in the 1950s, many schools feared (and some politicians hoped) they would price themselves out of the market. College fees did not rise quite as much as in fellow schools. Between 1966 and 1980, fees in HMC schools rose on average by 404 per cent, whereas Brighton day fees increased by 339 per cent, boarding fees by 367 per cent. Even so, survival seemed touch and go. The sale of the prep school Hawkhurst Court (at Wisborough Green), Clarendon Lodge and the College Road properties brought a capital inflow of £830,000 in 1983-84. Tough budgetary controls, periodic redundancies and the non-replacement of departing or retiring staff played their part. So too did a honing of the management's business skills.

When Chairman of the Council (1974-78), Harold Elliott determined to have what he defined as 'a first class business expert as a Bursar and I found what I was looking for in Ken Walker' (1975-81). He also brought onto the Council an accountant (Matthew Patient, 1952-57) and a stockbroker (Stephen Cockburn, 1953-58) to add to the bank-

er's skills of the self-effacing but tremendously influential Harold Myerscough (Treasurer 1967-78). That fiscal expertise sat easily on Bill Blackshaw should not be overlooked. Indeed, was the running of the business side of the school the thing he enjoyed most? 'Bill the Businessman' stresses 'the very forceful and energetic chairmanship of Harold. He ran the Council as he would run his business. We needed that.' But Blackshaw singles out the reforms of Matthew Patient while Chairman of F&GP (1975-79). 'He imposed proper budgetary accounting, building in provision for reserves, depreciation and a fund for repairs. He ended the system whereby the College spent what it got ... An accountant's approach was very necessary, and the sound lines he established made possible the developments of the '80s.'

Harold Myerscough

Ultimate salvation came, however, from the most unlikely of sources: the Labour government of 1974-79. Their decision to abolish the 11-plus and the direct grant (1976) coincided with the grimmest days of public school finances and created a whole new market for independent education.

*   *   *

As the 1960s get too much credit for forcing change, so the decades which preceded and followed get too little credit for nurturing a gentler and more effective liberalisation. Across the public schools, this wind of change blew in very piecemeal fashion. The speed of change varied greatly, but its results have become the new orthodoxy. Individual achievement is now seen as something to be encouraged, not restricted or even suppressed. A more relaxed relationship between pupils of different ages and between teachers and pupils (to say nothing of between senior and junior teachers) has developed. The treatment of VIth Formers as undergraduates, proposed by Stewart, is now partially realised. Pupils are no longer to be kept on the premises, and their parents off. The shifts from compulsion towards encouragement, and from obedience towards trust, have had profound consequences. Personal fagging and prefects with canes went long ago. The Deputy Headmaster hung his up on the appointment of

Public Speaking Competition, Open Day 1977

Maltings beer tokens

Rodney Fox (1985), while the Headmaster's was retired with Bill Blackshaw. Key elements of the foundation have thus been restored.

At the formal level, the shift of attitude is embodied in the replacing of Speech Day with Open Day (1977). Tradition must be flexible. The need for change is as vital as the need for continuity. A stout traditionalist, Blackshaw nonetheless understood the need to accommodate change so, seeking above all 'to avoid trauma', he tried, as he himself says, 'to have quiet change over a period'. His early years were especially significant: the establishing of a VIth Form Club which served beer and the opening of a special House in St George's Lodge for the Third Year Sixth (1972); they wore no uniform at all. Three years later came choice in jackets and ties for the rest of the VIth Form. Another reform much valued by pupils was his ending of formal House dining rooms and the advent of a cafeteria dining hall (1974).

School House in its Dining Room, 1968

Tennis in the Fives courts, *c.*1963

Curriculum diversification since the 1950s has, as we have seen, been matched in out of class activities. Its symbol is the building of a 'Sports Hall' in 1972-73, not a 'gymnasium'. Some of the old sports died. Boxing was abolished in 1965 and an VIII last competed in the Ashburton in 1969, while Fives had withered even before the courts were demolished to make way for tennis courts in 1966. That same year, Athletics was pushed from its primacy to make way for a 'minor sports' option system in the Lent Term. Association Football had already been revived (1965). Judo (1967) and Badminton (1970) added further variety. So did Hockey (1972); as Blackshaw's own speciality, however, it soon became the official major sport of the Lent Term. Most recently, co-education has brought netball and rounders to Brighton College.

Stewart considered the employment of a qualified specialist games master, but rejected the idea because 'such a man

Sailing, 1971

Just four of the Burstow Gallery's exhibitions

BRIGHTON COLLEGE
EASTERN ROAD, BRIGHTON. BN2 2AL

BURSTOW GALLERY

You are cordially invited to attend the

Private View of an exhibition of

recent and retrospective work by

JOHN WORSLEY

an artist of extraordinary versatility

official war artist - illustrator - sculptor
portrait painter - marine artist

INCLUDING LOANS FROM THE IMPERIAL WAR MUSEUM
THE NATIONAL MARITIME MUSEUM &

H.M. THE QUEEN

SUNDAY 7 OCTOBER at 11.30 am

in the presence of   ALBERT R.N.

WINE BAR

Exhibition open 8th - 28th October

daily 11.30 - 5.00   sundays 2.00 - 5.00

SHOP: Childrens books, prints and original illustrations

Brighton Festival 1983

Main Programme
THE BURSTOW GALLERY

The Raoul Wallenberg Exhibition

This man, one of the great heroes of the 2nd World War, saved 100,000 Hungarian Jews from the Nazis. His life story was recently featured on BBC's 'Man Alive'.

The Headmaster & Governors of Brighton College, the Director of the Burstow Gallery and the Raoul Wallenberg Committee cordially invite you to attend the private view and opening of The Raoul Wallenberg Exhibition by

LARS — ÅKE NILSSON
Political Counsellor to the Swedish Embassy

from 2.00 p.m — 3.00 p.m on

Monday 9th May 1983

in the Great Hall of Brighton College, adjacent to the Burstow Gallery.

R.S.V.P. Brighton College, Eastern Rd, Brighton. Tel: 697131

Exhibition Continues Tuesday 10 May — 21 May 1983
Open Daily 11am — 5pm; Sundays 2pm — 5pm.
Admission free — School parties welcome.
Sponsored by Highland Electronics PLC. & Levy Gee & Partners.
Patrons: Dame Flora Robson and Canon John Hester, Vicar of Brighton.

'Picasso and the Theatre' in the School Hall, 1982

The service in St Peter's Church inaugurating the Sesquicentenary, January 1995 [Photo: David Hollinshead]

would not scrub out the swimming bath, polish the floor of a gym or put up the boxing ring as required, all of which an ex-Army P.T.I. regards as part of his job'. Christie was, however, persuaded of the necessity and John Pope was appointed (1971 to date) 'to raise the standard of rugby and games generally'. That he has done with distinction. Never were XVs more successful, even in the golden 1920s. Under the coaching of Peter Perfect (1958-94), cricket was equally surefire. Squash too has held its renown, while the 'minor games' have been fostered thanks to a limited revival of the concept of option, just for the VIth Form initially, but later throughout. As Fred Hankins (then Director of Activities) notes, 'after we had the Sports Hall it was easy. Minor sports came of age!' Significant too was the relaxation in 1981 of half-holiday regulations when those not in teams, christened 'non- gladiators', were allowed to go home on Saturday afternoon.

That was 'a little bit of Hankins', to use Bill Blackshaw's phrase. So too was the creation in 1981 of the 'long lunch hour' on Wednesdays and Fridays which allowed all sorts of activities (especially choirs, ensembles and orchestras) to be fitted into the programme of what was effectively now a day school. Hankins was responsible also for the creation of the College's very own art gallery: the Burstow. Fitting well with Blackshaw's enthusiasm for the arts and his membership of the Brighton Festival Committee, the flair with which it has been run and the standard it has set (both due to Nick Bremer, Director of Art since 1969) have allowed pupils to experience painting and sculpture, to be inspired and outraged, in a most marvellous way. In 1984, the Front Quad became an open air sculpture park during the John Skelton exhibition. As for the 'Picasso and the Theatre' exhibition in 1982, it was the central event of that year's Festival and attracted 7,200 visitors to the College. 'The publicity is beyond price', the Headmaster proudly told the Council.

In the new environment, art, drama and music have thus gone from strength to strength. Arguably, the most important thing Blackshaw did in this field was to permit the concentration of creative and intellectual talent in one House, Hampden. A distinct exception to his policy of uniformity in policy and style among Houses, the potent amalgam which developed there stimulated the cultural life of the entire College and turned Hampden into a fountain of delight.

These last pages have concentrated exclusively on sketching the major planned changes of the past 25 years. Much that is important is barely touched on, or omitted altogether. That must be so if the evaluation and the context are to be trustworthy as well as candid. Truth is the daughter of time.

These chapters have demonstrated that the game is always afoot. When Bill Barr retired as President of the College in 1993, he described the last 40 years as feeling like 'one damned crisis after another'. His image holds good for most of the school's history. Bankrupt three times, on the brink of closure twice, it is nothing short of miraculous that Brighton College has survived to educate 13,000 pupils and celebrate its sesquicentenary. That it has done so is a tribute to the commitment of many of the people featured in these pages, for the reward of labour is life. As Clement Attlee observed in 1950, 'the British have the distinction above all others of being able to put new wine into old bottles without breaking them'.

Philip Burstow (founder of the College Archives
and author of the first College history)

Index

[compiled by Hilary Mortimer]

Index entries refer to page numbers, with relevant illustrated pages shown in bold type.

Eastern Brighton in 1845
[courtesy Stephen Cockburn]